Worker in the Cane

SIDNEY W. MINTZ

Worker in the Cane

A PUERTO RICAN LIFE HISTORY

W · W · NORTON & COMPANY
New York · London

W. W. Norton & Company, Inc., 500 Fifth Avenue, New York, NY 10110
W. W. Norton & Company Ltd, 10 Coptic Street, London WC1A 1PU

First published in the Norton Library 1974
by arrangement with Yale University Press

ISBN 0-393-00731-6

Books That Live
The Norton imprint on a book means that in the publisher's
estimation it is a book not for a single season but for the years.
W. W. Norton & Company, Inc.

Printed in the United States of America
0

For Eric Daniel and Elizabeth Rachel

Acknowledgments

I CARRIED OUT my first fieldwork in Puerto Rico in 1948–49, on a joint grant from the Centro de Investigaciones Sociales, Universidad de Puerto Rico, and the Rockefeller Foundation. The Study was part of a larger project, organized by the late Julian H. Steward; the director of the field phase was John V. Murra; to both these teachers I have a profound debt.

In the summer of 1953 I was able to return to Puerto Rico to undertake the particular research on which this book is based, supported by the Yale University Caribbean Program, with funds from the Wenner-Gren Foundation. In 1956 a second, shorter trip was made possible through the good offices of the late Edgar S. Furniss, then Provost of Yale University, and Leonard Doob, of Yale's department of psychology. My obligation to these institutions and persons is substantial.

I wrote the first draft of the book itself during the summer of 1957, while enjoying a Social Science Research Council Faculty Research Fellowship, and finished the work during the summer of 1958, while on a Guggenheim Fellowship.

In Puerto Rico I have a special debt to Charles C. Rosario. Sr. Rosario was ostensibly my "field assistant" in 1948–49; but it would be more accurate, I think, to say that he was my teacher. Rarely have I enjoyed the company and confidence of a person so generous, kind and wise as he, and my obligation to him cannot be measured.

Many other persons aided me greatly in my work, and it would be impossible adequately to thank them all; but I should at least mention Jack and Irene Delano; Pete and Ellen Hawes; Doña Constance Merrick de Rosario and the late Dn. José C. Rosario; Eric and Katia Wolf; the late Harriett Keeney Osgood and Cornelius Osgood; and my former wife, June Mintz.

Jane Olson, then of the Yale University Press, provided me

with painstaking editorial assistance and advice; Charles C. Rosario and Miss Carmen Irene Goyco de García helped me with the glossary; and Arline Diebold and Evelyn Middleton typed the final manuscript. I thank them all.

Finally, to the people of Barrio Jauca, Municipio de Santa Isabel, Puerto Rico—Taso, Elí, Cheo, Rosa, Pola, Berto, Santos and all the others—I can say nothing by way of thanks, for this is in truth their book, and not mine.

Preface

I FIRST BEGAN fieldwork in Puerto Rico in 1948, when I was twenty-five years old; the man whose story this book recounts was forty years old at that time. As I write this preface, I am preparing to return to his village, to talk with him at length once more, about his life and his perceptions. Among other things, I shall want to read to him some of his own commentary, spoken more than twenty years ago, to find out if he sees things in the same way now as he did at the time.

He is nearly sixty-six years old now, retired, and his eyesight is failing. A very great deal has changed for him, his family and his society since I first asked him to try to reconstruct with me his life experiences; and I shall be surprised if he finds nothing with which to disagree in his views of nearly a quarter of a century ago. I shall also want to hear how he describes—and how he feels about—the way his village has become different, during these years.

Perhaps I should hasten to point out that this man, "Taso" Zayas, is neither a public figure, nor a famous man, nor prestigious nor distinguished. In fact, except for his very unusual intelligence, Taso might be described as quite average in nearly every way. This, then, is the autobiography of an average man. But I tried to make clear when I first wrote the book that this emphatically does not mean that Taso is "typical," representative of others, or ordinary; and in these regards, the book— and Taso's own words—must stand on their own account.

Anthropologists have long had the habit of writing life-histories. But until quite recently, the persons such books dealt with—such books as Paul Radin's *Crashing Thunder*, Leo Simmons' *Sun Chief*, and Mary Smith's *Baba of Karo*—came from societies of the sort dubbed "primitive." When the present book first appeared nearly fifteen years ago, hardly any autobiographies of westernized working-class persons had been written by anthropologists. That is now much changed.

The book was preceded by some years by an anthropological study that I made of the community in which Taso lived, and lives. That community was composed almost entirely of rural proletarians—that is, of agricultural wage-earners who worked in the sugar-cane for wages—and who consumed hardly anything of what they personally produced, while producing almost nothing they could personally consume.

Resembling in very broad terms the industrial proletariats of Europe, these people nonetheless exhibited as well many of the characteristics of social life associated with the unindustrialized, rural, personalistic, non-western world, and were—and are—for this reason somewhat paradoxical sociologically. Anthropological studies of plantation communities and of rural proletariats were almost non-existent at the time. That, too, is now much changed.

The principal figure in this book played a role in the development of party-based political activity in the Puerto Rican countryside, and in the eventual coming to power of the Popular Party there. Long before becoming a Popular, however, Taso was a charter member of Puerto Rico's Socialist Party and, later, active in the sugarworkers' union as well. The importance of these experiences is revealed in his own narration, and one gets from this commentary some sense of the subtle psychosocial linkages that connect class membership, class consciousness, and political action. Such matters were not of consuming interest to anthropologists twenty years ago, but today political scientists and sociologists, together with anthropologists and historians, have become interested anew in the nature of class-based political movements, and in the history of such movements the world over. Here, again, there has been a noticeable shift in interest.

Rather late in his life—only shortly after I left the field for the first time, in 1949—Taso turned away from political activity (and, as the narration will reveal, from much else as well) and was converted to a Pentecostal religious sect. This immensely important change in his life-trajectory so caught me by surprise that it was a principal reason for my returning to the community to work with Taso on this book. Nothing that I thought I knew about him had prepared me in the slightest for his conversion. While anthropologists have long been interested in religious phenomena, relatively little was available in the literature of the time that dealt with religious conversion as an aspect of "modernization" or "westernization" among peoples who are not "primitive." This, then, is another aspect of Taso's story that has gained increasing attention over time.

Finally, this book is of course concerned in very fundamental ways with Puerto Rico and the Puerto Rican people, and with the situation in which they find themselves. At the time when my fieldwork began in 1948, interest in Puerto Rico on the part of North America was already substantial, due in some large measure to the post-World War II migration of Puerto Ricans to the mainland in search of improved economic opportunity. But there was not yet a large second generation of Puerto Ricans living in the United States, nor had the intense difficulties faced by the Puerto Rican people, both at home and on the mainland, been made part of the consciousness and sensibilities of North Americans. Moreover, the penetration of Puerto Rico itself by North American interests, already overpowering, was to become even more visible during the intervening twenty-five years. As this was happening, the heightened tempo of Caribbean migration to the United States, especially in the last decade, was increasing North American interest in the migrants themselves and in their homeland societies, just as these migrants—Puerto Ricans among them—were calling for attention to their own very particular problems in the urban North American setting. This is, perhaps, yet another way in which this book has a greater apparent relevance to the present than it had when it was first written. It is the same story, the same book; but the world in the context of which one may read it has become a little different.

When I wrote this book—which consists of Taso's story told mainly in his own words, with my comments and occasional interpretations—my main objective was to make available a rural proletarian's account of the experience of "westernization" (in this case, a North American colonial and imperialist species of westernization) in an agrarian, insular subtropical setting. While I sought to deal with the particular, local and individual in this instance, it did not escape me that, throughout Africa, Asia and Latin America, anthropologists were busily studying "tribal" peoples, while largely ignoring those who were being subjected to what were common and widespread processes of this kind. Thus I was dealing with a single case; but I believed it had extremely wide relevance in the modern world.

It was my hope that the remarkable intelligence and articulateness of the protagonist—a man who had very little formal education, and had lived a very hard life—would reveal itself successfully to the interested reader, and thus illuminate the immense human potential, often unrealized, that lies outside our reach because our social and economic system often destroys individual capacities before they can blossom. I have no fully confident belief that I succeeded in my intent; but I am entirely certain that my friend, Taso, in telling his own story, did. This remains, and is more than ever, his book.

Contents

List of Illustrations

Maps

FLOR DE CAÑA, *the flower of the sugar cane, is usually called* GUAJANA *in Puerto Rico. The sugar cane plant is very tall. The* GUAJANA *consists of feathery spikelets which blossom above it in the late fall, shimmering violet and silver when the breeze stirs them.*

The sugar cane itself, like most of the people who work in the cane in the Caribbean area today, is descended from Old World stock. But the name GUAJANA *is American Indian, Taino, and hence indigenously Caribbean. The flower of the cane is a symbol, then, of the mixture of peoples and cultures, of old and new. It is a fitting symbol for the people of Puerto Rico.*

Body page, chapter opening.

CHAPTER 1

Introduction

THIS BOOK is the story of a man's life. To relate that story as best I can, I must say something about why I was moved to try to record it. It is the life story of a highly sensitive and intelligent person who witnessed great changes in his culture as he grew to adulthood and changed himself, in fundamental ways, as he grew. While we worked together he did his best to reveal—and to justify—the personal solutions he had discovered for his problems. I had to try at the same time to distinguish between what seemed to be the objective truth and those aspects of what I was being told that were affected by the lens through which my friend was seeing his own past. This way of trying to record what really happened, or happens, is perilous because there are so many possible sources of distortion. The best one can do is to try to be aware of one's perceptual limitations, as well as of those of the informant. I have felt the need to interject myself into the story, not only to attempt to interpret what is being told but also to keep in view the limitations upon knowing the whole truth that are implicit in my role as recorder and reteller.

In January 1948 I went to Puerto Rico as a member of a group of graduate students in anthropology from Columbia University and the University of Chicago. We were to carry out community studies as part of a project organized by Julian H. Steward, under the sponsorship of the Centro de Investigaciones Sociales of the University of Puerto Rico, Columbia University, and the Rockefeller Foundation. Our aim was to select communities representative of major ways of life of the Puerto Rican people. I decided to select a community in the highly industrialized sugar cane area of the south coast. My

1

field assistant, Charles Rosario, and I settled in a small municipality named Santa Isabel and after living there for about five months we selected a rural *barrio*, or district, in which to continue our field work. This barrio seemed to us to be generally representative of rural life in the south coast area. The mayor of Santa Isabel provided us with the names of two barrio men who might help us get settled; both had helped the mayor in political campaigns.

I remember well our first serious visit to Barrio Jauca. The men we were to see were at work when we arrived, and we strolled up and down the village's single street as we waited for them to return home. People watched us curiously, and I can recall distinctly my feelings of nervousness. Though I had been doing field work for some months, my Spanish was still relatively poor. Moreover, I was a representative of something foreign—not just anything foreign, but something quite special: the United States. This area of Puerto Rico had caught the full economic impact of the United States Occupation as early as 1900. It was very poor and economically under the thumb of a single multimillion-dollar United States corporation. I was planning to live in this place for a year, to try to win the trust of the people there; I had to find out things from them, probably including some things they would hesitate to tell a friend, and some things they might never have tried to articulate. The anthropologist who remembers his first field trip will know what I mean when I say I was frightened.

The visit with our first "informant" was a failure. The name of the mayor did not provide entrée, and the man clearly wanted us to leave him as soon as possible. The interview ended in five minutes and of course left me feeling even more nervous than before. A few weeks later, after I was securely settled in Jauca, I learned that the man was a leading salesman of illegal lottery tickets. We became good friends, and he serenely sold me tickets twice a week, for nearly a year. I never won a penny.

At the house of the second man things went more smoothly. His name was Anastacio (actually, Eustaquio) Zayas Alvarado, and people called him "Don Taso." * When we mentioned the

* A full list of the major figures in this story and their identities appears on p. 279.

mayor's name, Don Taso brightened and listened attentively to our plans. If we were the mayor's friends, then everything would be all right. I wanted to live in the village? He knew a man—his nephew was married to the man's sister—in whose house I could probably live. His nephew's wife could prepare my meals. He did not seem surprised that I should want to live in Barrio Jauca, and when I told him my aim was to find out how people lived, that apparently struck him as reasonable. He did not assume, as had so many "better educated" people in town, that I was going to "improve conditions."

I recall how Taso looked that first afternoon. He was slight of build but his arms were heavily muscled and very tanned; his hands seemed almost grotesque, for he is a small-boned, delicate man, and his hands would have looked fitting on a person twice his weight and size. His face was very wrinkled; when I found out later how young he really was, I was shocked by the disparity I thought I saw between his age and his appearance. He had no teeth, and used a pair of badly fitting dentures with a lot of gold in them. He wore a white shirt—the badge of dignity of the Puerto Rican worker at rest—a rather natty but worn cream-colored fedora, shoes but no socks. We sat in the front room of his house—it was in fact a one-room house divided by partitions into four parts, with a cookhouse hung on the back—and I was able to look around as we talked. The walls were of unpainted pine and covered with pictures torn from magazines, a lithograph of San Espedito, a fragment of dried palm bent double and hooked on a nail, and many certificates marking the passage of a son from third grade to fourth or of a daughter from fifth grade to sixth. Taso's wife, Doña Elisabeth (Elí), stayed near the kitchen; she was pregnant, and held her youngest child in her arms. Children of all sizes moved quietly in and out of the house, keeping a respectful distance. We drank black coffee, heavily sweetened, out of china cups and ate soda crackers. I did not learn till later that the crackers had been sent for when we were invited into the house.

Don Taso talked freely about barrio politics, the union of sugar cane workers, work in the cane, life in the village. It was plain that he liked to talk. He managed somehow to understand my Spanish. He would rephrase my question to make it intelligible, check to see if I understood the rephrasing, and, if I did and nodded, answer it. I was struck by his ease, his intelligence, and his articulateness; it seemed to me almost immediately that he was a remarkable man.

In the following weeks, which stretched into months, and over a year, Don Taso and his family served as my main channel of contact with the people of Barrio Jauca—"the Jauqueños." As my mastery of the language and of the culture grew, I branched out more and more. I lived with Santos, and he taught me how to hoe the earth around the young cane plants. Lalo (Eladio), Taso's nephew, and his wife, Doña Pola (Hipólita), also taught and schooled me. Cheo (José), husband of Taso's niece, took me fishing for octopus and lobster. Don José Guilbé told me how people start stores in Jauca. From Aníbal, I learned about Jauca courtship. Don Gueni and Don Marcial, Don Tomás Torres and his wife Doña Enriqueta told me how things used to be in Jauca. And Roberto and Barbino and Oscar, Migdalia and Genoveva and Luz Divina, children of Jauca, showed me how to catch the tiny bivalves called *pichi pichi,* the land crabs, the mullet and crawfish that live in the irrigation ditches, how to build crab traps, and how to eat *grosellas* and *uvas del mar.* But Taso and his wife played a special role for me. I was always welcome in their house; Taso could come back from a blistering day of laying railroad ties and spend up to eight hours talking about everything that interested me, with patience, intelligence, and great passion for accuracy.

A year passed and I left Barrio Jauca to return to school and to write my dissertation. Dissertations aside, I can hardly say what I had learned during that year. Of course I learned how sugar cane is grown and cut. I learned what a modern corporate plantation is and how it operates. I learned how young people in the village fell in love and settled down and began to have children of their own. I learned some Puerto Rican songs, how to cast a throw-net, how to cook rice and beans properly. But what I regard as the bigger things I learned are hard for me to describe. In my growing friendship with Don Taso, and probably for the first time in my life, I learned to look down the corridor of time through which a man had walked. I found myself deeply stirred by what I could dimly understand. Taso, though only a few years older than I, had lived so differently, so hard, had suffered so much more, even in terms of the fundamentals of life, that knowing him and feeling his liking for me made me humble.

I had helped Taso's nephew Lalo get a job in the United States, and several months after my return to the mainland I saw him. He was flourishing in "El Norte," as the Puerto Ricans call the United States, and we had a sumptuous meal of chicken *asopao* (chicken and rice stew), pork chops, rice and beans, *viandas* (boiled starchy vegetables), and quantities of rum. When we reminisced about Barrio Jauca, Lalo told me that his uncle had become converted to the Pentecostal Church.

The news took me by surprise. Such a basic change did not seem to fit with what I thought I knew of Taso, and he had not mentioned the change in his letters to me. It is true that writing does not come easily to him, and his letters are usually no more than brief accounts of births, deaths, sickness, and the like. But I was surprised, all the same, that he had made no reference to so important an event. In my work with Taso during 1948–49 religion was one area where he had proved to be a very weak informant. Born a Catholic, he did not attend church and seemed uninterested in religious matters. He had expressed a mild contempt for the revivalist churches, and I had not intentionally disagreed with him. Unless he has some special reason, an anthropological field worker usually does not interject opinions contrary to those of his informant. But Taso was not just another informant for me, and I undoubtedly had expressed to him my own rather sour attitude toward the revivalist groups.

Now I believe that his reticence about admitting his conversion to me in a letter—for indeed he had become converted —sprang from his expectation that I would not understand, or that I might think less of him because of it. In short, Taso had not remained my informant, at least about himself; he had become my friend, as I had become his, and a wholly new element had been introduced into the relationship. So it was that I learned from Lalo that Taso had been converted, some months after the event; and soon there came a letter acknowledging the conversion. Surely Lalo had written to Taso saying he had seen me; Taso, realizing I would now know, wrote to tell me himself. "I have become converted to the Pentecostal Church of God," he wrote. "It is not true that you are tithed; one contributes what one wishes."

That was the point at which I decided to ask Taso to co-operate with me in writing down the story of his life. I saw him in the Christmas season of 1951, and he expressed eager-ness for me to return so that we might work together again. But I could not come back to Barrio Jauca until the summer of 1953. The present book is the result of our cooperation in 1953 and again in 1956, though some of the data, particularly on the village of Jauca, its history, people, and culture, come from my earlier work there.

The work Taso and I undertook together was predicated on mutual trust and esteem. I never paid Taso directly for his cooperation, nor would it have been possible to do so; we had become too good friends. And payment would have been inconsistent with Puerto Rican rural values in any case. What I was able to do was to buy occasional presents for the family and contribute toward dental care for the children, or toward house repairs. Taso trusts me enough now so that he feels free to ask for money when he is in dire need, and this is genuine evidence of the closeness we have achieved. In his own words, he would not "dare ask" if he were not sure I would respond; and my failure to do so, if it were a matter of free choice, would end our friendship. This powerful reciprocity works both ways: Taso would probably support me for an indefinite period if the need were mine.

Though we dealt with many of the most important events in Taso's life, we did so on a wholly declarative, question-and-answer basis. Some of the information that Taso supplied, it is true, came without direct questioning. But Taso's reactions

to my questions were sometimes guarded and highly discrim-
inating, even though I think he tried never to tell me anything
that was not true. The openness that marked our cooperation
sets the "pitch" or level on which the data are presented.
There was no attempt at psychoanalytic interviewing, and this
book pretends to no profound psychological interpretation.
What interpretation there is deals mainly with the society
in which Taso lives rather than with the man himself.

Taso's unusual matter-of-factness about my work in Barrio
Jauca, going back to the first day we met in 1948, was basic
to our common task. His restless and inquiring mind gets him
interested in almost anything another person may be doing.
Added to this was our friendship, and the fact that I felt it
important to set down his story. Among the circle of Taso's
friends and within his family, people simply accepted the
fact that I was continuing the work I had begun in an earlier
year, and no further explanations were necessary. People
knew that Taso and I sat down each night for hours to talk.
They were also aware that I had an electric machine that
recorded sound. Probably a few knew what we were recording.

Putting Taso's narrative in order was the most difficult
part of writing the book. When it came time to prepare the
materials for writing, I had to transcribe from wire to paper
more than five hundred typewritten pages of direct interviews.
Then I translated them into English and organized the information in them into formal categories so that I could tell
just how much there was on family life, political activity,
work, and so on. But the same materials also had to be divided according to the sequence of events in time. The data
were really being arranged on a grid, one axis being topical and
the other chronological. A substantial portion of the narrative
data could then be dropped out as minor, repetitive, or un-
certain. The remaining information, laid out chronologically,
provided the oral thread of Taso's story. For each segment of
the thread I have tried to write into the book background
material and some interpretation.

I emphasize the difficulty and the risks of this entire procedure, and the thoughtful reader will see why. The exact sequence of Taso's narration would reveal some clues to his character, but the sequence could not be entirely preserved if the final manuscript were to be read as autobiography. I believe one can learn much about Taso from reading his words as they stand. But I also want to make clear what this book is not, as well as what it is.

When Taso began describing some event with enthusiasm I tried to keep my questions to a minimum. Often, though—and sometimes unwisely—I would prod him with a new question, or even a series of questions; thus the text of the interviews varies from long uninterrupted passages to short dialogues. Although the "psychological validity" of the sequence is disturbed, I have never changed Taso's words or their meaning. Nor have I ever juxtaposed separate narrations without indicating a break. The dates of all events and the names of all localities are as accurate as I could make them. Nearly all the names of the people Taso mentions, and of course his own name, are genuine; the few minor exceptions to this were unavoidable.

Chapter 2 provides some background for the story of Taso's life: the past and the present in Barrio Jauca and what people do and think there. Chapter 3 consists of two written life-history statements which Taso prepared for me. The first, which was unsolicited, contains his comments on his life up to an arbitrary date; at a later time I asked him to carry the story forward in writing. Although these statements present a sometimes distorted and unclear picture of his life, they have been included to give the reader the flavor of Taso's own words and some idea of his own perspective on his experiences. Chapters 4, 5, and 6 present the major events in Taso's life in chronological order, though occasionally the data are not in wholly sequential form. Chapter 7 deals with the conversion, which looms as one of the most important experiences in the man's entire life. Here, as in one or two earlier chapters, I was able to use data taken from interviews with Taso's wife as well as data from interviews with him. In Chapter 8 I have tried to put the personal data on Taso into the context of his village and social group, and to suggest how he has changed as the culture around him was changing. Chapter 9 is an epilogue to Taso's story.

Taso is a superb informant in the anthropological or ethnographic sense. He is very perceptive and possesses a great capacity for examining the things about him and reflecting on them. He is cautious in his explanations, and many times when I would ask him how something was done, or what people thought about something, he would insist on telling me how *he* would do it, or how *he* thought about it. Early in our friendship I discovered after I had left the field that I had forgotten to collect an important and fairly complicated body of data from a sample of sixty informants. I asked Taso in a letter if he would try to do the job for me, and he agreed. I have saved the sheets of data he sent me; they are a model of intelligent data collection.

But Taso, all the same, makes a peculiar subject for a life history, for it is difficult for him to talk about himself for several complicated reasons. First of all, lower-class Puerto Rican males are at a disadvantage when asked how they feel about something; it is not culturally approved that they should reveal deep feelings, particularly in conversation. And so on many occasions my questions would be turned aside, often gracefully, but unanswered nonetheless. Second, Taso is revealed as a person with a great interest in maintaining restraint and control. Although such things are hard to measure, he seemed to be much less impulsive than many of his fellow Puerto Ricans and quite reserved in some ways. Thus his interviews are characterized by few slips of the tongue, few spontaneous expressions of feeling, and many half-completed sentences—where one can see him drawing back from what he was about to say. Third, there is the fact of our friendship and deep mutual regard. Very likely Taso told me many things he had never told anyone else; yet he must always have been on his guard to try to protect the image he would have me retain of him. This burden, of course, rested more heavily upon him than upon me, since it was his experiences and feelings that were being examined. All these things enter into the character of the data I have assembled, limit it, and give it one shape rather than another.

A quite refreshing contrast is provided by Taso's wife. Doña Elí served as my informant for only several hours' worth of material, but I feel these data are enormously valuable. I would have liked ideally to have spent as much time with Elí as with her husband. Elí, rather than being taught by her culture to suppress the expression of her feelings, is motivated to bare them; women are expectably "more emotional" in her group. But as with Taso, I do not feel Elí's manner is merely a reflection of the culture's values. Elí *likes* to express feeling and likes to suggest that forces move in her and about her over which she can exercise little control. Moreover, Elí is unsophisticated about what she recounts, and the meaning of the word is very clear here: she ignores or is unaware of secondary meanings, of the listener's capacities for inference, of the significance of association, and of the exposure of motives through symbols. Elí, describing to me some important personal experience over the hum of the recording machine, soon forgot that her narration was being recorded in permanent form. I doubt that Taso ever really forgot. So from some points of view Elí would actually have been a richer subject for a life history than her husband. Be that as it may, I have tried to use what both of them gave me to construct this story.

Though Taso and I worked intensively together, night after night, for several successive months in 1953 and 1956, and irregularly over the years, his story remains quite incomplete. This is not only because much of what I learned has no place here but also because there is much living still in store for Taso. Unlike most subjects for life histories, he is a relatively young man. I selected him for this task because he was my good friend and trusted me; because he seemed to possess a rare native brilliance and articulateness; and because the events in his life, particularly his conversion, seemed to be dramatic. But, as I say, the story is not all told. The narrative really ends with the year 1949, and a lot has happened to him even since then.

Certain things Taso and Elí taught me are true, no matter what may have been missed or distorted and no matter what happens to them now. As Taso revealed what he could of his life and how he tried to make sense of it, I became newly aware that most people in the world today still live and die without fulfillment. At the same time they are so muted by inexorable circumstance that the more fortunate of us are rarely compelled even for one moment to reflect upon the toll. And yet these human beings are not so thwarted as it might seem. They make do with what they have, and at times they can manifest a nobility and courage that I am awed by.

Taso is such a person. He is not an "average" anything— neither an average man, nor an average Puerto Rican, nor an average Puerto Rican lower-class sugar cane worker. He has lived just one life and not all of that. He doesn't think of himself as representative of anything, and he is right. His solutions to life's problems may not be the best ones, either, but he seems satisfied with his choices. I have tried to put down his story in the context of what I could understand about the circumstances under which he lived and lives.

CHAPTER 2

The Local Setting

FROM THE AIR, the narrow coastal plain of southern Puerto Rico looks like an irregular green ribbon. It contrasts sharply with the blues and azures of the sea to the south, and with the sere vegetation of the uplands to the north. The plain itself is covered with sugar cane. A road cuts through the cane, paralleling the sea, and linking towns along the coast. Most of the people live in rural areas rather than in the towns: in shacks that hug the shoulders of the road or stretch around the bays and inlets; in barracks and houses around the plazas of the old-time sugar haciendas; or in company towns built up near the monster cane-grinding mills. The mills are the most conspicuous landmarks from the air: their chimneys cast long shadows over the shacks and across the cane. From the air, the workers' shacks look regular and neat. There is a picturesqueness about the thatched roofs, the waving palms, and the nearness of the sea.

But walking through a village destroys such impressions. The ground is pounded hard and dusty, littered with tin cans, paper, coconut husks, and cane trash. The houses are patched with old Coca Cola signs, boards torn from packing cases, and cardboard. Only a few are painted. The seeming order dissolves into disorder and crowding. Large families are packed into tight living places. The houses are variously divided into two, three, or more sections by partitions which never reach the ceiling. The cooking is done in ramshackle lean-tos behind the living quarters. And all around the houses grows the cane.

Such a village is Jauca. The barrio called Jauca contains clusters of houses, some on the edge of the sea, some along the

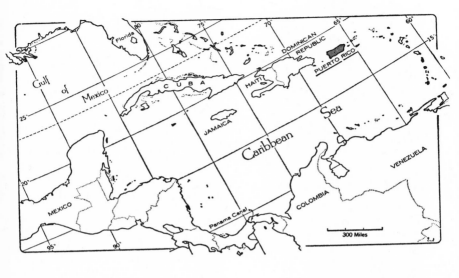

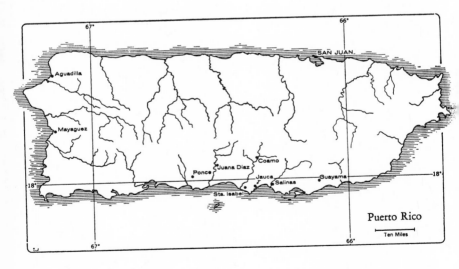

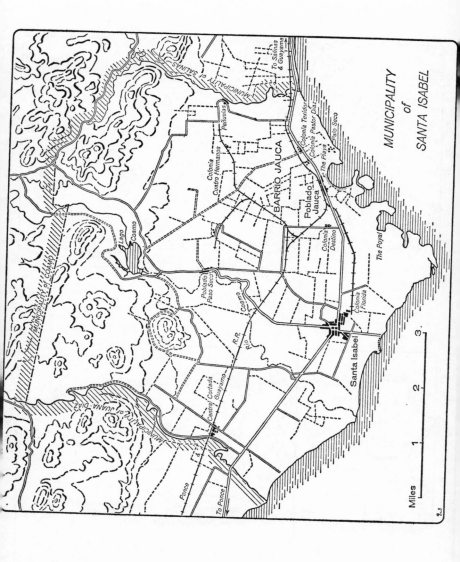

MUNICIPALITY
of
SANTA ISABEL

MUNICIPALITY of SALINAS

MUNICIPALITY of COAMO

MUNICIPALITY of JUANA-DIAZ

Peñuelas

Colonia
Cuatro Hermanos

Colonia Texidor
Colonia Pastor Díaz

BARRIO JAUCA

Poblado
Jauca

The Playa

Palo Seco

Lago
Coamo

Poblado
Paso Seco

Colonia
Destino

Rio
Coamo

R.R.

Santa Isabel

Colonia
Florida

The Poyal

Central Cortada
Guayama

Ponce
&

To Ponce

To Salinas
& Guayama

Miles   1   2   3

9.1

east-west highway, and others bunched around the centers of the *colonias*—the great farms of the corporations which control over 95 per cent of all the cultivated land in the municipality. In Barrio Jauca the largest aggregation of houses is along the highway; this village is called Poblado Jauca. The nearest large groupings are at the beach to the south and to the northwest near the plaza of the largest colonia in the barrio, Colonia Destino. There is a company store at Colonia Destino; 36 little two-room shacks provided rent free by the corporation to resident workers; a two-story house for the *mayordomo*, or overseer; two barracks left from slavery times and still occupied; and the ruined shell of the hacienda warehouse, now used to store machinery and fertilizer. The only trees in view are some palms growing near a point on the beach, the twin rows of tamarinds which line the approach to Colonia Destino, and a few scattered fruit trees among the houses of Poblado Jauca.

Poblado Jauca consists of a string of shacks lining the highway, and a substantial cluster of additional houses—on an acre plot of land called Palmas Orillanas—which extend from the road southward toward the sea. There are fewer than a dozen small stores and bars, two school buildings, and, at one end of the village, the crumbling mill and chimney of an old sugar hacienda. The village has standpipes along the road to supply its water, many of the houses are electrified, and the road which connects the village to the towns of Santa Isabel to the west and Salinas to the east is well surfaced. In its outward appearance, Poblado Jauca does not differ significantly from hundreds of other such "line" villages in the sugar areas of Puerto Rico.

At five o'clock in the morning Poblado Jauca is still and deserted-looking. An occasional touring car goes by on the coast road carrying passengers from Ponce to San Juan. The roosters crow and the dogs bark and the surf sounds softly. Every shack is shut tightly—the wooden shutters of the windows closed against the "night air," the doors barred. The cookhouses behind the shacks are cold; the sun is still low. An easterly breeze stirs the cane, rattles the Coca Cola signs, shakes loose a ripe nut in the palm grove near the water.

But by six o'clock the village comes to life. The first signs are the swinging back of the shutters that give on the back yard and the tendrils of smoke curling out of the stoves. The first need of the morning is food: the food, coffee. In the early morning the air has a deceptive chilly freshness. Everything is coolly damp and stimulating. In less than an hour the entire quality of the morning is transformed. By the time the men have drunk their coffee, tied their cuffs to their ankles with cords, and picked up machetes or hoes and the food for the midmorning breakfast, the sun is high and glittering; it weighs on the skin like something tangible, burns away the dampness from every surface, almost crackles as it grows hotter. The men leave the houses, carrying their breakfasts and tools and dressed in rough work clothes, wide-brimmed straw hats, and old shoes. They go to "defend themselves" (*se defienden*) in the cane, which is their phrase for the struggle of making a living. These men have lived with the cane, most of them, from the time they were born. It grows up to the edges of the house plots. When it is in full glory it stands fifteen feet high, and the villages are choked in it. It litters the roads; during harvest the smell of it fills the air, the "hair" of its surface works into the skin like peach fuzz. Men who work in the cane speak of "doing battle" (*bregando*) with it.

From the thatch shacks along the beach, from the wooden ones along the highway, the men move toward the plazas of the old haciendas to get their work orders for the day. Some will form the cutting lines; others will lay rails for the wagons that are loaded in the fields or will do the loading. There are cultivators and seeders, seed cutters and winch operators, ditchers and gang bosses. Most of the jobs can be done by nearly everyone, but individual workers have preferences and some have special skills. Old Don Tomás, like many of the oldest Negro people in the barrio, is a *palero*—a ditcher—the most skilled, the highest-paid, and the most prestigeful "dirt" job in the fields. The cutters come mainly from the shacks at the beach; they are white men, most of them named De Jesús, whose families migrated to the coast from nearby highlands.

The De Jesús are set somewhat apart by other Jauqueños. Some of them take their Catholicism seriously and go to church; they try to grow little vegetable gardens at the beach, and they fence their houses; they "marry cousin with cousin"; and unlike the old coastal working families, they prefer cane cutting on a piecework basis to most other jobs. Aníbal and Fredo are truck drivers; they were in the Army, and learned some skills there most Jauqueños, and especially the older ones, could never acquire. Truck driving pays relatively well and it is easy work compared to cutting or loading. Don Daniel likes to plant seed. It is a curious choice, for Don Daniel is very tall and seeding requires that one bend over continuously, setting and tapping the seed—which is not seed at all, but cuttings of cane stalk—into place.

By seven o'clock those who have work are out of the village. The children eat and start for school, or begin their jobs at home—toting pails of water, mopping the floors, tending the baby, ironing—or play in the yards with toys made of old tin cans and bits of wood. As the sun climbs, each woman begins to prepare the hot lunch which must be carried out to her man in the fields, no matter how far away he may be working. No Puerto Rican cane worker will settle for a cold midday meal. At nine o'clock he has his thermos of black coffee and a piece of bread smeared with margarine or topped with a slice of cheese or sausage—he feels it gives him the strength he needs to work till noon—but at noon someone must bring him a hot luncheon. Nests of pots hung on wire frames are the lunchboxes of the Puerto Rican countryside. Sometimes the pots hold noodle soup, or a quantity of starches such as boiled green bananas, taro, yams, and Irish potatoes; fish broths, cornmeal cakes, and salads mixed with bits of boiled salt cod are common. But no matter what else, one tin container is always full of rice, another of red or white beans in a mild sauce. Rice and beans are the staple of the lower-class Puerto Rican.

After lunch the cane workers pick up their machetes once more. Back home the wives are busy with the laundry. They scrub the clothes on washboards, remove stubborn dirt with scrapers fashioned from coconut shell, and hang the clean clothes on fences or stretch them over pieces of corrugated iron to dry. Then water is boiled for the afternoon coffee, and the youngest children must be bathed and dressed to await their fathers' return. By three or four o'clock the men have all returned, and the heat of the day has begun to abate slightly. The men bathe, crouching over the washtubs in the cookhouses or in showers fed from hand-filled tanks if they have them. It is in the late afternoon that the social life of the day begins. Men shave after their afternoon baths; young girls and boys put on their good clothes; the radios loudly announce the baseball scores, carry political discussions or Puerto Rican and other Latin American music.

Dinner is not eaten by the whole family seated at a table, but by each family member independently, down to the littlest, during a two-hour period. The father sits at the table and is served by his wife, who hovers about him, often with her youngest child in her arms. Again rice and beans and black coffee are the core of the meal, but there may also be cornmeal slabs in fish broth; or stewed goat or beef; or boiled salt cod. Children eat standing in the kitchen, or sitting in the yard and feeding the chickens from their spoons. The dogs and the chickens scour the floors and yards and follow the housewife about with friendly but cautious importunacy.

After dinner the street becomes the setting for conversation and flirting. Loafing groups gather in front of the small stores or in the yards of older men, where they squat and gossip; marriageable boys and girls promenade along the highway. Small groups form and dissolve in the bars. The women remain home; married couples rarely walk together, usually only on their way to revivalist prayer meetings. The more worldly young men—who have probably served in the Army and have a little money—may hail passing public cars and go to the movies in the nearby towns, or to see girls in neighboring villages. If it is a Tuesday or a Saturday night, illegal numbers-game sellers will be making their rounds, collecting bets placed on credit at an earlier time. The winning numbers (which are based on the winning numbers in the national *legal* lottery) will be announced the next morning over the radio, and nearly everyone in the village, knowing the favorite numbers of their fellows, will know who has won.

By nine o'clock—unless it is a Saturday—Jauca has grown quiet. Activity continues within the houses, the stores, and the Pentecostal chapel. Youths may prepare to hunt octopus and lobster on the cays, while their younger brothers are catching crabs in the cane fields, along the irrigation ditches. Couples in love say their good nights in the shadows. By ten even the stores are closed; one bar or two may still be open. The Pentecostals come home from their services. Only if there is a wake, a local political meeting, or a fight will activity continue outside the houses. The surf, scarcely noticeable during the noise of the day, can be heard again after ten o'clock, and the dogs and roosters vie with the gentle little croaking frogs—the *coquí*—in breaking the night's stillness.

During the course of the week the character of a day's activity varies. Saturdays are paydays, and Saturday nights are special. The nickelodeons play late into the night, and many people of all ages dance. Old Tomás Famanía, who has all his teeth and walks straight, though he carries a cane of *frescura* with a brass tip, and glories in his more than sixty years, comes up from his thatched shack at the beach to dance. He usually picks rumbas, and his partners will be Ceferino Hernández' daughters and granddaughters, none of them more than eight years old. The bachelors stand at the bar drinking their rum neat—each drink downed in a swallow from a tiny paper cup. The more affluent buy half pints of rum (called "Shirleys" after Shirley Temple) and finish them sitting at the tables. The teen-age males play pool on the much-ripped table in Cheo's bar and watch the girls walk by. Sometimes the barbecue pit at Cheo's will be going. A youth will crouch by the bed of hot charcoal, casually turning the long pole on which a whole pig is impaled.

On Saturday evenings during harvest the front doors of the houses are open. One can peer in to see the dimly lighted "parlor," which is separated from the "dining room" by a low wooden partition. There is the mother with one child nursing, another sleeping in her lap, a third perhaps drowsing at her feet or pulling at her skirt. The grandmother may be visiting, rocking in a chair, sometimes smoking a cigar. Conversation is animated and humorous: Don Fonso had to chase his mare two miles tonight down the main road; Barbino has nearly worn out the record called *Vuelve* (Return) at the bar, because his girl friend Wilma is leaving for "El Norte"; Don Fico hit on the *bolita* (numbers game) for $2,300 last Sunday; there is an elopement expected, or a revival meeting; how long will the *zafra* (harvest) last? The father returns from his visit to a *compadre* (godparent of one of his children) and greets his mother-in-law with respect and care. A man must maintain very good (but circumspect) relations with his mother-in-law. The children, those still awake, cling to him. He may put them to sleep by rocking and fondling them as the hours pass. When the front door is closed and the shutters are swung to, it is time for the parents to go to bed. One teen-age son may still be abroad; he will creep in after the house is dark, feast on the cold rice-and-bean leftovers from dinner, and crawl into bed, often alongside two or three brothers. And the bed may be a folding cot.

Sundays are quieter than weekdays, as Saturdays are noisier. The Pentecostal church has its day and its night services. Older people dress up on Sunday, though very few ever go to church. In the summer townspeople come to swim at the Jauca beach, to sit under the palms and drink soda or coconut water. Passing cars may stop in Jauca—a merchant or salesman seeks to purchase a dozen succulent land crabs to take home to San Juan. Jauqueños wander down to the beach to watch the townsmen swim. These are a different sort of people. They are not explicit about how they regard each other, but town and country are not quite the same, and the townsmen who come to swim or to buy crabs are not merely cane cutters who may live in town but storekeepers, civil servants, and teachers. And, parenthetically, it is not their color that sets them apart but their class.

Just as Saturday and Sunday differ from weekdays, so the harvest time differs from *el tiempo muerto*—dead time. From

Christmas until early summer the cane is cut, and much cane is planted. The fields are alive with activity. Long lines of men stand before the cane like soldiers before an enemy. The machetes sweep down and across the stalks, cutting them close to the ground. The leaves are lopped off, the stalk cut in halves or thirds and dropped behind. It is a beautiful thing to watch from a hundred yards' distance. The men seem tiny but implacable, moving steadily against a green forest which recedes before them. When the cane has been piled and then scooped up, either by men who load it on carts brought into the fields on movable tracks, or by the new *arañas* (spiders), machines that load it on rubber-wheeled carts, the oxen may graze among the trash. And soon the field may be cleared for planting a new crop, which will be sprouting within weeks of the harvest.

From a distance, the scene is toylike and wholesome. Up close it is neither. The men sweat freely; the cane chokes off the breeze, and the pace of cutting is awesome. The men's shirts hang loose and drip sweat continuously. The hair of the cane pierces the skin and works its way down the neck. The ground is furrowed and makes footing difficult, and the soil gives off heat like an oven. The mayordomo sits astride a roan mare and supervises the field operations. He wears khakis and cordovan riding accessories. To see him ride past a line of men bent over and dripping sweat, to hear the sounds of the oxen in the fields behind, the human and animal grunting, and to feel the waves of heat billowing out of the ground and cane evoke images of other times. The men of Jauca grow drawn in the first two weeks of the harvest. This is the time to make the money to pay debts from the past dead time and to prepare for the next. It is a way of life that can make menial jobs in the continental United States seem like sinecures.

When the cane is entirely cut the intense activity ceases. The last trainload of cane, from the westernmost plantations serviced by the Machete and Aguirre mills, is pulled through Jauca by the little engine to the accompaniment of an unceasing whistling. The train is crying; the next day the whistles of Machete and Aguirre will cry. And then, people joke sourly, the people will cry. The nickelodeons play less. The drinkers of bottled rum turn back to *cañita*—"the little cane," the illegal white rum. Don Tomás has no more dancing partners, because there are fewer nickels. The little account books each Puerto Rican family has for its food purchases begin to carry more unpaid entries. *Fia'o*—credit—gets extended two weeks instead of one, or four instead of two. Back before World War II, when Puerto Rico was much poorer, dead time was marked by a sharp increase in infant mortality, supposedly from a disease diagnosed as gastroenteritis; the correlation with the cessation of income does not seem to have been a coincidence.

In dead time one hears more reminiscence, there is more fishing, the ways to turn an extra penny are given more thought. Around the houses one notices little treasures that were overlooked before because they mean much less during the harvest: the bedraggled chickens, a melancholy goat, perhaps even a duck. There is a lime tree behind Don Cosme's house, and it will yield large quantities of lime drink. And if coffee is really short, one can brew *hedionda*, which grows all over. Headache powders may be better, but some headaches do pass if you crush a leaf of *naranja*, dip it in oil, and press it to the brow. Cheo has a hive of bees; and if one has a compadre who is a fisherman, he may make a present of the *carey* (turtle meat) that he could not sell or use this morning. A little cornmeal will make the land crabs fatter, and one's sons keep the crab traps going throughout the rainy season. The land is crowded with the growing cane and the yards are dry and sterile, but there is a tree here and a bush there, one hen still is laying, and octopuses live in the rocks of the cay. Everything belongs to Corporation Aguirre, it seems; but there is a little left that belongs to the people.

The feast day of the patron saint of Santa Isabel—who is not Saint Elizabeth, despite the town's name, but Santiago Apóstol—comes in the summer, at a time when money is scarce. (Some wags have suggested that the town fathers should pick a new saint, preferably one whose birth may be commemorated during the harvest.) In October and November there is some work in the fields, for this is the planting period for the *gran cultura* (big growth) cane, which is allowed to stand fifteen or even eighteen months before it is cut. Some Novembers there are elections. The baseball season gets into swing. And when Christmas comes, the harvest is near once more. The year begins and ends with the swish of the machetes.

The round of life varies also with exceptional happenings, natural and man-made: elections, hurricanes, war. Yet the outside observer who will stay and watch long enough gets a strong feeling of continuity, stability, fulfilled expectation. A full year of watching reveals the circle of events. But it is only in looking at the history of a village like Jauca, and at the individual histories of its people, that one may see the tremendous changes in local life over the past half century. The lives of people and the life of the community unwind backward through time: the village gets a tarred road, its first car; standpipes replace the stagnant surface well. People are born, grow up, marry, have children. They learn to use a machete while they are still toddling, to pick medicinal plants and to catch land crabs in their early childhood, to cut the cane or to do the family cooking while in their teens. The village grows "modern": the people get electric lights and radios.

Since history is, among other things, the accumulation of ideas and objects over time, it is not surprising that in the life of Barrio Jauca one can see Puerto Rican history revealed. Puerto Rico was one of Spain's first New World colonies. It was inhabited by American Indians at the time of contact, and this part of the island background lives on in the faces of Jauca people and in place names and the names for some plants and objects. Well within the confines of Barrio Jauca there is a sugar cane field where aboriginal pottery sherds can be turned up with one's heel.

The island became Spanish late in the fifteenth century, and remained so until the American Occupation in 1898–99. The early history of Spanish rule of Puerto Rico—then known as San Juan Bautista—was marked by vigorous colonization and the rapid decimation of the Indian population in gold-mining enterprises. But by the middle of the sixteenth century, Spanish interest in Puerto Rico and the other Antilles had declined. The attraction of the Andean and highland Mexican areas had overshadowed the islands, and from then until the start of the nineteenth century Puerto Rico remained largely cut off from the currents of trade and empire of the Western world. As the nineteenth century opened, Puerto Rico once more was subject to rapid growth. Spain's strength had diminished and her New World colonies were beginning to slip away.

In the first decades of the nineteenth century the Crown made efforts to encourage the development of new enterprises in Puerto Rico, and the sugar economy in particular received strong support. The south coast of the island felt this impetus directly. Literally hundreds of small new sugar haciendas were founded, and both slavery and legal coercion of the landless were used to push up production. These haciendas created a particular social tradition. They were owned by single families, resident in nearby towns or on the haciendas themselves. Though they produced a world-market crop, they were largely self-contained, with their own food-producing land, their resident slaves and forced laborers, and their own social structures. Such "family-type" haciendas took on a characteristic shape in the first decades of the nineteenth century which was preserved largely intact until the American Occupation. It was marked by sharp divisions between owners and managerial staffs on the one hand and workers on the other. Relationships were paternalistic and arbitrary from the top down, submissive and deferential from the bottom upward.

Though these haciendas were capitalistic enterprises they had many features more commonly associated with non-capitalistic industrial structure: forced labor, little use of cash, traditional and conventional bases for behavior, distinctions based on inherited rank, and so on. Again, though they were capitalistic economically, the family-type haciendas were not expansive. Little wealth was ever invested in expanding or intensifying production, new mechanical devices were rarely introduced, and the owner or *hacendado* was usually content to live on whatever profit his enterprise brought him. By the later decades of the nineteenth century the Puerto Rican sugar hacienda was becoming more and more outmoded as a productive unit. The end of slavery and forced labor in 1873 may have hastened the deterioration. By the 1880's many of these haciendas had gone out of production, and some had become cattle farms or ranches.

When the American Occupation took place sugar was no longer Puerto Rico's main crop. But then American capital flowed heavily into the sugar industry and transformed it completely. This process was especially marked in the south coast region. Great grinding mills—*centrales*—were built, and the lands of scores of small haciendas were bought up to form the "farms" of such mills. These new centrales were very modern in economic and industrial organization, enormous in scale, and a symbol of the kinds of changes in Puerto Rican life wrought by the Americans. The hacendado class of the south coast, as elsewhere in the island, sold out its holdings to the Americans and moved away. The towns and the countryside thus lost most of their educated middle- and upper-class citizens, and the hacienda shells became pure worker villages.

This transformation was accomplished at a high human cost. Though the United States government introduced many beneficial measures in Puerto Rican life, the private sugar interests did at least as much harm as good. Political activity was sternly suppressed on the plantations by coercion, blacklisting, and economic control of workers through company stores and company housing. The traditional standards of work were replaced by piecework and labor recruiting, and some of the related practices were unpardonably harsh. Puerto Rico thus became one of the few examples of clear-cut American colonialism, unhidden by nominal political sovereignty for the colony.

In the 1930's and 1940's the picture changed sharply once more. The wave of new thinking which marked American political life in that period was strongly felt in Puerto Rico and was synthesized with local political developments. The

Partido Popular Democrático, a kind of New Deal party, came to power in the 1940's, and successfully challenged and limited the power of the sugar corporations. The Popular party also introduced the notion of sponsored industrial development, and in the intervening years it has significantly bettered the position of the Puerto Rican economy and of the average Puerto Rican workingman.

So very much has been written of the past twenty years of the island's history that it is hardly necessary to examine this period in detail here. But it must be noted that Taso's life spans the years immediately after the American Occupation to the recent past. His society and culture were in rapid flux during the very years he was growing to manhood. The large changes in Puerto Rican life and in the relationships of Puerto Rico to the United States were impinging daily upon his consciousness and upon that of his neighbors. From older people Taso learned what life was like before the Americans came; in his childhood he saw the immediate effects of the Occupation; and in his youth and maturity he played his own role in the change.

The changes of the past fifty years seem slow in the eyes of one man, until he looks back to childhood and sets his recollections alongside his life today. When I first went to Jauca it was the history of the village and the relation of that history to the present which I tried to understand. When I went back it was to try to follow the thread of a single man's existence in the fabric of village history. Except for a short period in his early manhood, Taso lived his experiences within the narrow compass of Barrio Jauca, where he was born. The barrio defines what might be called his life-space, though it never became the limit of his horizons until he reached middle age. His is the story of a man who learns that he must accept a finite environment, like a finite personal history, even while the boundaries of inner experience may approach infinity.

CHAPTER 3

Taso's Written Autobiographical Statements

"IN THE YEAR 1908, at the age of ten months, I was left fatherless with my mother, one sister, and two brothers."

Thus begins the life history of Eustaquio Zayas Alvarado. When I started to collect Taso's life history in the summer of 1953, I asked him first simply to tell me the story of his life as he remembered it. He asked for time to think about it, and I did not turn on the recording machine that first night. The following evening when we sat down together again, he produced from his pocket several sheets of lined paper, torn from a child's notebook, on which he had written down his story. Though few events in his written text were dated, I could establish that it covered a period from his birth (1908) up to 1945. So the formal gathering of the data on Taso's life began with a written statement, and the life history begins with it here.

In 1956 when I returned to Jauca to check for inaccuracies in the information I had already gathered, I asked Taso first of all if he would write down the remainder of his story, to cover the years 1945–56. I wanted him to do this, if possible, before we discussed anything else, to permit him again to select in his own mind those events which ought to be mentioned for these later years. Again he asked for a day to think about it, and once more he produced a brief written statement.

The first statement runs to about 850 words; the second is about 780 words long. I think they are probably the longest things Taso has ever written. Although the story is ragged, the emphases unexpected, and the continuity almost imperceptible at times to the reader, I have chosen to include the statements here as they stand. Granting all the limitations implicit in the task I posed for Taso, the texts are as purely expressive of the man and his retrospect as anything that came out of our work together. The events referred to take on meaning and continuity as the later interviews give depth and detail.

The reader may note that the second statement is more concerned with dating events. I believe this was not only because the period covered was more easily recalled but also because of my insistence on chronology during our 1953 work. The second statement seems rather more self-conscious than the first. Though we had not worked together for nearly three full years, my constant probings during the summer of 1953 may have had their effect. Yet the second statement, almost as much as the first, is marked by a curious running-together of events, some of them deeply serious, others seemingly trivial. Occasionally, as later chapters reveal, life-and-death problems are ignored altogether or referred to in understatement.

These are documents written by a man unused to writing, and particularly unused to writing of those events, sentiments, and emotions which are close to one's self. Taso, if he needs to express some fundamental idea or feeling, does so most spontaneously by acting; only rarely would he do it by speaking; and by writing, never. These are the words of the man himself, picking and choosing items out of more than half a lifetime of living that he regards as worthy of record. There is much more he will say before even this part of his story is told. These are its beginnings.

In the year 1908, at the age of ten months, I was left fatherless with my mother, one sister, and two brothers. Later on my older brother went to the town of Guayama. At that time my mother was working sewing clothes, washing, and ironing to make a living. At the age of about eight years I began working, earning thirty cents [a day]. Then my mother sent me to school, and in order to be able to get to the fourth grade I had to go to school for about five or six years. What would happen was, I used to have to quit school because of the economic situation. I would usually go to school half of the day and the other half of the day I'd be working. Yet I was never able to finish the fourth grade. Later, my sister married and my other brother left home, and we remained alone, Mama and I. Then my sister came back home; she separated from her husband. Right away she went and got married again; and again my mother and I were alone. Around 1920, my mother died. Then I went to live with my sister and my brother-in-law. By that time my sister had two children already, Rosaura [Rosa] the older and Eladio [Lalo] the younger. Then in about three or four years, more or less, my sister became pregnant again, and she died as a consequence of that birth. And there remained the two of us along with the three infants. At that time my brother-in-law was an irrigation foreman in the cane, and I was working with him. We took the smallest infant, the one to which Tomasa gave birth before she died, to a lady to take care of, and we used to pay for this. And we had to carry the other two to work and put them somewhere nearby until the afternoon, when we returned to the house. After, my brother-in-law began to board at someone's house; but not I. About two weeks later, we were coming home from a burial and he invited me to eat where he was eating and I went with him. Then the lady of the house and her husband told me that if I wanted, they would make meals [for me, too]. I accepted, and I began paying $1.50 [a week]. But when I saw how they treated me, I always paid more after. Soon they invited me to live in their house, and I went. Then I had great relief because they did everything for me in the house. And I was with them a long time, until I became a young man. Later on, though, I fell in love with the wife I have today, and I began another, different life. Then I went to live with my wife in her mother's house. At the time I was working in Colonia Cuatro Hermanos, about three kilometers from here. Then my wife's mother bought us a little house of the flat-roofed type, which was on the land of another person who was not the owner of the house. I improved the house; but later on I had to take it apart because they wanted me to pay an amount for [the use of] the lot which was more than the house was worth. So I returned again to the house of my wife's mother until I was able to get a lot where I could put up the house. And I had to wait a long time because no one wanted to rent lots. Then a boy who grew up with me told me I should speak with his mother to see if she might rent me a lot. I went, and after a great effort and with the help of my friend, I got the lot. Then my wife's father, who was a carpenter, began to build the house. It turned out that we needed [material for] a wall because we made the house bigger. Then I went to a friend of mine and borrowed $15, and I bought the lumber and finished the house. By that time my wife already had two children and was pregnant with another. When that one was born, my wife had a serious illness—for four days she knew no one, and we watched over her day and night. Dr. Vélez told me that she would not live. Yet after four days she recovered from that illness. At that time I was working on the railroad; I earned $5.10 weekly. By then, I had been given $43 credit in the store in which I traded, and I went along paying it off out of that same $5.10, and with [the sale of] some animals we were raising. At that time my brother-in-law, the father of Rosaura and Eladio, was located in Aguadilla, and I thought to go there to improve [my situation]. While I was there I received a letter from Guayama from my older brother, saying that his wife had died and that he was ill. Then I went to Guayama and took him [back with me] to Aguadilla. But there it was worse. At that time a man was earning only 50 cents [a day] in Aguadilla, and I decided to return to my house [i.e. to Barrio Jauca] again. My brother was already well and he went back to Guayama again. Then my wife got sick again and her mother told me to move my house to the lot where her house was, so that she would be able to attend to her. I would work during the day and when I came home I worked moving the house, until at last I finished.

The 1932 political campaign approached. Because I was a

Socialist they left me without work and at that time I suffered a lot. I had been working in the campaign but I did not get any protection from them [the Socialist party]. After, I returned to work at Colonia Destino. During all those times they were working by piecework on the colonias. If one agreed to a quantity of work for $1.50, and the work turned out badly so that you had to spend a whole week on it, then what you earned for the week was $1.50. Because of family differences I resolved to seek a place to which to move my house again. I went to the mayor and solicited a lot that the municipality had in the barrio. It was one single lot and there were two requests. Then we agreed to divide it between the two of us, and we did. And here I am, in the midst of so many inconveniences and fights, raising my family—my wife, and I, and our eight children.

Here is the second written statement.

Around 1945 they had already begun to eliminate the system of irrigation which had been used before in Colonia Destino—that is, making *maclaines* [irrigation cross channels] and irrigation ditches [by hand]. It was changed for a system that they call "oil-line." They used machines for this new system; and so our work was finished, it was reduced to almost nothing. Then there arose certain differences in the CGT union [Confederación General de Trabajadores], and in 1946 they set up the independent union here, in which I worked as treasurer of the Barrio Jauca subcommittee. Later, that [union] failed, too. On July 18, 1946, I began working [again] on the railway brigade. During the year 1945 I had had many difficulties with Carmen and Pablín [his oldest children] and their schooling, and they lost a whole year of school for lack of teachers. In the following year Pablín wanted to continue going to school but Carmen didn't. At the time one didn't have to worry about the money for trips to school because there was a bus that used to come to get the children. But later on they stopped the bus and then one had to pay travel costs so that the children would be able to go to school in town.

At that time we had seven men in the railway brigade. At the end of the harvest of 1947–48, they [the corporation] ordered that only five men be kept on the brigade. At that time Elí was reaching the end of her pregnancy with Anastacia, which was going to mean a pretty bad situation for me. They also ordered that the men go to work only four days—that is, twenty day-salaries per week. Then I claimed that they should give me [work] also out of those twenty day-salaries. And they did it that way. When Elí began labor to bear Anastacia I had to get a public car to go to look for the midwife whom they call Fermina, at the Quinta [quarters] of Colonia Alomar. I did not find her there and I had to go to the beach of Santa Isabel [to find her]. I brought her back with me, and Elí had a pretty good delivery. Already at that time [1948] the political campaign was on, and certain differences arose in the matter of the slate [of Popular party candidates] and they held some meetings which were rather tumultuous. But everything came out all right. At that time we had bought a little bicycle for Pablín, who was continuing with school in town, from a cousin of Pablín's who had sent it from San Francisco.

Around the end of 1950 Elí decided to make a profession of faith [i.e. be converted to the Pentecostal Church], and after, I [was converted] too. But Blanca had done so before anyone else. Things went along, and in the year 1952 Pablín was graduated [from high school]. At that point I had to get together the help of Alejandro, my half brother by our father, and Cheo [Rosa's husband], and my own efforts to buy a suit and the other things for the graduation. Then Pablín was at home not doing anything. Later, there was an opportunity to work and he worked about four or five weeks. With what he earned he bought Elí a stove and some other things. Then once again he had nothing to do, and he secretly sent to ask travel money from Lalo to emigrate, and when Elí found out she had a nervous attack such that he [decided he] did not want to leave. He did want to go on studying, but it was

1. Don Taso

2. Doña Elí

3. Taso and Elí with five of their ten living children

En el Año 1908 a la edad de
10 meses. quedo huerfano con
mi mamá, una hermana mujer.
y dos Varones luego despues. mi
hermano mayor se fué al pueblo
de Guayama Tara ese entonces y
mi mamá trabajaba lociendo
ropa, lavando y aplanchando
Tara las necesidades de nosotros
y ella; Como a la edad de 8
años empese a trabajar Guanando
30 centavos entonces mi
mamá me apunto de la
escuela, y para Juedo llegar
hasta el cuarto Grado estuve
yendo a la escuela mas o meno
de 5 a 6 años, puque Casi

impossible. I could not pay the costs. Then Cheo sent him to the Percy [Secretarial] School [in Ponce] to take a course. Before he could finish, the Army called him, May 13, 1953. At that time my niece Rosa had emigrated, and Cheo had the bad luck of getting sick with the chicken pox and he was hospitalized at San Lucas [Hospital, in Ponce]. Then I moved from my house to theirs to look after the store and the house. Later Cheo came out and we moved back to the house again. And in 1953 Noél was born. For that delivery a brother in the faith, Benjamín, was the one who went to find the midwife. At that time there was none in the barrio, and he brought her from Paso Seco. When Pablín set out for Korea, afterward he sent Elí from there $65 a month with which we added two rooms to the house, because we were already quite uncomfortable. But that was a sad period in the house for the lack of him.

In this period of time, from the year 1945 till today, I have lived more tranquilly. Although during this time I suffered twice from a sickness which at the outset seemed dangerous, it was only a simple infection of a gland in the prostate. And regarding my situation now, it is much better. For example, Carmen sews and from what she earns she buys clothes for the [younger] children and at times she buys them for Blanca, and even for us ourselves. Also Pablín at times helps out. In those other [earlier] years they were not able to help me and I had to supply everything. And regarding the benefits of the church, I am very appreciative. For example, my girls are at home and even the littlest ones are being taught good precepts, to keep them far from juvenile delinquency, and to have respect for God. So that all this has come to be a great help to me. I feel more serene. I do not live a life as desperate as it was in the years before. And also, I earn a little more. In short any problem I have now I can resolve better.

These statements raise many questions. The individuals to whom Taso refers, the half-explained events, the jobs held and lost, the place names, politics, union activities, religion, children—as Taso elaborates his story in later chapters these

things become more significant and familiar. Many of the
basic events are immediately understandable. But he refers
only in passing to his conversion, and this event emerges as
of profound importance in the later interviews. He says hardly
anything of the children, except to mention their problems in
school and the help they come to give him. Again, it turns out
that the children—nine living, three dead—are of crucial emotional importance to him. And there is very little about his
wife, with whom he has worked out a highly successful relationship at the cost of great suffering to them both. These
are all things Taso deals with in later talks. They are highly
personal matters, the stuff of one man's life. At this point, the
lens through which they may be examined increases in magni-
fication and narrows in scope.

CHAPTER 4

Childhood and Adolescence

MY MOTHER was originally from the town of Juana Díaz. I don't know what town my father came from. Nor can I tell you anything about their families. When I was ten months old my father was drowned. Then I remained with Mama, but soon she too was gone. So I know nothing of their backgrounds, nor of their ancestors—because I didn't know them, either. I know my parents were married, but I don't know if it was a civil marriage or a church marriage. After my mother was widowed she remained alone until she died. I don't know if my father was married before. [He later recalls, however, that his father had a mistress and had two sons by her. Taso knew his half brothers, and they visited freely in his mother's house when he was a child.]

The only thing I know of my grandparents is of my mother's side. The one time I visited them they were living in a barrio called Sabana Llana in the municipality of Salinas. At the time I came to know them, I had gone with my mother to their house. My mother used to know how to string tobacco for curing, and she went to do this at my grandfather's house. That was the only time I saw my grandfather. After my mother had strung tobacco for a time at his house, we returned to Jauca. He died after that, and I didn't get to see him again. He was the only one of my grandparents that I came to know. He had a lot of land. I don't know if it was his own property or if he had rented it, but I know he managed a lot of land there. In some parts he had food crops, in others he had tobacco. He used to harvest a lot of tobacco. I don't remember exactly, but at the time I must have been less than ten years old, something like that—I remember I was good and small.

I don't know much of what my father used to do. Those who knew him have told me, and my mother also used to tell me, that he had a store here in the barrio. Also he was the jailer in Santa Isabel. I don't know if he did both things at the same time. Perhaps he would work part of the time in the jail and part of the time in the store. Those, people have told me, were his jobs; I don't know if he might have had any others before. I am telling you this because Mama used to tell it to us, and people are still here who used to know him. The things I know are from what people say: "Your father was like that, he was this way." It makes one think. Usually one doesn't have a person who will tell one, "Your father was this way"; and being so little at the time he died, well, one forgets. I only remember that they have told me that my father was a short man, that he had blue eyes, things like that.

And was there no one in your childhood who was to you as a father—a godfather or someone like that?

No, I always remained only with my mother. I was with my brothers and sister and my mother until Mother died. As to godparents, well, I have nothing to say about that, because I told you before what my religious position used to be—it's different now—it seems to me that my parents would have been more or less the same, because in 80 per cent of the cases that is how one is religious here in Jauca. I can never remember that Mother told me she was going to church, or that she told me anything about that, see? But I was baptized by the articles of baptism, yes. I had one godmother who died, who was called Juanita Valentina. She lived and died here in Jauca. And her husband was my godfather; he was named Mere Suárez. Also I had other godparents. Because that system—they used it and there came the moment in which I used it, too, though now I don't—they used what they call here in Puerto Rico pouring water on the child [an unofficial and unsanctioned lay baptism], and there also they were accustomed to have a male godparent and a female. That other was called Rosa Malavet. She poured water. Then the other they called Telefo Godineaux, a ditcher. They also died many years ago. All of them died.

Of my childhood, what I can tell you is the following. When I was left only with Mama—or better, when I began to have the use of reason, or to have knowledge—that is, when I began to help her—I know that I began by helping her about the house. I used to help Mama carry the water— we used to go to Palo Seco to get it. And my mother always had lots of animals at home, goats and pigs and different things, and I would busy myself in helping Mama look after them. Our house was a pretty big one, but it was an old house. It was roofed with galvanized iron sheets, and it had three rooms—two bedrooms and rather a large living room, with one part as a dining room; then the kitchen—it was separate, behind the house, independent of the house. There were five windows and three doors: one to the front, one to the kitchen, and a third to the side.

At that time [while Taso was still very young] my eldest brother Pablo had already gone to Guayama. And there remained my sister Tomasa, my brother Eugenio, and I. My brother and I used to sleep in one room, and my sister and mother slept in the other. Pablo, who went to Guayama, was the oldest. According to what my mother told me, she had had eleven or twelve children. When Papa was drowned, one of my brothers was drowned with him. My other brothers and sisters died as a consequence of illness. I remember well my brother Pablo, and Eugenio, and Tomasa—they were the ones I really came to know. I was the youngest.

Tomasa, when I first remember her, was already a big girl. She also helped in the house. I remember that when I used to go for water she used to go too; and gathering tinder and washing the floor, these things she did as a girl, as Blanca does with us.

What sort of girl was she—was she simpática?
Simpática just as I am! [He smiles.] She was short, white,

had freckles on her face, just as you see Blanca—that was Tomasa, my sister. Of course one loves all one's brothers and sisters—but I loved that sister of mine very much. I can tell you something about that. I don't know if it's a thing only among us Puerto Ricans or if it's true everywhere, but they say here that the brothers and sisters who love each other dearly are the ones who are always fighting. She and I always used to be like that. We used to have fights, but in a moment we were together once more. And I can tell you more of her. When she was a *señorita* and I still a boy, I was always watchful (*pendiente*) where she was concerned. I was continually jealous, because I didn't want her to leave my side. But there came a time when she left—

Now about school. At the beginning when a boy goes to school, say in the first month, he never feels comfortable. The school I went to was the one down the road there in the barrio; not the same one, because the one I went to was blown down by San Felipe [the 1928 hurricane]. Later they built the one that is there now. I left school and went a long time without schooling. Then, after I went back again, I went to a school in a house rented from Don Nicolasita by the Government. I went there for four or five months. I returned again, then I left again. That was a common thing, see, since at that time there were no [child labor] laws such as they have today, so that when the corporations used to need boys they could just put them to work. The Aguirre Corporation now owns Colonia Texidor and other colonias in different parts; but at that time, no. Texidor was administered by the Texidors; Colonia Pastor Díaz by the Díaz themselves; the colonia of Don Clotilde Santiago was administered by the same Don Clotilde Santiago, and so on. The corporations didn't have the control that they have now. And in those times they used to use boys and women. There were lots of jobs then for women. The women used to work in the spreading of manure. And they used to carry sacks of seed on their backs and distribute the seed.

Well, things have changed. Now they don't use animal manure in the cane fields any more, and the spreading of seed the men do. And the boys, through certain laws that they have now, well, it's difficult for them to get work. You saw what happened to José Miguel [his son]. Already José Miguel has the body of a man, and in spite of this he is still not permitted to work. In that time, there was none of that. Whatever boy wanted to work and found work, worked. And although they made some threats to the school-age boys, the boys always used to work. I remember one time there was a teacher who dragged me from the yoke of oxen there in the corral and took me to school, but as necessity compelled me to abandon school, well, I went back to work again.

Now, what I earned I came and put into my mother's hands. At that time, I was already a boy of nine years or more, and I used to like the movies. Mama always gave me 50 or 75 cents, and with this I'd go to the movies; the rest she took care of. But always, always, until her death, whatever I earned I would come and put into her hands. She had certain habits that I'll always remember. For instance, when I worked I used to get paid on Saturday, and always, when I would come home, she would be waiting for me at the door with my meal at her side. That indeed was one of Mama's customs. I would go to get paid there at Colonia Pastor Díaz, when I was working with Elario Godineaux, and there they had a system—a bell was rung to signal it was time to get paid. At times the bell was rung at five, and at 9 P.M. they still hadn't paid. That one [Pastor Díaz, a hated hacendado] used to look at the payrolls, tear them up, and after he tore them up suspend payment till the next day. And when he didn't do that, it would be nine at night before he would pay. Then when I'd come home I'd find my mother waiting for me at the door with my dinner.

Can you remember being sick as a child?
The first illness I had that I remember was called *perniciosa*. That was when I was still quite a kid. I was perhaps twelve years old. It was around 8 P.M. I was playing, after the custom of kids, and suddenly I felt a little sick and I went and lay down. And that same night I had attacks. And according

to my mother, she said that the attacks were such that I lost consciousness. I say this because afterward Mama would sometimes tell neighbors about that illness of mine. Mother told me that they had to go to town right away and bring the doctor. And the doctor certified that they were attacks of perniciosa. [Taso later described this illness more specifically: there is a sudden high fever, convulsions, and blood is passed in the urine. I have been unable to identify the sickness more specifically.] There were several attacks, according to the way they explained it to me, and they reduced them with injections and other things—they cut down the attacks. Afterward I went to bed; I didn't know anything until later about what happens with such an attack; I can speak of this now, though, because three of my children have had such attacks, and two of my children died with those attacks.

After that time I suffered a lot with toothache. That was an illness which tormented me terribly while I was a child. There were times when I was working and I had to leave the job and come home so that Mama could make me one of the remedies she was accustomed to fix for me in order to give me relief from the pain. She used different things for toothache. She would make gargles of rum that she gave me to hold in my mouth; other times it was alcohol in compresses, with cotton; and Guayacol, which you buy at the pharmacy, and they put in compresses to burn the spot where the tooth hurts. And they also would use extract of *guayacán* [the tree *Guaiacum officinalis*], which was a very strong thing. People always said it would weaken the dentition, and they didn't use it much. But when one was very tormented, then they would use it. We would put it in a gargle or in compresses, wetting a piece of cotton and putting it on the tooth. It's the resin of the guayacán one gets by making a cut in the bark; it flows forth, they mix it with rum, and it is a very strong thing that one gargles. And if you spit it anywhere, well, wherever you spit, it takes on a blue color for a long while. It is something wholly powerful, and it is my understanding that it loosens the dentition. I believe it contributed to my losing my teeth prematurely.

I also suffered during childhood with malaria (*paludismo*). It would be a matter of several chills, and then fever which at times would last two, three, four hours. And while one had this fever what one's stomach asked of one was water; and it was with fear that one drank. One would be willing to die drinking that water; and later on, if the water didn't settle, then came the vomiting, and then one vomited all of the water; and afterward the fever passed and one was left with a normal appetite. Everything they gave one, one would eat. It was in this way that they knew what was and what is malaria, they would say. They would say, "That is malaria because after the fever goes he eats a lot." I don't know the explanation they had concerning it, but I remember well that after the fever passed, if it passed before lunch, afterward I would take my lunch and eat it. Very different from when it is another illness, when there are times that one loses one's appetite, and there are weeks and weeks that one has no appetite. In this case it was just the opposite. As soon as it passed, I and many, in the majority, would eat whatever there was.

In that time here in the barrio it was rare to find a house in which there were no people with malaria. You could walk into any house, and always find someone shivering and fevered and vomiting, especially among the children. It was an illness that attacked the kids a lot. You would find cases, lots of cases, of adults, but it abounded among the children. And I believe that at that time the people did not know what caused malaria. It seems to me they did not know that the mosquito produced it. I believe the people didn't have knowledge of that then, and this is a barrio where the mosquitoes abounded excessively. In later years people came to use nets a lot, but in the beginning, no. It could be that at first it was a question of the economic situation, things were a little hard; but in any case at first there were not many mosquito nets.

I remember that Mother always had this treatment for

malaria. There was a medicine they called Tónico Ferruginosa
Leonardi, which was a syrup with lots of quinine. If you
didn't shake it, the quinine remained at the top of the bottle.
To use it you had to shake it; and then when they put it in
a tablespoon, a great quantity of the quinine seeds would be
taken in the doses one drank. It was my mother's favorite, and
my bane! It was a very sweet thing, and I don't like very
sweet things at all. And she would always give it to us during
the morning before the coffee. And I had a terrible hatred of
it. And they had a tea, too, and that was a terrible thing.
They took nine grains of green coffee, of those they call the
male coffee (*café macho*), the big round grains, and they got
a plant that they call here *rascomoños,* and there are little
buds on the plant; then they broke these into three pieces
and put them to boil, and that was the sourest thing in the
world. And Mama would give that tea to us, the brew of
coffee and rascomoños. And they also used a purgative called
Carabaña. That also was a terrible thing. I believe those were
two of the worst things I have ever taken, that tea Mama
would give us and Carabaña water. As soon as we—as soon
as she would see that we were feeling signs of fever, well,
she would immediately come up with these remedies. As soon
as she saw that we were beginning to tremble, to get chills,
she would regard it as a sign of fever, and she would come
immediately with that treatment.

*Do you remember ever having a tantrum when you were
a child, such as we saw Benjamin's son having today?*

[He smiles.] I remember. One time my mother went out
to look for kindling, and I wanted to go with her. She didn't
want me to. She wanted me to stay behind and look after the
house. And under no circumstances did I want to stay behind.
I got myself into a really enraged state. And there where the
aqueduct is now, there was a road that went out as far as the
lake at Colonia Valdivieso. And the part back of this lake,
which is now cane land, used to be bush, and that was where
we used to look for kindling. And when she began to walk, I
began to walk behind her. And when she stopped, I stopped.

But when she began to walk again, I began to walk again, crying with great anger. But when we were well along, Mama stopped and turned back. And when she started back, I started back ahead of her. And then when she got back home she gave me a good hiding. Before she whipped me, I ran off—I climbed through a window. And when she came outside, I took off down the street. Now, I have a brother by my father—now I remember that before you asked me if my father had had any other woman, and now I remember! I have two other brothers by my father!—and when I came running, one of my brothers by my father was standing there to the side where Cosme Mora lives, and my mother yelled to him to catch me. When he grabbed me I hit him with a rock, but he held on. Then Mama came, and she gave me my whipping. I remember that that was one big tantrum I had. I was a school-age kid at the time. There could have been other times that that happened, but this one I remember well.

Now, I can't remember this ever happening to my sister. My sister was a completely humble woman, and she remained a completely humble woman. I never remember her being beaten. Now, with me, yes, she and I used to have our troubles, but apart from that, I don't remember her ever being whipped. Now, she and I [he smiles]—we used to put on the gloves. And in school, too, there were times when I used to fight a lot. We used to fight over any foolishness, any misdeed that one did to another.

The only fight, though, that I remember as more important was one time when I was standing on top of the school steps. And a pupil came along, sweeping, and when she got to me she struck me with the broom and knocked me to the ground face down. I was standing, and she hit me and I fell on my mouth, and when I fell on my mouth I cut it. And when I got up from there I went after her. I was really angry, because she split my lips, and as I wasn't expecting it when she pushed me, I fell and cut my mouth.

And another time as well—but that was a question of ignorance, you see. We went to the ocean to swim, and a boy who is now abroad [*embarcado:* used to refer to the U.S.], who left here when he was a kid and never came back to Puerto Rico—we were hitting him with a jellyfish. We found this thing—it's like a container of blue water—and we caught him naked and hit him repeatedly with it, and we almost killed him with that jellyfish [contact with it causes painful burns]. It was a question of a fight anywhere; and moreover we had to fight with a brother of his afterward!

Can you tell me about your mother's death?

When Mama died, I was at home. Mama died of pneumonia. Her sickness was a question of a week. And the doctor who saw her was—Montalvo—he treated her. She died around 1920. I remember the burial. What I cannot remember exactly is where the money came from for the expenses; it would have had to come from my brother-in-law, because he was the man of the house. When that happened, Tomasa had already left her first husband and was living with the second, Cornelio. We were all living together when my mother died, and he was the man of the house. And afterward there was a *velorio* [wake]. The velorio is a thing that—I know that you have seen them in Puerto Rico—in the velorio, people drink coffee and eat crackers, and tell stories and such things; they used to have them almost exactly the same before—almost the same.

You mention Tomasa's first husband [Nico Suárez]. *Can you tell me more about him?*

Well, I knew him; he was a local man who had a business. He was a seller of viandas. He lived off that. He had a horse and cart, and lived off that business.

But there were no children from the marriage?

No. Well—look, I'm going to mention something—I was mistaken in this. Rosa—she—comes of the first husband. I didn't recall that she was Nico Suárez'—since she was born in the possession of Cornelio. Cornelio always said she was his own daughter, understand, because she was born in his possession. But, in spite of this, he—as we say—Nico is the father because he made her. But she was born in Cornelio's power, and it was Cornelio who registered her birth and who made her a daughter. I had forgotten this. Lalo and Rosa are really children of the same mother, yes. And see, I am clarifying matters that I had forgotten, since they lived together so little, and Rosa was born when Tomasa was already living with Cornelio. And for us, he was already her father, and the other matter never passes through one's mind. And always we speak of him as the father of Rosa, see—you have evidence also in that you can ask Rosa: "And who was your father?" "Cornelio."

Now, I can tell you of Tomasa's first love, eh—with that husband of whom we were speaking, of whom I told you that Mama did not approve, nor I either, though I was a child. At that time the man had already had other women here, and Mama and I had seen also that his mother interfered considerably in his marriages with those other women. And, almost continuously, they were fighting about it. The mother was always in the middle of it—stuck in the middle of the couple. And when my mother cunningly inferred (*maliciaba*) this, then she tried to prevent the marriage. It was for this reason that Mama was not in accord. It did not concern any other matter, you see, but rather trying to avoid having the same thing happen with her [Tomasa]; that's what I thought too. But it was not worth the effort it took for Mama to call it to Tomasa's attention, or to put forth her point of view. The moment came anyway when she went away, and afterward she had those very problems with him. And when she came back home, nothing was more just than that Mama should say that that was a thing that she had already told her, and if it came to happen it was not for lack of warning. So Mama did not hesitate to reproach her severely. And I also felt like saying something to her, though I was much younger than she; I also felt a little angry, because it was a thing she had been warned about at home, and if it fell through it came from not doing what Mama told her.

Eh—the night on which he carried her off we were in the

old house, and as it was the custom, you see, for girls to go out walking around here, well, she went out. But when time for bed came, Mama called her, and she didn't appear. And Mama took a walk around and we looked to see if we would find her in the barrio. But one knows pretty well already what has happened; and one says, "Well [he laughs], let her go!" One knows already. One looks in the places where the girl might be—and in those times it wasn't like it is now; by eight-thirty or nine a girl had to be in her house—if from then on she didn't appear, she had probably eloped with her sweetheart. Now it is very different, because now at times there are girls walking out here until dawn, and it is difficult for one to know what is happening without waiting till the next day. But not then; one could be sure that if by nine she had not appeared she had gone off with her lover.

Women, especially mothers, get angry and talk—but in the end they have to resign themselves! [He laughs.] And Mama stayed quiet [i.e. did not insist on a legal marriage]. Perhaps she thought the marriage would last only a little while, and then afterward there would not be the trouble of getting a divorce in the midst of everything, which would be a little difficult. And Mama would be one to think about that, you see? That is my opinion, and in truth Mama stayed silent [he laughs again] and did nothing. When Tomasa left him she returned home pregnant, and then at once Mama was worried; she knew it was her responsibility to look after her, you see.

Well, then—I cannot say when, because women always begin to fall in love in secret, you see, so one does not know, and afterward, when one comes to look into the matter [he laughs]—God knows if it was a couple of weeks or half of that when Cornelio and Tomasa began falling in love! But little time passed.

When that happened, you see, when Mama knew that they were in love—when after, more or less, one knows—well, then Mama didn't want to intervene more in it, you see. We knew Cornelio already; at the time at least he had no commitment to anyone; he had nothing with anyone, and he was a man of work, and a man of whom nothing could be said adversely here. And so then Mama simply left things alone. It was a matter of Tomasa's now being a woman. Mother didn't interfere.

Eh, at the time, we had the old house, and there was a flat-roofed shack on this side of the old house. Then when he carried her off, he took her there, and afterward they came to live in the house. After they lived there a while—it was only a little while—they asked to live in the house; and then we all were living together in the house. There was no problem regarding that. They came to live in the house, we had several rooms, and then Mama—when that happened we were alone, Mother and I—then Mama and I had one room and they had the rest of the house. Mama and Cornelio never had quarrels.

Now, after—Cornelio and Tomasa—they had fights, but that was later when he began— [he chuckles] when he began to take women and so on. The fights they had were on account of jealousy. There were jealousies because—afterward he would get such passions for women, and he was very fond of women (*bien mujeriego*), and the question of jealousy would provoke a fight between them. And one time they separated for a week or so, and Tomasa went to live in the house of—of Alejandro, my half brother. At the time Mother had already died, and I went with Tomasa; we were there a couple of weeks. But then Tomasa and Cornelio got back together again and became contented with each other once more, and we moved back to the old house.

When she went off that way it humbled Cornelio, and he regretted it [he laughs]; but with that and with everything, he always continued with— [he laughs again]. At the time Tomasa had borne Rosa; I don't recall if she had borne Lalo already, but she definitely had Rosa. Wherever she went, she went burdened. That—when they broke off, it was a matter of a week or so; she returned soon, and they settled things.

She knew his ways and always had things in order, so when he came home, concerning the rest there was no problem. But their problem always was the question of jealousy, you see. And he—at the same time she would be telling him these things, almost immediately after— [he chuckles]. Yet Tomasa, I never saw her dance or—what is more—I don't remember that—after Tomasa took a husband, I never even saw her walking for pleasure on the road of the village. Tomasa was a woman who was always at home, and she never went out anywhere. So that— [he chuckles] I don't ever remember him being jealous; the fights over jealousy were on her part, yes.

Regarding that, I felt a little sad, because it gave me pain that my sister was suffering so much in that regard. When I was already a pretty big boy, I myself used to see at times that he—when I would pass by—I would see him talking to women in different places. And I knew already that they were women that— [he sighs] that he had on the side. And I never, never said anything to Tomasa because of wanting to avoid fights and things at home. But I really suffered, because my sister used to have to suffer all of that; but if I were to tell a story of that at home, well then it would be one fight more, and one I was provoking. I would see these things and I would turn my gaze away.

Now, Cornelio, while he was living with Tomasa my sister, carried off another girl [Nenita]. Then they made him marry her—they denounced him [i.e. brought him to court], and then they made them marry. But he remained living with my sister. There was a time when he stayed with his legal wife when he was married, and so they were together a little while, when he settled down; but he never neglected his obligation to our house, see?

Cornelio had this about him, that he could fall in love with another woman, you see? For example, he fell in love with that lady he carried off, living at the time with my sister. I remember when they fell in love. And the night he carried her off he took her to a house in a part that is called Cayures, a house that is there all alone. And that was a Saturday. And on Monday he came home to see Tomasa my sister. And they had their words. And afterward he went again where she [Nenita] was, and came back Sunday to the house to wait for a peddler named Don Cayetano, from whom he had bought on trust. He waited for him until about 6 P.M., which was the hour Don Cayetano was accustomed to come down here in a two-wheeled carriage. And after he paid him he went back again to the house where he had left her [Nenita]. And by this time she had run out of the house and was waiting for him in ambush on a path in the cane. And when he passed by, she attacked him with a knife. And they fell to fighting, and according to what he told us afterward, he said he struck her, and she went head over heels. She went running from there, along what we call a maclaine in the cane field. And he turned around and came back to our house with a knife wound in his palm. There in the fight they had she had also managed to bite him, and then he came back to our home to cure himself. And at that time I was already a big boy. I remember that, and I was even present at some of the different fights he and Tomasa had during her life. Finally, my sister died, and she [Nenita] remained then in Santa Isabel. Now she is as placid as she was wild; now she is completely tame.

I never told Tomasa of anything I saw. Actually one doesn't say anything in order to avoid discord between married people. Because fights begin, and if it is a man who likes to use his hands, well, it goes badly with the woman; and avoiding that kind of foolishness, well, at times one keeps one's mouth closed. And one never thought—I never thought—it would get to the point where he would carry off that other girl, too —that it could be a thing that—I thought it was a matter of making love and nothing more, and as we say, everyone comes to pass such a time. I never thought that it would come to such an extreme. But actually he did carry her off. And when he came back home, well, he and Tomasa, they didn't have a fight but rather, as they were already a married couple, they had their little quarrels. But in this regard my sister was a different kind of person, you see. As he continued living at home, and as Rosa had already been born at the time, well, she never— And he was—a few nights in the house, and then he would go to Cayures where he had the other. And she had gone to another place that they call the "street" of Cayures, to the house of a sister that she had there, another separate place, and there they were a while. And after that, he came to live here in my father's house, here in the barrio.

And thus they were a long while, living thus, Nenita and Cornelio, they would get along, and other days they would have fights. She would lie in wait for him, and he would beat her up, and thus they were. But he always continued living at our home while my sister was alive. He would go away for two or three days—but he never gave up coming to the house. To such an extent that when Nenita began having his children, the children would come to our house—yes—and in the house—think of it—Tomasa after—after feeding them even dressed them up. They would eat, and then she would send them back home.

It is a kind of situation that leaves one feeling a little uncomfortable, you see? When you have a sister, and the husband of your sister carries off another woman, one feels a little uncomfortable about that, you see? That someone would do this sort of thing to one's sister. But if your sister continues living with him—oh, one is not able to take a hand then—it is their pleasure—and as later he always continued living with my sister, always giving her what she needed, there was no one who could say to her, "Leave him, leave him be, whatever may happen." That is a difficult matter regarding married couples. Because I know certain women here, their husband gives them a beating in the morning, and another at noon, and a third in the evening, and in spite of it they die living with him. I don't know if it is a question of love or what, but they don't leave him because of it. Now if Tomasa had left Cornelio, he would have been well left! There was no one who would have said to her that she ought not to have left him.

Now, concerning Tomasa's illness at the time she died. On that occasion Tomasa had a completely good delivery; she came out well from the birth. But it happened that before the end of the *cuarentena* [the traditional forty-day postnatal sexual abstention period] a lady came to visit the house who was a niece of Cornelio's. She came from Santa Catalina [a barrio of a municipality north of Santa Isabel]. She came at about three in the afternoon or later, and Tomasa went out of the house to the kitchen, which was back about 20 or 25 feet from the house. And the floor of the kitchen was earthen; it was a kitchen without a wood floor. She set about roasting coffee, in order to serve coffee to this lady who had arrived. And when the coffee was roasted, she took the pot off the fire and put it on the ground, and she squatted at the side of the pot to stir the coffee, from which the smoke was rising.

When you roast coffee in a pot like that, there is a whole lot of smoke; and in order that the taste of the smoke not remain, she continued moving the grains about in the pot, squatting on the ground while the smoke was present. And it seems that it was this way that my sister caught her illness. As soon as she got up from there, she felt pain. She said it was a pain in this place [he points to his ribs on the left side]. She finished making the coffee, and after she served it she went and lay down, and she continued during the night with that pain, and the next day she got a fever. And she continued with the fever. And people said, as they used to imagine, that it was *pasmo* [literally, "spasm"] and they began to give her medical treatment in accord with its being assumed to be pasmo—remedies that the people here knew.

I remember one remedy; I don't know the others. It was when I was a boy that they used these things; they would take what they called the *comején*, that is, the lump of wood where the comején [termite] lives; they take that and boil it, and they give the water to drink to those whom they believe to be suffering from pasmo.

Pasmo comes when one goes out suddenly like that, from inside a house, and the air outside is cold, and this cold that one catches, that's what they call pasmo. And people attributed it to her roasting coffee, which is a pasmo-producing thing—that is, it is a little dangerous. And so they treated her two or three days with those domestic remedies. Then Cornelio brought a doctor, and he prescribed some medicine, but the medicines didn't arrive at first and then the fever came too. When the doctor came she already had fever, and they gave her medicines. And the medicine didn't stop the fever or the pain. And then the doctor said it was puerperal fever that she had, and they continued giving her the doctor's medicines. And it seems to me, if I am not mistaken, that he came back and prescribed again. And since the medicines didn't help, there came the comments that it was pasmo, and they continued with certain household remedies.

And then after six or seven days there came what they call a *síncope* [literally, "swooning"]. It was a sweat such as I have only seen one person have in my entire life. It was a sweat that ran from the body as if you were to take a person and pour water over his head. I recall well that we wrapped her in a sheet, and in five or ten minutes you would take off the sheet and wring it out in wash basins. And there were three or four mortars, those little ones, in the house, and people were at those mortars grinding cinnamon day and night, to crush it into cinnamon powder to be used to powder her with, trying to absorb the sweat. And it was terrible the way one would no sooner apply the powder to her face than the sweat would carry it off. And they made many other remedies, trying to cut the sweat; and it was not possible.

In the midst of the spasm and everything, she was speaking with us as we are talking now, without loss of consciousness. I remember well how she would direct us, "Anoint me here, anoint me there"—she herself, speaking with us. At that time there were many neighbors helping, and at the time Monse —Pablo's woman, my brother's woman—was also helping in the house during Tomasa's illness. And from Colonia Destino there were some, and others entering and going out since by then we were staying up all night struggling with her. Especially those that were older—I who was still a child, sometimes I was up and sometimes I'd be sleeping. But I have never seen a thing like that, an illness like that one, a sweat so tremendous that it was impossible to reduce it. Until finally one morning at about ten she died, speaking thus with us.

So it was—all that sickness which caused her death. The doctor said it was puerperal fever. But I know she caught her illness, because she was completely recovered from her delivery. And as soon as she roasted that coffee and put it out to cool and stirred it, she felt that pain. She finished the coffee and went to lie down, and she did not get up again.

And the newborn baby was given over to another woman, and they kept it fed with milk and with teas. They used to give a lot of teas to the children in those days; that is what they did with him until finally Tomasa died. And after she died we had to solve problems. At one point Doña Petra had him; and at other times Doña Agustina had him. She was a woman of considerable age, and she had him a little while; but as he was still very small he bothered her a lot at night, you see, and as he lacked the mother's breast, well, she decided to turn him over once more to Cornelio. And after that he took the infant to Petra again, and she had him a little while, and later she returned him; and so he was passed from hand to hand. Nenita had him, she who was also Cornelio's woman, and so he was until when he was already a boy of about two years and a half he also died.

When Tomasa died, as is the custom, they held a velorio, as they do now—you have seen them here, chanting [*rezando:* telling the rosary] and giving coffee and crackers to the people. Then they used to tell stories a lot at the velorios—stories that the people would tell, stories that they knew. And I heard many Biblical stories; that's why I say that there are people who have read the Scriptures with those ends in mind, some to be able to sing and others to explain them as stories at velorios. I recall that there was a man here called Manuel and I heard him many times telling the story of Samson in velorios that way. And so the people entertained themselves during the night until it grew light, and sometimes they would continue until time to leave for the burial.

Now, I put myself in Cornelio's place. When a man loses

his woman he feels completely sad, to see his companion lost. And I could see it in him, though we were all sad, he particularly was grieving at the time. Particularly a man left with little children, and you could say that there was no family here to look after them, so the man felt a little sad. I continued there with him for a while, working and living there, and afterward he began looking about because it was a little hard for him. After that he had the child in the house of Doña Agustina, and he went to eat at Doña Lola's house. But I didn't go with him to board at Doña Lola's at that time. I remained alone at home.

One day we went to a burial in Santa Isabel. And while we were coming back home Don Epifanio, Doña Lola's husband, invited me to enter and to eat. He knew I had no sure place to eat. And I accepted, and entered to eat there. And when we were sitting at the table and eating, Lola proposed that if I wished they, seeing our situation—that if I wished, she could make meals for both of us. And so I began eating there. And then I asked her the price of the meals, as those were critical times and one earned little. I was always thinking of keeping up good relations. I asked her, and she told me it was a question of $1.50 [per week], and I accepted. And then I saw the way that she looked after me, her behavior; and I never paid her $1.50, but $2 or something more. And as they saw how I conducted myself with them and how they got along with me, when he [Epifanio] went to work at Cortada [a neighboring sugar mill], they invited me to live with them in their house there. When they made me this proposal I went, and paid more money. In this way I resolved most of my problems—I didn't have to worry about having to buy clothes, or about having to fix my bed, because she [Lola] took care of everything. She would come, straighten the bed and make it, take care of my dirty clothes, repair my work clothes, and I didn't have to worry about any of that. I resolved most of my problems.

At that time we used to get about 80 cents a day at work. And we worked seven days. We earned $5.60. Out of that I would pay $2, $3, $3.50, for board, and the rest remained for other necessities. I continued this way there, until finally in that house I was made my first pair of long pants. Then after that they went to live at Colonia Texidor. And I too— I moved there with them. They were there a little while, and then I came back to live in the barrio; but I always used to go to eat at their house. They were there a little while, and then they moved back to the barrio, and when they moved back I moved into their house again. And so I remained until I fell in love with Elisabeth. And I was in their house until I married her. Then I moved away from there; I left them. Then I came to make a different life. Then I began to start a home of my own.

You have told me a great deal about Tomasa. Now can you tell me about your brothers?

Well, while I was still quite small my brother Pablo went off to Guayama. And my brother Eugenio remained at home with Mother. Later he went to work at a pump station they had here in Jauca, and he was there a while. And at times he would leave that job and work as a plowman. Sometimes he was in that work, sometimes he would go off and he would come back, and so he worked three or four different times at that job. After our mother died he took a wife from here, named Antonia, and he lived with her several months—a question of several months—and after that time they had a baby boy who died when he was about a year and half old. After that she went to live at Coamo, and Eugenio used to go week ends to visit her there. And then she took ill, and one afternoon they brought him the news that she had died, quite suddenly. They came and told him she had died; and after she died he remained here a short while. Then he went to La Torre de Ponce [a district in the municipality of Ponce, west of Santa Isabel] where we have an uncle, a brother of my father, and then he was working there, doing the work we call *atierro*, breaking land—hauling the plows with oxen. He went there first, and then I went there where he was to stay, and I was there some months. When he lived with his wife, our mother was already dead—she had died some time before. And afterward, when he went to that place to work, as Mother had died, then I also went to live there.

At that time you were living here with Cornelio?

Yes. They were here, you see, Cornelio and Tomasa. Then I lived for several months in his [Eugenio's] home here. Then after he went to La Torre I came back again to the house of Tomasa. And from there, then I went to La Torre, to my uncle's house. He [Eugenio] was already doing the work that I mentioned to you before. And my uncle there wanted me to stay there with him, because Mother had already died, and the only one that was left was Tomasa. And I did get used to being there in one way, but in another I didn't, because I missed Tomasa very much.

Beyond that, I liked it a lot there, because at that time in the barrio of La Torre there were very many different fruits and things. You know that when boys fall into such places, that is a delicious thing. I was enchanted by that, I was always roaming about there, and there were many mango farms and such, and it was a delight; but I missed Tomasa. And I suppose it was about three months, something like that, and Tomasa came to see me there. They were there, if I'm not mistaken, something like from one day to the next, before making the return trip. And I wanted to return with Tomasa, but my uncle didn't want to let me come. And I secretly got ready to make the trip, and when they left to catch the train they had to go quite a distance, a kilometer or something more. Well, they left and I hid myself, and when they were arriving at the station, then I came out by another route to where they were. And Tomasa my sister said nothing, because she missed me too. She let me come, and we took the train and I returned to Jauca.

Then after a while my brother Eugenio came back here and brought me my clothes. He came that time with the idea of staying in Jauca again. Then he was here a while working at different jobs in the cane, and then he returned to work again at the pump station. Then he came to live in a house belonging to his mother-in-law, and it was at that time that he took ill and his death came in a matter of a week. It was pneumonia. I went to the velorio; they [Cornelio and Tomasa] were the ones who took charge of that, as older people of greater experience, so with regard to that I never had to carry out any responsibilities. They were older people who knew what they had to do. I did not know what had to be done with regard to the velorio, only that I was there as an attendant to my brother. The next day we went to the burial —we went and buried him—and I went every night to the ceremonies they had for him until they celebrated the ninth night (*novenario*), which is the last service they used to hold for people who died. Thus ended his span of life. He was bringing up a little girl at the time, in Coamo, and after he died I saw no more of her. After a long time—long after he had died—she came back here to Jauca; I got to see her, but since then I have never seen her again.

My brother Eugenio was a man of my build, more or less, with the difference that he was stockier, he was fuller, in spite of which his stature was like mine. Eugenio was different from my brother Pablo. My brother Pablo was a whiter man; but their eyes were very similar. And in behavior, well, Pablo was one way with regard to jobs and my brother Eugenio was another. My brother Eugenio was—that brother always liked to work in the cane, in the pump stations, and in different kinds of work, while the other brother, my brother Pablo, well, he never liked to work with his hands.

For me, they were pretty much the same, because I did not have to depend on them, you see? The same liking I had for one I had for the other. But Eugenio was always more at our side than Pablo. Pablo went off to Guayama when I was little, and then he used to visit us occasionally. Eugenio was with us a lot during Mother's life. Although he worked in different places, it would be some place near; he was always here. When he went to La Torre, Mother had already died at the time, and it was the only time that he went away so far from us.

Can we go back again to when you began to work? Did the men you worked for play any part in forming your ideals?

You mean were they interested in how one behaved? Look, I worked for a mayordomo called Enrique Martínez here in Colonia Pastor Díaz. And before that I worked for another there whose name I can't remember. But in any case, their problem was whether one could do the quantity of work for which they paid you. They weren't interested in anything else.

I must have been about nine or ten years old, more or less, when I began to work. It was then that I began to work in *work*, where you earn a wage. And there were occasions when I would be going to school at the same time. I remember the first work I did was picking corn. They paid me 35 cents a day. That was what they paid then. This corn wasn't for eating. They used to plant corn there in Colonia Usera for the use of the colonia [i.e. for feed and fodder]. It was a matter of a few weeks' work. And after that I went on to do other work, work they used to have plenty of here for the kids—all of this work has now been eliminated—I went on to feed (*darles rabos*) the oxen in the cane fields. While the carters were filling the wagons with cane, each carter had a lad feeding the oxen. I spent lots of time working at this also. And after that I went on to struggle with the oxen; I used to handle two yokes of oxen, bringing the carts out of the cane fields and leading them to the railway siding.

At the time I am speaking of now, in this colonia of Don Pastor Díaz there was cane only in the swampy lowland, and a little bit in that upland part called Cayures. Those uplands were in brush, and there were many *húcar* and *tachuelo* trees, which are among the best woods they have here in Puerto Rico. And they used a great number of people for uprooting those trees and converting the wood into charcoal in order to clear the brushland. And when those lands were clear of all that wood, then the plowing work was begun. I would go with Elario Godineaux, who was my plowman—and there were other plowmen with other plows—to prepare those lands. They gave those lands a first plowing and then one plowing more, which they called "crossing." And afterward they passed a harrow over the land to break it up, and then they did the squaring-off (*banqueo*), that is, marking the rows so as to be able to come back later with a special plow (*bombo*) to make the rows and to finish them off.

These ox plows consisted of four yokes of oxen managed by two boys; the one who took care of the two forward they called the *cuartero*, and the one who managed the two behind they called the *tronquero*. I used to manage two of those teams, and another boy would manage the other two. The plowman would use a whip to assist the tronquero when one got to the main furrows, so that the hindmost yoke of oxen might get as close as possible to the main furrow (*callejón*) before the three yokes in front turned about. That way the furrows would reach right to the main furrow, and it wouldn't be necessary to lay down many cross furrows at the edge of the main furrow. And so there we were in that part, Cayures, until they had broken open a large amount of brushland in that area. I worked a long time in that work there. And not I alone; at times they had three, four, five plows working, for at that time the preparation of the land went so slowly, and it took a lot of plows to speed up the work a little.

At that time the colonia had a tremendous number of oxen. There was an ox corral where one could see 125 or 150 oxen, or more. And at Colonia Destino, many more, because it was a much bigger colonia and they had to use more plows. And then there was the loading and moving of cane, which was a terrible job. The number of oxen they used to need was tremendous. And particularly the colonias where they had the system of changing the teams of oxen. Because the yokes of oxen were not supposed to work all day, except those used for carrying the cane. The hour of changing the teams was from eleven to twelve. At eleven they would turn the boys loose and we would come and change the oxen. But in the cane-carrying it was difficult because there were times when at that hour most of the carts were in the cane fields being filled, and it was not possible to change the teams. Then sometimes the oxen used by the wagonmen would work the whole day. But the plow oxen would always be changed at midday for a new team.

Here in this colonia of which we are speaking [Pastor Díaz] they had had a place for raising animals, and besides that they bought young animals to break in. They carried out these tasks during dead time. The wagonmen would load up with rocks and manure for the fields, and then they would take these calves and begin to train them for when the harvest would begin, so that by then they would be broken in. And after they mashed them up a little with the carts—we used to call the first yokings "to mash them up"—then they'd use them with the plows for a little while. Then those oxen could be used with the wagons to carry cane. To be used for carrying cane they had to be gentle oxen, because if they bucked or anything like that, then they would throw out the loads of cane. So by the time they used them to work with the wagons, they would have to be completely tame.

At the colonia, they always had what they called an ox-herd—the colonias always had to have someone, an older person—and apart from that there were times when they would have two or three boys also busy with that work. Because during the harvest they were accustomed to take the oxen to feed in the fields they were cutting, in the part they had already cut. The boys would be there to see that the oxen didn't go into the part where the [uncut] cane was without turning them back, and if there were small plots of cane nearby, to see that they didn't go off and eat them. So there was not only the oxherd, but also other people were employed to care for the stock. And during the night sometimes they would carry cane stalks to the corrals so that the oxen could eat them during the night. And other times they would move them to the enclosures, to the pastures, and they would feed during the night, and at 4:30 A.M. the oxherd would come and lead those animals to the corral so that when the carters arrived they would have all the animals together in the corral. As for the animals which could no longer work because they were old or injured, they had the custom of taking them to sell in Salinas, to the butcher shop, or to Santa Isabel or one of those towns, and there they would sell them for meat since the ox—well—could no longer work. That was their pay [he smiles].

What sorts of recreation did you have as a boy?
Concerning these things, there was one that I used to do from the time that we were very little boys, from the time my mother was alive—and that I continued to do even after I was living with Elisabeth. After we would work through the day, we used to go to the sea, to the part we call El Cayo [The Cay]. And we used to go with a person who could cast a throw-net. From here in the barrio we would carry the viandas. They would get the firewood there; they would get rocks—those rocks from the cay there. They would make a fireplace, and on it they would put a five-gallon tin (*latón*), and they would peel the viandas, and they would put them on to boil, and we would go to cast the throw-net, and there we used to catch fish—lobster and all kinds of fish. You caught *jarea*, you caught *robalo*, you caught *jayao*, you caught *mero* —different kinds of fish. But always there were plenty of jarea above all.

One night, we were in just such a *serenata* [an evening's enjoyment or meal]; and those who remained at the fireside wanted to play a trick on those of us who went to fish. That night we went with a boy named Guillo Alicea, who was the one throwing the throw-net. At the entrance to the cay he made a cast, and he caught about twelve jarea, but good big ones. That was before entering the cay. When we got to the cay, the others remained behind cooking viandas, and they came and cooked the jarea, and ate them up. And we—well— meanwhile we were walking and fishing. But we made a great catch that night after we entered the cay; we caught a fish that they call here a *vieja* [literally, "old female one"] that weighed about eight pounds, and another that weighed about six, and beyond that, a great quantity of other fish and lobsters, and so on. And when we came with the catch we had made, those who had stayed behind were laughing at what they had done. And then Guillo Alicea, who was a slightly smart-alecky fellow, said: "Look how they have finished with all the fish cooked here tonight! I am not going to give so much as a raw fish to any of them."

And we went to work and prepared all those fish, and put them in a fish can to cook; and the viandas were already cooked, and we ate what we could, but the others were left without any more fish. And we ate fish until we were stuffed. From there to the barrio I brought a lard can full of cooked fish so that they would not be wasted. We who had kept on fishing brought back whole cans full—a matter of greed—nothing more than what Guillo did out of his shamelessness, because of the way he felt when he saw that they had cooked all the first catch of fish and had saved us none. And at the time I was already living with Elisabeth. When I arrived home, I called Joaquín, Elisabeth's father, and Elisabeth, and we sat down on the bed with that serenata that we brought.

And I went fishing like that from the time I was a boy. I continued to do that until finally people did it no more. I'll tell you especially when they were giving up that custom. At the time of the war [World War II] they prohibited so many things, and you couldn't be with lights in those places [i.e. along the beach]. And then the people lost the custom, until now I don't know anyone who goes to the sea to make such a serenata.

There was also another night when a funny thing happened to us in one of those serenatas. We went to the cay from here, actually from Palo Seco [a mangrove swamp on the beach]. And with us that night went Don Bache, Cheo's father—older people would go with the boys. And that night we left Don Bache cooking on the outer shore. And we went and walked through all of Palo Seco. And on our way back from there we caught a little barracuda of about a half pound. Don Bache remained there cooking and ate the barracuda with a plate of viandas, and then though we walked the whole cay we didn't catch anything else. What we were left with that night was pure viandas with oil and vinegar. When we went out that night we thought we would eat some fish with oil and vinegar, but the viandas were all we ate that night!

We used to carry on that activity as a sport, you see, because we used to eat our regular meal at night. But this we did really because we liked the night fishing so much—catching the fish—and we did it as a sport and for enjoyment at the same time. We never did it in order to sell the fish. When we held one of those serenatas it was to eat the fish there that way; if it was a big fish then people would bring back a couple of pounds of fish to their homes, but we never did it with the end in mind of selling the fish. In recent years people would go especially to catch lobster and such and sell them; but when it was for a serenata it was exclusively to eat, a matter of a fiesta and such. There were times when one used to drink one's little bottle too, and give out shots there.

Then there were the movies; as I've told you before, I used to like them a great deal. Many more people used to go to the movies then. One gentleman—a black man, not *trigueño* [literally, "wheat-colored"]—would go from here who was called Ventura Antonetti. And he was obsessed with the movies. If he didn't go to Santa Isabel he would go to Salinas [a municipality a few miles east of Santa Isabel]—and on foot; at that time there was none of this car business. And we would make up a group among us boys and older people: Ventura, María Rosa Malvet, and Dolores Alomar, those are people of color from where compadre Gueni lives. Then, from here in the barrio I would go, and Adolfo Davíd. And from Boca Chica [a nearby colonia] an endless number of people would go. A great mob would go to the movies, on foot. And sometimes we would do that up to three times a week. Then, later on, we used to go twice a week.

The enthusiasm was tremendous; at the time they showed lots of serials, and when one of those started, one wouldn't want to miss a single episode. It was so serious that one would have to be dying to be willing to miss one of those shows. And so we went on for a long time. But afterward—I myself cannot explain how it came about—we began to give up that habit, little by little, little by little, until at last we went no more. But at the time I'm telling you about, it was remarkable the number of people who used to go to the movies on foot. And when we came out of the show everyone would have saved his nickel, and we would go to the bakery that used to be on the Calle de Guayama, and there each one of us would buy a pound of bread, and then we'd spend the rest of the trip [walking home], each of us eating his pound of bread.

And one time I recall that we went to the movies during a strike in the cane fields [1920], and with us went a boy from Colonia Pastor Díaz, a boy named Bartolo who used to work in the house of Don Pastor as an errand boy, and Adolfo David. And those two boys were always hostile to each other—wherever they were they were fighting. And that night we went to the movies, and when we came out they began to quarrel, and they quarreled and quarreled. And when we got to the entrance to Colonia Alomar, well, then we said, "Good, if you're going to fight, then fight; let's have the fight right here." And we made a great ring, a ring of boys; and we put them in the middle. I remember that Adolfo had a cup which Doña Antonia had entrusted to him and he gave it to me to guard for him. And Bartolo was carrying something else that he gave to someone to hold. And they fell to it with punches. And while they were beating each other up and we were raising a great noise, as if it were a cockfight—the police were hidden in the cane, watching the entrance there [expecting some trouble in the strike]. And when we raised that great roar there, they came bursting out of the cane—and they were left standing in the road, without a single boy remaining behind! We didn't stop running until we got to the entrance to Colonia Destino, and we weren't fooling in that race!

We used to see many pictures that were exciting. Lots of us used to like the cowboy pictures, and I remember a picture of which I didn't miss a single episode, a picture that was called *Breaking the Barricade;* and another called *The Road of Iron;* and I don't remember all the others. I do know there were pictures of which I didn't miss a single one of the episodes; and if there were fifteen episodes it was fifteen that I saw. The print was in Spanish; we read it. Now I don't know where the pictures came from. They were silent pictures; there were no talkies then. That came later, many years later. Later, I gave up the custom of going to the movies. It seems to me when I began going to the dances, as I became more attracted by the dances and so on, then I gradually began giving up the pictures. At the time I was going to the movies I was still a little boy—I wasn't dancing or any of that. Then I got to like the dances more, and then I lost my love for the movies. Until at last I gave up the movies and was left with dancing.

Can you tell me about any of your friendships then?
Well, the friendship I had with Guillo Alomar became quite close. Guillo *Alomar,* because before we were speaking of another Guillo. There was a time when nearly all the boys of the barrio here would get together at night in that place where "they" used to live that was almost a little barrio. And almost all who lived there were people of color, and there were lots of little boys, little boys of color. Boys like us, averaging about eight, nine, ten years, or so. And they would take big cans and use them to play on. Felix Godineaux, who lives with Adela—he was one of those who would take up *palos* [sticks, used here to mean instruments for beating rhythm], and at times tambourines, and others would imitate the sounds of instruments with their mouths; and we would make up some terrific dances among ourselves, you know? And that was a regular custom. Every night we would be mixed in with those there.

And so we went along developing that [friendship], or at least I in particular was acquiring it with that boy. And he had—it was not his mama—I don't remember well, but it seems to me it wasn't his mama—a lady that was named Baldomera, who was raising him, and another who was named Dolores—well, those two women were intimate friends of Mama, and they would show me very great affection when I went there. And there were times when I would arrive quite early in the afternoon, and they would call and invite me to eat in the house, and I was there almost all the time, and then we used to share his dinners. Different times he would give me some of his own dinner. And they used to eat a thing that I liked very much—probably you have not eaten it. Here in the sea when they fished a lot they used to catch a little fish that we called *pelaillo*. It is a little fish; and when you cut off the head, off with the head come the insides, and it doesn't have scales or anything. Then you salt it and you put it to dry in the sun. After it is dried, they would prepare flour and put the fish in that softened flour, and then put it to fry that way—as fried codfish is made, as Elí makes *bacalao* [salt cod]. And that fish dinner was the best. And I used to enjoy myself very much at their house. And as they knew how very much I liked that, if I wasn't there when she was making it, Baldomera would always save me my portion. And if I didn't come, they would send to look for me so that I might come to get my portion there.

In the evening that place was like an amusement park for us. All the kids would get together there. That project was an every-night one—to play, to dance; we always would run to the same place. It would be a night of big noise there. And in that place of which I am speaking, all, all the people were of color; there were no whites at all. All the families were people of color.

And the others got along well with them?
[Somewhat impatiently.] Yes, that was no problem.
Now, regarding the dances. I got to be so crazy for the dances that there were times that after leaving work, working all day, we would go to a dance in Coamo [a municipality to the north]. And together he and I, Guillermo Alomar and I, we would go on foot, from here in the center, as far as Usera, Las Flores, and even to Coamo, and dance there until four in the morning, and then return here from there, to be here in the barrio for work—and to work through another day. But that was when we were older.

What other friends from childhood could you mention?
The first time I came to know Compadre Berto was when we were boys and used to handle oxen, there in the colonia

of Don Pastor Díaz. And there we became friends and work-mates. Sometimes we didn't work from noon on, and we would go to Boca de Caballo [a nearby inlet], which is a place where there are many sea grapes. There were some tremendous trees, and we would take the oxen there, and we would go to eat the grapes. And there was a gentleman named Tomás Ríos, and we would go to his place there also. We used to eat the melons he cultivated—he had a lot of melons and we would eat them too.

Paying for them?

We didn't pay anything! He used to grow a great many, and we used to take them, and cane, and so on, being boys— And there is a coconut grove in the same part of Boca de Caballo where the trees were very low, and you can reach the coconuts from the ground. And we would spend the afternoons there, drinking coconut water and eating sugar cane. That was something we used to do often.

And we also had another custom. If we went to the corral in the morning to yoke up, and if for any reason they weren't working there, we would continue our trip and go to the cay of Palo Seco and there we would set out to catch octopus, and in those days they used to catch a lot. There were times when we would leave there each one with twelve or fourteen or fifteen octopuses. Those we would carry to our homes, his to his house, and I would carry mine to mine. And we didn't sell those—they were used in the family.

Compadre Berto has always been much enamored of fishing. His father used to fish a lot with hook and line. We continued that friendship as children; and later on at the dances there were many times that we were dancing with girls at the same dance, and so we came to have that friendship we still have today.

Now I'm going to tell you how it was that I learned the work of the *pala* [ditching shovel]. My brother-in-law Cornelio was a palero, and he used to work a lot here in the *poyal* [swamp] of Colonia Pastor Díaz. At that time the poyales were plowed and furrowed in sections for cultivation, consisting of seed beds for two or four pieces of seed cane. That is, where the poyal was very wet, where there was a lot of ground water, we made hills to accommodate two pieces, and, where the terrain was dryer, four pieces. His work at that time was that of ditcher, working with the pala. I used to go with my sister Tomasa to bring him lunch and breakfast. Tomasa was a strong woman; and at that time they used to make ditches as deep as two shovel lengths, and as wide as two shovel widths. And then my sister would take the pala, and she would fold over her dress in front and catch it between her legs, take the pala and start to dig the second [deeper] shovel length. And I too put myself to practicing it. They used what we called a *botalón,* a long-handled pala, to collect the dirt that remains in the ditch—the fine earth, as we call it. At times she would go behind Cornelio seconding him, and I behind her, with the botalón, finishing up the job of removing the earth that was left. Afterward my brother-in-law would come back, recut the ditch on each side, and back we would come, she and I, and clean up this earth. This we used to do for half an hour or an hour when we would go there, especially at the lunch hour, because at breakfast we could do little since she had to come back home in order to prepare lunch. So that was how I came to learn to do pala work. Then I came to do it on my own account, earning money, later on.

Then my brother-in-law was put in charge of irrigation at Colonia Pastor Díaz; he was *encabezado* [a kind of foreman]. And then I used to have to go at night with a lantern to illuminate the work of the irrigators during the night, sometimes half the night, and sometimes the whole night through. I would go along lighting the way for the irrigators as they went along doing the work. And I used to see how they did the work, and sometimes when they put their palas down I would grab one and put myself to doing their work. That's how I learned to do irrigation. At that time I was a kid—just a kid. I was a few years old, and already I used to lose whole nights lighting the way for them.

They had that practice because then the colonia didn't have a pond in which to keep its water supply. The water it received was government water, and that water was being supplied day and night. So in order to make the most of the water they used to work it that way. Although there was also another way. When they weren't able to irrigate at night, then they would prepare what we used to call regulators (*arregladeros*) of water, and we could arrange the water so that it would be working by itself the whole night [i.e. without irrigators working, by gravity feed]. But they used to use the night workers because then they could get more benefit from the water. And in the times of serious drought they would do that especially—providing either all-night or at times half-night workers. That was when they used to employ me, lighting the irrigators' way by night. I remember that in those days they used to grow corn in the cane banks, here and there. And at night we would roast ears of corn from the plants they were growing on the pathways through the cane. And then one irrigator would go off and prepare chocolate, crackers, and that sort of thing, and it would be ready for us to eat about 9:30 or 10; because we used to have to be in water all night long.

It was during this time, too, that I first felt the pain of a hernia which I have told you about before. I felt that when I was still a boy. I was already working. Yes, I was working already. I was lighting the way of the irrigators, and calling the oxen, and doing various tasks. But when I began to feel that pain, I was mostly struggling with irrigation work, at times taking the pala, too. And I would set about learning to make the proper movements for irrigation work and so on. When I first began to feel that pain, it was not frequent. But as time went by it became more common—to the extreme that recently [i.e. in the past ten or fifteen years of his life] there were times when once or twice a month I would be laid up with that pain. And when it came it would put me down so that I could not stir from bed. I would have to be in bed until the pain passed. It gave me pain first in the higher parts, and later the pain slid to the testicles. I felt it more on the left side and then, when I had a lot of pain, I felt it on both sides;

but at first I felt it on the left side, and when the soreness was very great, I would feel pain in both places. It hurt me most when it descended to the testicles; then it bothered me very much. Then I could not move. And as soon as I was touched there it hurt me excessively.

Anyway, that was the way I learned about irrigation. And as I was about to tell you, then I got work as an irrigator there with my brother-in-law. We had varying prices with regard to irrigation work; it would depend on the job. For wetting down seed—the first wetting you give the seed after planting —at that time if I remember rightly they were paying $1.50 a *cuerda* [approximately nine-tenths of an acre]. And fertilizer [i.e. irrigating fertilized soil] paid at $1.60, something like that, more or less. And regular irrigation (*el riego corrido*) they used to pay at 90 cents or a dollar. The wages were by the piece. So for regular irrigation, when there is neither fertilizer nor seed, if the piece rate were 90 cents, and you wet down two cuerdas a day, or three, that was what you were paid for. At the time the work was done that way, I was quite shrewd about irrigation work and I used to do all right for myself. I always earned $18 or $20 [weekly], which in those days was a real bonanza. That was the way I learned to do irrigation, and the prices for which I would work.

Now I also used to work by a day rate, at 80 and 85 cents a day at Colonia Texidor, where they paid a dollar for a day and a quarter, or 80 cents a day; so I've done this work in various forms, by day and by piece. At the time when I used to earn $18 or $20, the [regular] wages were 80, 85, 90 cents— a dollar a day at the most. The prices varied, and by piece-work one could earn something more. Now I can tell you more about this. The owners of the colonias never wanted one to earn much money. There were times when I used to earn my $18 or $20, and my very own brother-in-law would never give me this whole amount on my account. If I had earned $20, well, he'd put down $15, and then leave $5 until the next week's accounting. And they used to practice this system, you see. In fact the week after I left the job I went to collect $7 or $8 that I had worked for before and had earned before.

They wanted to conceal from the owners that a worker was making that sum of money; and this was the way they would try to conceal it in irrigation work.

Earlier, as I told you, Guillo Alomar and I were feeding the oxen part of the time, and afterward, still as boys in short pants, we used to load carts with cane, too. This was work that the men used to do, but we also used to do it. And in one colonia—the colonia that used to belong to the family Valdivieso—we two always loaded cane, with another boy who was also a friend of mine—not like Guillo, but I always regarded him as a friend too—called Claudio. The three of us and another boy who came on later whose name I can't remember were always the ones who loaded the cane at that colonia. And we did different jobs; when dead time came we were irrigating. And in those days they used to carry gravel from the river or from the seaside to throw in the *callejones* [paths between the cane fields]. They used carts that were worn out. We also did that work during dead time. Actually we did any kind of agricultural work there was. They also used to load carts with manure, and we did that work too in dead time. When there were very big droughts and not much food for the cattle, we also used to load certain carts that were especially adapted, that they called *pajeras*. We used them to carry straw from the cane fields to the corrals. There women would take the straw and pour molasses and a little water over it, and the cattle would come there and eat in the evening. In short, we were employed in all the jobs that were connected with the cultivation of cane. In dead time, we did every kind of job.

Now, about the dances in my youth—I used to look upon them somewhat timidly, because we were not allowed to take part at first. Although I wanted to, it wasn't possible. I had to wait until I was bigger. And even so, at times they used to throw us out of the dances. The organizers of the dances didn't let us boys in. Some times they told us we couldn't go in the dance; they wouldn't allow boys in short pants to be at the dances. And sometimes, although they would throw us out, we would insist that we wanted to be there until the end, and we would begin to dance a couple of numbers, and they went along letting us stay and letting us stay, until finally there we were dancing the whole dance. When I asked Lola Lebrón to make me long pants, it was in order to go to the dances. With long pants we would be able to enter more easily, understand. Those who already had long pants had less trouble in this regard, while those who didn't—the ones in short pants—well, the organizers of the dances didn't want to let them stay.

What were the dances like?

I am going to tell you about a dance in a house a little beyond where Tomás Torres lives [a nearby section of the barrio]. At that time José María Silva and his wife Alcilia lived in that house. She is still living; he is dead. Dances used to be given there on Saturdays—called commercial dances. That is, they were held with the end in mind of making money. I can name some of the girls with whom I danced there. There was a girl named Santía; Juana, who was her sister; another girl they used to call Juana of Destino; eh—Marcola used to dance. Many girls came from Destino, and afterward left Destino—one that was called Julia, another that was called Rosa; in short, many girls, señoritas, were at those dances. At those dances, almost always a man called Inginio played, and he was a good accordion player, but good, good; and the other instruments were the tambourine, a *güiro* [an incised gourd which is used as a rasp], and guitar—those were the things they used in those days. And the admission fees for those dances might be a dollar, or 75 cents, or 50 cents—that depended on how much money was around, how the situation was.

At those dances they might sell cold salt cod with creole vegetables, and sometimes rice and chicken, and other times viandas and salt cod and tomato, and things like that. Around 11 P.M. and on, these different foods were prepared, and they were for the escorts to buy to give to the girls or to friends, and to eat oneself as well. That was aside from the fee. The

fee was a dollar, or whatever, and that was only for the dance
itself. The other expenses one had to pay separately. If one
asked for a plate of rice and chicken—well, it would cost 30
or 40 cents, an inexpensive matter; and if it were viandas,
25 cents. Also they made coffee and sold it, and almost always
they sold drinks, too. And you asked me once if the girls used
cosmetics on their mouths and faces—the women here have
always used those things.

Those dances almost always used to begin as it got dark,
around 8 P.M. or before, and they would be dancing until the
sun rose. There were times when it was already daytime, the
sun up, and the musicians would get ready to leave to go to
their homes, and those still dancing would get together and
collect $1 or $1.25, and we would go and give it to the musicians so that they would play a bit longer. And so we used
to continue dancing thus until 8 A.M. or 8:30, even until 9 in
the morning. There were times when some of the parents
would come and watch for a while and then leave. Those
who held the dances had to go first to the parents of the girls
in order to get permission for them to go to those dances. It
is different now—now you don't have to invite partners; now
they come to a place where there is a nickelodeon and they
dance. Then you couldn't do that. The person who was going
to have a dance first had to reckon beforehand with the matter
of partners, and there were times when they gave dances here
with girls from Coamo.

Tole [Doña Antolina, Taso's mother-in-law] did that. As
the young people here were more enthusiastic then, she would
go to Coamo and invite partners from there. And she had to
rent a car or a truck, and it would bring them here to the
barrio, to her house. Then she would feed them, you see, in
the afternoon, and during the dance the expenses were the
partners'. Now the next day she had the obligation of sending
them off again to Coamo at her own expense. So they had no
expenses whatever for transportation. That was the obligation
of the manager of the dance. That was another way they had
[of arranging it]; instead of having all the dances here with
the girls from here, sometimes they would get girls from an-

other place for the dance. Thus they would change the partners and the people here liked it—dancing with partners from Coamo, lots of good partners. And really one enjoyed himself a lot at those dances—and now they have been disappearing. I believe it is a question of modern times (*modernismo*)—the facilities that they have now when they want to dance. They come to a place where there is a jukebox and they don't have to ask anyone's permission.

In those dances I was telling you about just before, in the house of José María Silva, there was no electric light. They lighted the place with kerosene lamps, and in the kitchen they used lanterns—they used them in the kitchen because of the wind—and the kerosene lamps, which were more easily extinguished, would be put in the dance hall, in places where there was not much wind. The lanterns were used in the kitchen because there were times when they had to take them by the handle and move them from one place to another, and the kerosene lamps were less easy to handle.

And at those dances there was not only dancing but almost always outside there would be a big game, also—dice or cards. One would dance a while and gamble a while. Thus one would pass the night at those dances, gambling part of the time and dancing the rest. The pieces they used to play a a whole lot then were the *plena,* and the foxtrot, and the bolero accompanied by the accordion. And there were many other kinds of dances—one called the Charleston—and no end of dances. At the dance there would be people of color, and white, and whatever. There were no problems in the dances.

But at times at those dances one would have to struggle with different—problems. I remember I had a problem at a dance with a first cousin of mine. And it was over a dancing partner; she still lives here—is a sister in the [Pentecostal] faith. I remember it well. He was dancing with her, and I went to cut in, to dance with her, and he refused to give me his partner. And I came back and insisted that he give her to me, and he continued to refuse. And then one feels a little ashamed of it—in the midst of the other girls and the other

men, and I threw a punch at him, and—we wrestled, and we
fell through the open door to the ground, the two of us in a
fury. We fought until they intervened and separated us, and
I had a grudge against that boy, though he was of our family
—to the extreme that I lay in wait for him (*le velaba*) [he
laughs], and it was not with a good end in mind. But afterward he himself recognized that he ought not to have done
that. I went one night to buy a beverage there where Colo's
store is now, and he was there. When he saw me enter he came
and offered his hand and said, "Cousin, quit this!" He asked
my pardon, and we became friends once more. At that time
I must have been at least fifteen or sixteen years old, something like that, because I had already been dancing quite a
while, when I was still a boy in short pants.

You were not in love with that girl you fought over?
No, no, we were not in love. It was just that she was one of
the dancing partners; we danced with everyone. I don't know
whether he was half in love with her, or what. But when I
asked to dance with his partner, he insisted on not giving her
to me, and a second time also. And here [i.e. in Puerto Rico]
especially—I don't know about other places—but in the dances
here that is not something one can do much. For there are
those who, refused on one occasion, well—that was enough
[for a fight]. And it's something one doesn't like because to
be left standing in the middle of the dance hall—it is like a
slight, you see? And it reveals an attitude which is a little
disagreeable.
Boys here begin falling in love with girls from the time
they are little. I remember that in school, still a school boy,
I fell in love with a girl they called Guadelupe. We were
little kids—school kids. Then there was another girl, called
Teresa, who was also a schoolgirl; but these were kid things.
When I was already a big boy, already *mozito* [a youth],
then I fell in love with Herminia, and I fell in love with Luisa,
and [he smiles] other girls besides. Luisa was a girl I got to
know well at a dance. I fell in love with her. And really, when
one is that age one is always in love with this one and in love

with that one, see. As we say in this country, we are like the
hummingbirds. And it was a pretty happy life. One falls in love
with the girls at the dances, and has an opportunity at the
dances to enjoy oneself fully, because the girl herself seeks one
out to dance in the dances. Well, I had some trouble at times
when I had to avoid a dance because more than one of my
girl friends was at it. And almost always—and that is why
I would prefer not to have my daughters dance—it's at the
dances that there's the most opportunity for the man to—con-
quer the woman. That's why I would prefer to have my daughters avoid the dances—although it's a natural thing, and there
comes a time when they have to fall in love and take husbands.
But it would please me if they would avoid the dances, where
things happen that—ought not to happen. The day that they
fall in love, let them fall in love in the house; they have to
marry, so let them marry in that way. But let it not be at a
dance. Because I remember through my own experience that
it is very easy to make a girl fall in love at a dance. It is one
of the easiest ways to do it. Because there are parents here
who are very strict with their daughters, and they don't let
any man come near them with the end of falling in love
[making love]. And in spite of that, the girl goes to a dance
and then it is very easy for one to make love to that girl.

And thus I was with the girls in the dances, for that was
the best opportunity to get to know them; because one is close
to [*pegado,* literally "stuck to"] one's partner while you are
dancing with her, and it's the best opportunity to talk to her.
While apart from that it is a little difficult. Sometimes a man
is not agreeable to a parent, and he can't talk with the girl
easily, you see—it's difficult for him. While at the dance he
comes and it's an easy thing; already they're together. And
when a piece ends they can sit together, and there is no one
to intervene in this, because even if the parent himself is
watching, he has to remain quiet.

Can you remember the first time you kissed a girl?
[He laughs nervously.] In a dance that is difficult. Now
see, if one leaves with her, there are times when one walks

about with her—well, one at times can go that far, but at a dance it's difficult. Many times I saw fights at a dance here on account of that. A boy kisses his partner, and this has brought about grave consequences at the dances. Because it is not that the girl gives him the opportunity, but rather that he takes the satisfaction of doing it. And that has provoked great fights at the dances. Although it has not been a common thing, there have been cases of it also. I don't remember kissing a partner at a dance. Away from the dance, yes [he laughs], I kissed them at times. That—you know how things are with those in love—one begins by taking the girl's hand, and thus little by little you go along till you have her trust, and that is the way. You had to avoid her family [he laughs] —for if one came— I don't remember—let me see—the first time. Now later, other times, yes, but the first time was when I was a little boy—imagine. Now after that, I remember, especially that girl Guadelupe who is not here now; she is in El Norte. I remember the night I kissed her. We were little kids; well, that night we were secretly holding hands (*jugando de manos*) and then I invited her to kiss me, and I kissed her [he laughs]. I felt very proud.

And you didn't say anything about it to the other boys?

No, that one always holds back—that is, understand, I— because through one's speaking of it it can get back to her family, and then that's the worst. I have always been a little reserved about my affairs. I know they talk a lot about those things. There are times when one has a friend and one tells him secrets, and as soon as he is able he goes and talks, you believing that he is not going to say anything, and that's the way it goes. Because of that, whatever anyone confides to me remains a secret for me.

Can you remember when you got to do more than kiss a girl?

Well, that was when I was a boy, I did that when I was still in short pants, perhaps about seventeen years old. It was this way [he indicates money in a characteristic gesture with his fingers]. I'll tell you this way. [He writes "75¢" on a pad on the table.] That type of woman. I was working. I was working at the time, and my mother was already dead. They gave a dance here, and they brought—someone here—they brought women—from Salinas. They would bring them from Ponce and from Santa Isabel. And after that I backed away a little from that, because of certain cases that I saw happen here, especially with a friend of mine, Moncho, who later emigrated. That boy had an illness that was almost a death case. I got further away from that.

How did you know what a man was supposed to do?
That is a thing I can't explain, because—because no one taught me and I didn't see anyone doing it! [He laughs.] That is a little difficult! I don't know where it [such knowledge] could come from. Right now I know that most of the little kids you see around here—I know that they know—now how they learn, or how it happens, that is a little hard to know. It could be from watching the animals, or whatever. I am sure that with regard to seeing people—here that is a little difficult, a little difficult. Because they can see a pair of sweethearts kissing, and holding hands and other things, but regarding that, it's a little difficult for a child to see it. So there has to be another way in which they are able to learn, to come to have this cunning (*malicia*). But with regard to that, you have seen how it is here in the barrio. And at home I regard it as equally impossible for a child to learn, for whoever is the parent, or whatever the crowding, he will always hide as much as possible, especially from his children. So I don't know how they are able to learn, to get this idea. I am very sure it is not in the family; most surely it is not within the family.

And can you remember as a child being curious about where babies came from?
Well, not I—at least it's as if I always knew they must come through this act.

Yes, but you have no memory of seeing animals for the first time, or—

That is something so common here; it's a thing a child is accustomed to seeing.

Then that was the first time. And how did you know that woman?

That was one of the dances they were giving in that place. One knew they were giving those dances [i.e. with prostitutes] here, and that kind of dance was the kind they especially prohibited boys from entering. So the boy in short pants always remained outside, below. And the young boy watches— you know what a boy is like—how they [the women] dress, and walk, and come and go, and that is where those who can take the opportunity, and the women are what they look for.

How did you come to know the price?

One always asks that.

Of her?

Yes.

And you went to the dance with that intention?

[He laughs.] Yes. Yes, especially because when they come to those places, that is their aim; to dance and to do that. One always—especially when a boy is becoming a youth— goes to such a place, and sees their movement; and in the male that desire is growing. He sees their ways, how they behave with the other men there; and then this ambition grows in the man.

At that time Moncho and I were both beginning. But soon I backed away from that—see, on seeing his experience. But he continued many years, continued with that business. I gave up the habit, because of the sufferings I saw him go through. He was nearly killed by a sickness from that, and I got frightened and gave it up. Oh, that boy was very sick. And if he lost his health, still, and in spite of it, he continued with that.

Where do you suppose the impulse comes from that pushes the boy to do that?

Well, there's the conversation of one boy with another. And apart from that—for instance, take a boy like José Miguel [Taso's second living son, sixteen years old]. They do not have those dances now—but suppose they were giving them —well, that boy, there he is in the doorway, and he is watching the behavior, how they are, the men with them; then the boy also gets this ambition—"Could I do that too?" And that way the boy goes along with growing cunning. I am talking to you about how it happened in those times, although now it doesn't happen just that way, see. But in those times, well, a young boy was able to acquire cunning in that manner because he had an easy opportunity to see that. Now it is a little difficult, because giving that kind of dance is hard now. But I believe that is the way the boys have the easiest chance, if they are in the doorway watching those women and how the men are with them, behaving as if they were completely lost. The boy goes along acquiring that cunning and the desire to do just what the others are doing there. And a boy like José Miguel, although he isn't yet 17, you can say he is a man already. He goes along thinking, with the ambition to do what the others do.

Can you remember the second time?

Yes, but it was a woman who had had a husband, and he had left her. She was alone. She was a woman older than I— although she was still quite a young woman. She was not from here; she had come here. I don't know where she came from. And I as a young boy—well, at times, a woman falls in love with one, and that is the opportunity one is given; that was the job I accomplished [he chuckles]. It only happened once. It was different from the other times because she was a woman who—she was not like those before. She was a woman who—she was not like those others. She was less dangerous. It could be that she fell in love, see, believing she would be able to corrupt a boy, see? And that occurred at a time almost right after that first experience I told you about. After that I don't remember whether there were other times because in a short while I fell in love with Elisabeth.

And with Elisabeth that was not possible until you married? [He laughs goodhumoredly, but in astonishment.] No!

Then a very frank question—tell me if you don't want to answer: Did you want to do that with Elí before you got married?

Well, when I fell in love with her, I did so with the hope that she would become my woman. Then I had to show a little more consideration. And if the woman doesn't give one the opportunity, it is difficult. For you can see cases where a person falls in love with a woman, and if he goes where the woman is and possesses her before making himself responsible to her, and then gets the desire to go away, he leaves her and the woman loses her chance [to marry]. So that also depends on the opportunity that a woman provides one. When a woman doesn't give one the opportunity that isn't possible. Because the woman thinks that one might do some bad thing [i.e. desert her before establishing a *de facto* marriage], you see, and therefore the woman always holds the man back. It is not possible; you may find those cases too, but it is difficult. And when I married Elisabeth, there was no one else.

These narrations cover the period from Taso's birth in 1908 until his marriage in 1927, when he was nineteen years old. Almost all the information from the recorded interviews concerning these years is included in the preceding sections. But the story can be filled out with data that I gathered during other visits, especially my first and longest stay in the village.

On one occasion when we were discussing the weaning of his children, Taso made a humorous reference to his own childhood. He was, he had been told, weaned after he was three years old. A neighbor named Sixto Rivera used to tease him when he was a child because he had been weaned so late. It would make him feel ashamed to be teased about it, he told me.

Taso was able to give little information concerning his mother's appearance. She was tall, he says, taller than his wife. Her hair was black and her eyes brown, unlike Elí, who has blue eyes and dark blond hair. His mother always wore long dresses with sleeves that came to the wrist. At no point in his description of his mother or of his relationship with her did I sense any special reserve or hostility; she is remembered with reverence and with very clear longing, although without much detail.

Taso's memories of his sister seem to be quite complete and detailed. In 1956 I tried to get some specific information from him on sex typing—the differences in training, in the kind of tasks given a male child which enable him to distinguish himself from girls. Taso harked back immediately to his own and Tomasa's childhood. Tomasa did the ironing and washed the woodwork and the floor. Taso cared for the family's goats, taking them to pasture, carrying water for them at noon, giving them grass in the late afternoon, and bringing them back at dusk. He was charged with collecting the kindling, and often he made the food purchases for the house. Both his sister and he would get water for the house. Palo Seco, the nickname for that stretch of marshy mangrove swamp, near the Jauca beach, where the brackish surface springs were that used to provide the barrio's water supply, was still littered in 1956 with broken bits of glass from the jugs people formerly carried there to get water.

Taso described himself at the age of about nine years old as wearing knickers, long knee socks, a *bombacho* (a shirt which slipped over the head, hung outside the pants, and was tied about the waist with a cord), and over-ankle shoes. People, he says, did not worry so much about having shoes then. (This was a real problem when I first went to Jauca in 1948. One might send a boy to school without shoes—though it was done with shame—but never a girl.) In the years of Taso's childhood most of the clothes children wore were khaki-colored, possibly a reflection of the American Occupation. Even in recent years some older men, particularly in the uplands, still affect the old-style cavalry hats of the United States Army, and mayordomos and their assistants still commonly wear khakis.

Taso says he liked school. When I asked him in 1956 why he had not made more efforts to continue his schooling and whether he had not had aspirations to become trained in some particular craft or profession, he answered that he had wanted to continue his schooling but constant economic need pressed upon him. He aspired to little because he knew of little to which to aspire: that is, there were few models of a different life which he could look up to realistically. He did well in school, particularly, he says, in mathematics. He also did well in Spanish, in hygiene, in writing, and in "agriculture" and geography. His worst subject, he said with a smile, was English. When he was about twelve or thirteen, a teacher who was very fond of him often invited Taso to join him in lunch. The teacher wanted to take Taso with him when he left Jauca for a job in a different school. Taso would not go. He had to work, he said, and he did not want to exchange the familiar for the unfamiliar. His formal education ended before he finished the fourth grade.

Of the house he was born in and lived in most of the time until he began boarding with Doña Lola Lebrón, Taso says that it was one of the better ones in the barrio, but that it was ramshackle and old. It was wooden, unlike the majority of houses, and had a wooden floor, also uncommon. The beds in the house were of wood, with springs and mattresses, and with canopies overhead. One senses that Taso's family probably had known better times. Most of the houses had earthen floors and very little furniture, with beds woven of maguey fiber or cloth, without mattresses. Hammocks were common then, too.

His early memories for the most part are dim and miscellaneous, but the basic facts are here, and it may be worth noting them again. Taso was born in Barrio Jauca, Santa Isabel municipality, in 1908. His father was a merchant of

limited means, a native of Barrio Jauca; his mother was the
daughter of a landholder or tenant farmer in the highlands
of Salinas, who apparently came originally from Juana Díaz.
Taso's father and an elder brother were drowned when Taso
was less than a year old, leaving Taso and two brothers and
a sister, all older than Taso by some years. I have recon-
structed some of this information: Pablo, the eldest, was born
about 1884 (died 1947); Eugenio was born about 1898 (died
1922); Tomasa was born in 1900 (died 1923). Taso's mother,
whose age could not be determined, died in 1920 when Taso
was twelve. In addition to the brothers and sister mentioned
here, Taso has at least two half brothers, Alejandro and
Hermelindo Cruz, sons of his father by a mistress, who are
somewhat older than he and who took their mother's surname.

Taso began school when he was about seven or eight years
old, and started to work at nearly the same time. He tells
how sometimes he would go to school half a day, and then
work half a day; on occasion, the schoolmaster would come
and get him and other truant little boys at their jobs and take
them back to the schoolhouse. It didn't matter; the next day
they would be at work again. The jobs were in the cane, on
the colonias nearest to Jauca village. Taso worked mostly with
the oxen at first, assisting the plowmen. Later on he acquired
new skills in the cane, earning more money and increasing
his mastery as he grew.

He tells in some detail of his feelings for his mother and
sister, of his sister Tomasa's first common-law marriage, and
how such things were handled. Shortly after this marriage
ended his sister married again, pregnant with a child from
her first union. In 1920 when his mother died Taso became
in effect his sister's ward. Soon his sister died and he and
Cornelio struggled with the care of the three children, two
of whom have survived to adulthood.

The years 1923–25 seem to have been particularly difficult
for Taso. He was still young—fifteen years old in 1923—and
already bereft of all his close relatives. The emotional tone
of his relationship with Cornelio is not fully evoked, but Taso
seems to have been lonely and worried in those years. When

he began boarding at the Lebrón's, some of the problems of physical existence were resolved for him, but he seems to have lacked any wholly dependable and continuous source of personal warmth and security. In 1925 he got his first pair of long pants. Two years later he was married by common law, and a new period in his life began.

This record has many implications which the interviews themselves only suggest. One is struck, for instance, by the serious deprivation which seems to have marked Taso's earlier years. He had no father; while he was still quite small, his mother died. Three years later he lost his sister as well. At the same time that his sources of security were taken away from him, Taso was compelled to cope with more and more difficult problems—of fending for himself, of satisfying his own growing needs, and of being partly responsible for the needs of others, particularly Cornelio's infant children. This deprivation appears to be of special importance with regard to his lack of a male figure upon whom he could model himself, and to whom he might look for reassurance and guidance. Cornelio was undoubtedly the most important adult male in Taso's childhood. But Taso's feelings about Cornelio must have been very mixed. He never refers to Cornelio with much warmth, and the record suggests how Taso must have resented Cornelio's philandering while Tomasa was alive. At the same time, Cornelio was one of the few people to whom Taso could turn for help or advice. Cornelio was a self-sufficient man; he held fairly responsible jobs and had high earning power. He never neglected his economic responsibilities to Tomasa, and he cared lovingly for their children after her death.

The other men to whom Taso could have turned for guidance were his brothers Pablo and Eugenio and Don Epifanio, Doña Lola's husband. Pablo moved away while Taso was still a little boy, and Taso saw him only irregularly. Eugenio died when Taso was fourteen. And whatever real intimacy there may have been between Taso and Epifanio seems to have become attenuated when Taso took a wife. That Taso's relationship with Cornelio continued is evidenced in later inter-

views describing his move to Aguadilla, where Cornelio had
gone, and the help Cornelio gave him there. Cornelio was
still a boss, able to muster resources and help for Taso and
his growing family. Today Taso maintains very warm relations with his nephew Eladio and with his niece Rosaura.
After Cornelio died they spent much of the time of their
own growing-up in and around Taso's house.

Cornelio's treatment of Tomasa must have colored Taso's
view of adult male-female relationships. But Cornelio's behavior, while perhaps unusual in its openness, was not sharply
deviant within his social environment. Obviously Taso did
not retain a completely negative attitude toward Cornelio's
behavior, however much he indicates his disapproval at the
way Cornelio acted. As he suggests, it took two to perpetuate
a situation such as Cornelio's and Tomasa's, once it had been
created.

Taso's own words show how hard it must have been for
him to live without his mother and sister after their deaths.
His problems were not only emotional, however. Taso was
doing the work of a man by the time he was twelve years
old, but there was no woman to satisfy his practical, let alone
his emotional, needs after Tomasa's death. It is important to
stress that a working man of Taso's social group is supposed
to have a woman at his side—mother, sister, wife or other.
The division of work between men and women fits this expectation. That Taso lacked someone to prepare his meals,
mend his clothes, care for his quarters, and attend to his other
practical needs made life very difficult for him. That is why
he stresses his feeling of relief when Doña Lola undertook
to look after him. At least on the practical level, she succeeded
in giving him the feeling that he was at last living once more
in a home, and that his daily needs would no longer over-
whelm him. Taso talked at times about the problem of having
one's clothes washed. Occasionally, before he began living in
Lola's house, he would leave his work clothes with a laundress
only to find that they were not ready when he went to pick
them up before the day's work began. There was no one to
make his bed or to cook his food. And these tasks are not

supposed to be done by men—in fact, many men of Taso's group will quite seriously insist that they are constitutionally incapable of cooking or of washing clothes.

It is easy to see then why Taso might have felt disoriented during the period between Tomasa's death and his residence in Doña Lola's house. He did such things because he had to, and washing and cooking and house tending must at least have depressed him; at the worst, they could have threatened his sense of identity. It was Doña Lola who made Taso his first pair of long pants. As he puts it, "*Me hize hombre en la casa de ellos*" (I became a man in their house). Thus he was living with Epifanio and Lola at the time he himself views as transitional between boyhood and young manhood. He had been interested in girls before then and had even had his first sexual experience. But his long pants are a symbol of his manhood, and they did in fact make him more grown-up in the eyes of others, as his discussion of the dances reveals.

It is of interest that Taso refers several times to his own children in recounting his childhood experiences and that the references are made in connection with dances and with the onset of heterosexual experimentation. At the same time that he reveals a certain boastfulness in discussing his own exploits, he expresses anxiety about his daughters attending dances. This swift moving back and forth from his own experiences and sensations to fears about his children, and a certain primness concerning them, occurs again and again in the verbatim record. It necessarily has to do with the way Taso sees himself, now and as a young man, and with the way he sees his own children. Moreover the narration reveals that the ways children experienced adolescence and took on their status as marriageable young men and women in Taso's group has changed with time.

Taso's reminiscences about his childhood illnesses require no special notice except for two items. The inguinal weakness or hernia he describes seems to be associated in his thinking with the learning of harder jobs, part of his maturation under Cornelio's guidance. His fear of venereal disease, after watching a young friend's suffering, also relates clearly to the growing-up process. But the symbolic significance of these things need not be discussed here.

One other item in the narration ought to be recalled. Taso describes his fight with a cousin, occasioned by a slight he suffered at a dance. The point of interest is Taso's statement, *"al estremo que yo le velaba"* (to the extreme that I lay in wait for him). The verb *velar,* "to watch over, to keep a vigil," is laden with special meaning in this connection, for it implies "to lie in wait with the intent to commit violence." Every language has its repertory of affect-heavy terms of this sort. In Puerto Rican Spanish, *guardar* ("to keep, guard, protect") can mean to hold a serious grudge, or to keep resentment alive. The verb *maliciar* ("to suspect") is often used particularly to mean "to suspect sexual misbehavior," and the noun *malicia* ("cunning") frequently refers to precocious sexual impulses. The adjective *pendiente* ("hanging, clinging") means "watchfully waiting," again often with sexual overtones. The terms *velar, guardar, aguantar,* and a number of others are used in patterned ways to refer particularly to violent behavior or the possibility of such behavior. Taso himself has never been a violent man and apparently fought little physically during his life. But the record is marked by the violence around him (as in the story of the relationship between Cornelio and his legal wife Nenita). His story about himself and his cousin, however, is the only one he recounted from his adolescence in which serious violence might have been a possible outcome.

From Taso's description of domestic arrangements—Cornelio's wives, his own father's mistress, and so on—and of his feelings about such things, it might seem that there were no rules for conduct in Barrio Jauca for these areas of life. Nothing could be further from the truth. That the rules are different from those familiar, say, to middle-class North Americans, however, goes without saying. This is not the place to survey thoroughly the conventions of courtship, marriage, residence, and household organization in Taso's village. But something must be said of these things, since the patterns of

social behavior and the social structure differ so strikingly
from what is familiar to most outsiders, and since so much of
what Taso says has to do with these arrangements of life.

Courtship among the people of Barrio Jauca is usually
conducted in secrecy. It is expected that young ladies will
not speak to young men or have anything to do with them
socially except in the presence of some other person. But
young people chafe under constant chaperonage and seek to
escape it. They do so, however, with the collusion of a
chaperon who serves as a go-between. Thus small groups
of young men and women strolling on the road may stop
by covert agreement so that a boy and a girl can talk together, off to one side and in relative privacy. At dances a boy
and a girl may sit together briefly in front of everyone and
talk, or perhaps even hold hands. In the evening a young
couple may be seen conversing in the shadows. Sometimes
a young man may "steal a kiss." But invariably someone
will be standing nearby. The "secrecy" of courtship, then, implies the presence of a third party. This suggests a powerful
force for social control at work, to prevent young couples
from consorting privately; and young people apparently bend,
though reluctantly, to this form of control. In this group,
"dating" in the United States sense does not occur. One is
led to assume that people in Barrio Jauca rule out privacy
in courtship because they fear the possible consequences.

This assumption appears to be confirmed by the character
of marriage in Taso's social group. Of the 183 marital unions
that I tabulated in the Barrio Jauca population, 134 were
based on common law; of the 134, *all* involving previously
unmarried girls were initiated by elopement. The form of
elopement is so standard that it can be described precisely
and holds for all but the most unusual cases. The young couple
secretly agree upon the occasion to elope. The young man
communicates—again secretly—with a relative (or, rarely, a
trusted older friend) living in another village or town, and
arranges hospitality for himself and his wife-to-be for a two-
or three-day period. The act of separating a girl physically
from her family in this way establishes the fact of marriage.

Thus, unless the couple later marry by civil or sacramental ceremony, elopement and marriage come to mean the same thing. The families of the newlyweds only rarely interfere in the arrangements, however much they may resent them. The girl's parents, however, may insist that their new son-in-law marry their daughter by civil ceremony. In this way they establish the wife's legal claim upon him in the event that there are children and the two separate afterward. The young man can be compelled to marry the girl if he is not already legally or sacramentally married and if the girl has not lived in a previous union of any kind. The compulsion has a legal basis, but usually the threat of being taken to court is sufficient. Jauqueños say that the use of legal threats has increased in the past two decades, but I have no statistical evidence that this is so.

It will be seen that the previous marital status of both parties, particularly that of the girl, is socially as well as legally relevant in local thinking. A woman is either a *señorita* or a *mujer de estado*. A mujer de estado has lived in some sort of marital arrangement; she is no longer virginal. The rules governing her behavior and her social person are different. If she marries a second time she need not elope. And public opinion does not control her behavior with such strictness, though a mujer de estado will also seek to conform by not meeting in private with a suitor. Particularly because she is not a señorita, she must be careful not to compromise herself. Parents do not attempt with the same zeal to compel a suitor to marry their daughter if she is not a señorita; legally, it is much more difficult to do so anyway.

One final point may be made emphatically in this regard. Though most marriages are established by elopement and remain common law, it is certain that pre-elopement sexual relationships between a young suitor and his girl are extremely rare. In other words, the seeming informality of the predominant marriage arrangement must not blind one to the fact that this social group values premarital chastity highly and manages to enforce this value with remarkable success. The same assertion may not hold so firmly for a mujer de estado. I think this is because after a señorita becomes a mujer de estado, she is thought to be much more responsible personally for her own behavior—she is "grown up." In the view of many young men an unattached mujer de estado is fair game, while a señorita is not.

Que se casa pa' su casa is a pun which means "He who marries should have his own house." Residence for those who elope is ideally away from relatives on either side in Barrio Jauca; if one elopes, he should have his own hut, however humble, to return to with his wife. The privacy which is denied young people during their courtship is insisted upon when the fact of their marriage has been publicly acknowledged. Independent residence is an ideal which cannot always be realized, however. When a young man cannot immediately provide his bride with her own house, the next best choice is residence with the girl's family. There seem to be several underlying assumptions here. It is assumed that a man will be able to deal successfully with his wife's mother; it is also assumed that his wife will not be able to deal successfully with his mother. A man's relations with his mother-in-law are likely to be circumspect and somewhat distant, but very important. If he has trouble with his wife, his mother-in-law may prove an effective intermediary. Moreover, if the marriage fails, it is to her mother's house that his wife is likely to move. The mother-daughter tie is hence a very important one. The mother-son tie is much less so, once the son has married. Food and gifts are much more likely to move from daughter to mother than from son to mother, unless the son is still resident in his mother's house and unmarried.

A son who brings his wife into his mother's house is courting trouble. This is the third residential alternative, and by far the least preferable. A man who brings his wife home to live after eloping runs the risk of being thought babyish and immature, as well as economically unresourceful. People believe a daughter-in-law cannot get on well with her husband's mother; perhaps it is not surprising that the belief is usually confirmed when the two women share the same house.

The picture is not so simple when the woman is a mujer

de estado rather than a señorita. Courtship of an unattached mujer de estado is not so delicate; elopement is not culturally required, and residence—at least initially—may be matrilocal or patrilocal, but it is much more commonly the former. Everyone aspires to an independent household. Ideally, there would not be a single case in which three generations would be found in the same household. In practice, independent residence is heavily predominant.

Marriage signifies social approval of a relationship which will come to have economic, sexual, reproductive, and socializing functions. Sexual activity immediately after elopement literally legitimizes the relationship. The economic function begins to be fulfilled as soon as the young people set up housekeeping. Everyone hopes for a child as soon as possible, and reproductive and socializing functions are thereby brought into operation. But the marriage relationship in Barrio Jauca is very brittle. In my 1948 sample of 60 couples, counting a marriage by each individual as one, there had been 183 unions—on the average each marriage partner had been married one and one-half times. Successive unions were usually common law, though in a few cases an individual who married the first time by civil ceremony would later marry another spouse by common law (without a divorce), and the opposite also occurs in my sample. Children usually remain with their mother, while she frequently returns to her parents' home until she marries again. Seriatim marriages characterize some individuals of both sexes, and there are many half brothers and half sisters in a village like Jauca. It obviously need not be pointed out that these patterned aspects of Jauca life are not tantamount to immorality, promiscuity, wantonness, or anything of the kind. Jauqueños have their own quite principled conception of immoral behavior.

I do not have adequate data to assert this definitely, but it appears that the brittleness of marriage declines with advancing years and the birth of children. People in their midforties do not often dissolve their marriages, though the marriage may be the second or third for one or both partners. Marriages between persons of very different ages—that is, more than about six years' difference—are rare. Since a man's economic status and power do not usually improve significantly with advancing age in this rural proletarian community, he cannot readily contract marriage with a much younger woman through blandishments of wealth or promised luxury. It is considered pathetic for a mature man to be without a wife—a woman to cook for him, care for his house, bear and raise his children. Thus young people who may experience several marriages of short duration in their late teens or early twenties often settle into a more lasting relationship within ten or fifteen years. It is possible that the increased migration to the United States may have affected still further the fluidity of marriage relationships, but I have no statistical confirmation.

A young man usually has his first heterosexual experiences well before he is twenty years old, often as early as fifteen. His sexual partner may be a prostitute, or an older unattached mujer de estado. Adultery, between a younger unmarried male and a married woman, or between married persons, is rare and also extremely dangerous. By the time he is seventeen years old a young man begins to think seriously of secret courtship and elopement, as I have described these. A young woman may have her first heterosexual experiences at an even earlier age than a young man—there are marriages in my sample contracted when a girl was thirteen years old—but her first experience usually occurs in an elopement, and not before. A girl who has a sexual relation with her secret suitor before elopement is very likely to lose her chance for elopement, and hence the public acknowledgment of marriage. She is ruined (*dañada*—literally, "damaged"), and has become a mujer de estado in the sense of no longer being virginal, but she does not have the attributes of a woman who has passed into and out of a socially legitimized relationship.

It sometimes happens that a man who is living in a common-law relationship may elope with another girl. If her parents then compel him to marry her, the obligations of his legal marriage take precedence over the obligations of his common-law relationship. It is easy to see why the parents of a señorita will seek to guard her from young men and to compel a suitor to marry her by civil ceremony if possible. At the same time, there are cases where a man lives simultaneously in two relationships, one common law and the other civil, as was true of Taso's brother-in-law, Cornelio. Such arrangements are rare, however, and ought not to be confused with the practice of having a wife and a mistress, more frequent at a higher class level. No Jauqueño would have dreamed of speaking of Taso's sister Tomasa as Cornelio's mistress (*querida*). Yet such situations are poorly thought of by Jauca people. They feel both women are at a disadvantage in such circumstances. At the same time, they feel strongly that the prerogative to terminate such an arrangement rests with the woman, and that if a woman stays in such a relationship it is her own responsibility.

In recent years, a few young Jauca men have contracted marriage by civil ceremony, preceded by public visits to the house of the girl of their choice. Also, some young men, particularly those who have had army service, have married by civil or Protestant ceremony, sometimes to legitimize further a common-law relationship, sometimes to initiate a first marriage. This trend partly has the quality of acculturation to middle-class Puerto Rican and North American standards. It also suggests—particularly in view of the apparent increased inclination of parents to compel a man to marry their daughter after an elopement—a decline of the power of local community norms and a tendency to depend more on the institutional controls of the wider society.

Taso's comments about his childhood friendships, and the references to color in this connection, have historical as well as sociological meaning. Taso himself is a "white" man. There is no noticeable physical trait which would suggest any other kind of background, and he knew of no other genetic strain in his family. Barrio Jauca, however, and most of the south coast of Puerto Rico, is populated by people who are frequently of more complicated ancestry. The range of physical appearance in a rural south coast community is bewildering, running from a Negroid phenotypical extreme to a Caucasoid phenotypical extreme, with physical suggestions of American Indian ancestry as well appearing in many individuals (for example, Taso's wife and their daughter Lilian). While there is high consciousness of physical differences, there is little race prejudice as it is known in the United States. Marriages between persons of dramatically different phenotype are common; physical type probably does enter into the choice of a mate, but its priority as a consideration seems to be very low.

So matter-of-fact is the racial egalitarianism of a person such as Taso that questions about the social relations between persons of different physical appearance did not stimulate him; instead they usually caused him to become mildly impatient or quizzical. It is not that there is no feeling about race in Barrio Jauca; but it was difficult to get interview descriptions of race relations since, in Taso's view, there is nothing to be described. This is, of course, not altogether true. For instance, in addition to many euphemisms of social description, there is a stock of chauvinistic terms referring to physical characteristics which are never used publicly. That there is feeling about color is also revealed by certain commonly held stereotypes.

There is no question but that the people of color of Puerto Rico have not had wholly equal opportunity in the island's history. And it is impressionistically correct that persons of extreme Negroid appearance remain concentrated in the lower social and economic echelons of Puerto Rican society. But the most important feature of the relationship of people of color to the total social system is the fact that they are not confined to any social category that might be considered castelike in character; when they rise in the social and economic structure, they discover that it is in fact a single structure, with few vertical barriers separating them from their social and economic equals of purely Caucasoid ancestry. Though there is color awareness, race consciousness, and some race prejudice in the lower class, race feeling hardly has any consequences in daily social life. In Taso's case, the circle of his friends, compadres, and kinfolk represents the gamut of physical types.

Taso's references to his religious training are clear. Throughout his childhood and half of his adult life, religion was of no importance. He was born a Catholic and was baptized. But his Catholicism had no emotional or ideological significance. And, as he says, "In 80 per cent of the cases that is how one is religious here in Jauca." In Puerto Rico the original content of Catholicism appears to have been seriously eroded in the centuries of isolation and ecclesiastical unconcern. Devout Catholicism persists mainly in the upper class and in the highland municipalities. Among the lower-class people of the coasts, Catholicism is generally not an effective part of life, and every sacrament and rule, except with regard to baptism, is observed only in the breach. This situation has great relevance for the later chapters of Taso's life.

Taso's descriptions of his early work experiences point up some significant facts about life in Barrio Jauca in the earlier decades of this century and about the ways in which it has changed. In describing various places and events and in his references to the breaking of new ground for cane, he provides evidence from his childhood that the region of which Barrio Jauca is a part was going through an agricultural transformation in the 1920's. Land that had never been cultivated before was being thrown into sugar production on a grand scale. The uplands in particular, which could be employed for cane cultivation only when an artificial water supply was assured through irrigation, were coming under the plow by the thousands of acres.

Taso makes plain that there were no enforced laws affecting the labor of children. As the United States corporations expanded their control, buying outmoded haciendas and putting land into cultivation, boys as young as nine or ten years of age were employed in large numbers to feed and manage the oxen and for other jobs. Only in the 1940's did laws affecting the labor of children come into effect. The cessation of employment of women and boys in the fields was accompanied by a progressive mechanization of the field operations. The large numbers of oxen were gradually reduced, to be replaced by machines. Standardization of field jobs also came about, as later texts reveal. Thus with reference to work, Taso was growing up in a period of vigorous and significant change. The economic and technological changes naturally affected the social qualities of life, and the impact of these changes was felt even in the most intimate areas of living.

Education was of minimal importance for the lower-class children who were Taso's contemporaries. Today compulsory education is much more a reality in Puerto Rico—though many children still receive inadequate schooling. One of the difficulties with school training formerly was the lack of any realistic opportunities to which the child could aspire. With few models to stimulate his effort, economic need as a constant goad to give up school, and little evidence that education could lead to a better or fuller life, it is not surprising that most of Taso's contemporaries got no more schooling than he did.

Taso mentions that when he was a child people walked to the movie houses in Santa Isabel and in Salinas—"At that time there was none of this car business." In his earlier years, he would go with his mother or sister to Palo Seco to get water for the house. The roads are now good in the south coast region. Automobile and bus transportation is swift and readily accessible. Standpipes replaced the surface springs of Palo Seco as a source of water in 1935. And electrification is now common to almost all the houses and shacks in the barrio. These are not the only areas of life in which public works and technology have eased effort and have brought the village more into the modern world, but they are of the greatest importance to local people. Kerosene stoves, when they can be afforded, save time from tinder gathering. Electricity can mean the use of electric or even steam irons. Refrigerators had begun to appear in the period 1945–50, and by 1956 there was a television set in the barrio. Such devices as electric mixers, washers, dryers, electric or gas stoves, and the like, are still unknown—not even aspired to. But even without these, the mechanical changes as well as the advancements in public works have been part of the revolutionary remaking of the barrio since the second and third decades of the century.

The description of Tomasa's death from malaria and Taso's references to his own childhood illnesses and the deaths of some of his children lead into another important area of change in Jauca life. Even when Taso was a child, doctors were called in Jauca and their ministrations were respected. But in the case of Tomasa's death, it is plain that there was still a struggle in progress between modern scientific and folk medicine. The commonness of malaria (which persisted in Jauca until the 1940's) and of other diseases (such as schistosomiasis, amoebic dysentery, and gonorrhea) to which Taso does not refer indicates that as late as the 1930's the awareness of modern medicine did not mean an opportunity to take full advantage of medical techniques. Fundamental improvement in health and health conditions in Jauca and in scores of other villages like it began only in the 1940's. Before then, lower-class Puerto Ricans were barely able to benefit from what was known of diseases and their control.

In these many areas of life the first half of the century brought about vast and rapid change. This is the background against which the events in Taso's life must be viewed.

CHAPTER 5

Manhood: The Early Years (1927–39)

I GOT MARRIED in—it seems to me it was in 1927. Yes, '27; because I remember that when Elisabeth was pregnant with our first child—which was after we'd lived together for about a year—the hurricane of San Felipe struck [1928].

We men paint a beautiful panorama for a girl. It's true that at times we don't provide them with what we've promised. But we aim at winning the girl, and we make a great number of offers. And finally we dominate! When I began to fall in love with Elisabeth, it was at a dance. I remember it as if it were now, and I even remember the house where I began to fall in love with her. The dance they were giving that night was being held in the house of Santiago Alvarado, here in the barrio. And it was at that dance that I began to fall in love with Elisabeth. I had seen her before. Our love was kept secret for a long time. After a while it seems that they [Elí's family] got some idea that we were in love. But that was never a problem for me, understand. They saw what I was like—and it seems they didn't really disapprove. Even so, one night I was taking her home—she was living at Cuatro Hermanos [a nearby colonia]—and I was taking her there to her house. I turned back before we got to her house, and it seems that she caught something when she got home! [Elí's mother saw Taso with her, and Elí was scolded for walking unchaperoned with him.]

Elí was married before. She was a mujer de estado. I don't really know anything about her first husband, not even his surname. He was called Eusebio. He was not from here, but from Guayama. I saw him only a few times. He was a short man, a white man. He was here at the time, and then he went

99

to Guayama and I never saw him again. I knew Elí from before, though. Like the other boys in the barrio, one makes the acquaintance of the girls here—but it was not a question of our having a close friendship before. Rather, one always says something [flirtatious] to the girls one meets. In the midst of that, she went off with him. Then they broke off and she came back here to the barrio. It was when she came back—after perhaps a year—that I began to fall in love with her once more, and then the thing became serious. Now, while they were living together they lived in Guayama. I don't know who left whom—but after that, they came back here and then they separated. He went back to Guayama and she stayed here with her mother, living in a house her mother had near Colonia Valdivieso. Then they moved to a place near Comadre Paula Godineaux.

About eight or nine months passed by. I was not concerned about Elí's having been married before, because I already knew her from before that. I knew she had had another husband. I don't know how others might see it, but for me it made no difference, particularly since that man never returned here. After he left here, he never came back. And she and I never discussed her marriage. Our jealousies came later —hers of me and other girls and the like—but never regarding that. I have never been jealous of my woman. The day my woman makes me jealous I'll leave her. That is my opinion. One must think about that beforehand. Because if a man knows that a woman has had another husband [and it makes him jealous] perhaps he ought not to marry her.

Now, as I told you before, when I began to fall in love with Elisabeth it was at a dance. After that, when she accepted me, then I went to live with her. At the time I was living in that house there of ours [i.e. his mother's house] and I went to live in the room that Elí had in her mother's house. She had a separate room, and it was the one we then came to occupy. At that time Antolina [Elí's mother] was living alone. Then after some time she began to live with Sico [her third husband]; he moved into the house. There was a period of some two or three months that we lived in a house belonging to Comadre Paula, a house located beside Antolina's house. And then we began living in a little house that Antolina bought for us. Beside her house on adjoining land there was a little house for sale, and Tole [Antolina] bought it for us for $15. In those days you could buy a little house like that for such a price. Afterward, I went and talked to the owner of the land. I told him that if he would let me keep that little house, if he would let me fix it up a little, I would agree to help him in anything I knew about. He told me that there was no problem, and that I wouldn't have to pay him anything. I proceeded to fix up my house there, and seeing what he had told me, I was quite contented, you see? Then I had my family's old house in another place, and I went and dismantled it. I turned over part of the lumber to Cornelio, and I took the rest and repaired the new little house. But then the landowner wanted me to pay a sum [as rent for the land] which was impossible—and this after he had told me I wouldn't have to pay anything. I gave him an argument, saying that I had not committed myself to anything of the sort. What he asked at the time was impossible for me to pay: $12 a year. I told him it wasn't right and we had words. Then I decided to take the house apart. I dismantled it and put the lumber in Antolina's house. So I was left without a house of my own again; I had to move back into Tole's house once more.

And at that time—in fact even before—my troubles with Elí began, because of other women whom she knew I had been in love with before. There was one case in particular, and it is only very recently that I became convinced that she had at last given up that obsession. The girl is called Luisa, a trigueña, and she lives in a nearby town. I had been in love with that girl in the past, and Elisabeth never wanted to make peace with her. On different occasions they almost came to blows here because of Elí's jealousy. And one time I nearly had a real problem with a member of that girl's family. What happened was that the girl's mother came to the house to humiliate Elisabeth. And as Elisabeth has this tremendous spirit (*genio*), and jealousy at the same time, she came out of the house carrying a shotgun. Nothing happened, luckily. But there was a man in that girl's family called Don Chago. That man hadn't lived here before, but then he moved here. He was of the family of Compadre Colo. And when he found out about the dispute, he said he was going to wait for me and I was going to have something to settle with him, because it concerned his family. But there was a friend who hurried to where I was working and told me what was happening, and that I should be careful when I got home. I remember it as if it were now; I was working with the portable rails, either filling wagons or laying rails—one of those two jobs. And I took a pick and took out one of the things we call a shoe, for joining the rails. And I had taken a coat in the morning to protect me from the cold. And then I put on the coat and put this shoe in my pocket, and walked with my hand in my pocket, holding the shoe, until I arrived at the house. When I passed by where he lived, he was seated in the doorway. And I passed by expecting him to call to me. But I passed by and came to the house and he said nothing. After I bathed myself in the afternoon, I was walking around the barrio and in the yard of the house, and he never called my attention to what had happened.

But Elisabeth was a thoroughly jealous woman—not only of some particular girl but of any woman with whom I might be talking. That would be enough for a fight, and a vicious one. I remember one night there was a wake there where Alvarado lives. Sarita, whose sister had died, and I had come from town. I don't remember on what errand I'd gone but I went and came home. And as custom has it, I said, "Well, I'm going to the wake," and I went to the wake. Elí stayed at home, and she—it seems she went out to the road to watch me, as a jealous woman will. I stayed awhile at the wake, and when I left I went out on the road and returned home. At that time we were living next to Tole's house. And I left the wake on the side by the railroad, but when I got home Elí insisted that she saw me come away from the sea side. You see what kind of thing was going on? And when I got home, well, nothing else but a fight, at that hour.

And so we were fighting for years, and it was a terrible struggle, what with her jealousy. That began almost from the moment we started to live together. That was about 1927, and in the 1940's Elisabeth was still that way. Now, as we have had a family and so on—she is old, and I am a little old —well, that has ended. She was completely different from me, because Elisabeth could not say that I ever had doubts about my woman. I believe that the day I would have to live in jealousy of my woman, I would say, "Well, you take your road and I'll take mine," because I am not that way. Now a woman is not like that.

And in that period of time I suffered greatly, and so did she. That, that was a regular war. If I got home feeling calm the woman would be invidious, and then there would be a fight. It was one of our greatest problems. As she knew there were girls I had fallen for in the past, she believed that at any moment, well—as you know, there are so many cases here where a man carries off a girl now. And then his woman [i.e. a prior common-law wife] is left behind. And there are so many cases in which a man has carried off a girl, and for whatever reason they haven't made him marry her. And after a while he carries off another girl, and then they make him marry that one, and then this one here is left. And I believe it's from that that her madness came.

During that time, a girl I knew was out walking with another girl from here, and I took her to Ramos' store and paid for several beverages for them there. And Conrado, who is of Elisabeth's family, saw me when I paid for the refreshments. And he ran and told her right away, and when I left there I was immediately embroiled in a fight with her. And that, well, it was more of what she was most expecting, you see? Because he went and told her he had seen this and he had seen that, and then the woman became even more rebellious.

Now, I never had children with another woman, only those I have had with Elisabeth. But there are cases also in which men have their wives and have had children with other women like that. To know other women, though having a

wife—that's a thing that happens here all the time. I don't
know if it is like that over there [in the U.S.], but here, yes.
Now, there are women, prostitutes, whom anyone can use for
whatever purpose. But there are also other women who don't
have their husbands, who live alone, and they too—well, as
we say, each one of us defends himself. There are also those
who have their husbands. Of course that is a bit dangerous.
But these, too, may lend their little favors. And here there
are those men who have more opportunity, not like those of
us who have it rarely, not persons such as I am, always at
home, tied firmly to my family. There are those who pay no
attention to their situation or to anything, but rather are
watchful for whatever presents itself. And there are even cases
where a man will have children with another woman. And
afterward that creates serious problems. There are those who
don't take that into account, who don't take care with regard
to that. And especially where there may be a fight afterward
with a jealous woman—one must also be careful to avoid such
disputes. Particularly in my own case, where I had a woman
who was a little hot-tempered in such matters! One must
avoid these things, and it is not so easy. And after one has
one's wife, where the woman accepts one thinking he is a
committed man, that children may come, it is a little difficult
unless the man makes a proposal which is false, fools another
woman, and is able to succeed. But it is a little difficult after
a man is committed, although there are those cases, too—I am
not going to make a comment on that! [He laughs and stops
talking abruptly.]

*I introduce here materials from my interviews with Elisa-
beth, Taso's wife, wherein she describes her marriage to Taso.*

My first husband had gone off. I had thrown him out and
hardly remembered him any more. During this time I remained working with my mother. I was working and buying
all of my own necessities. And after much time, well then
Taso, as I was then alone, well, he began to—I would pass

by and he would say something to me, to flirt as they make love to girls here. I was still very young, and recently had left that other. I only lived with him eight months, nothing more, and I was the same as when I had gone off with him. I used to go to dances with my mother. Mama went, and she used to take me. I went to a dance, and I know it was at that dance that he fell in love with me. It seems to me that was —there was a man here they used to call Nene—Nene Alvarado, and there was a dance given at his house, and it was there Taso fell in love with me, in that house, at that dance.

Mother knew Taso from the time he was a little boy, and my mother always used to say, "You see, since he is a boy raised in the barrio, the barrio knows him." We noticed that Taso, from the time he was little, was good with his mother, and that he was hard-working. From the time when he was little he would go to work, keeping up the house, and keeping up the obligations of a grown man. I recall when his sister died. I was still a little girl and I got to see the wake for his sister. I went to the velorio that night. In other words, we had reasons for knowing the life of Taso's family, you see. We knew their life, and we saw their behavior; we saw how they conducted themselves, and we saw it was a family that got along well, brother with brother. He always lived with his family, and he always worked to help his family out. He was always working only for his family, and he was a boy without vices. What happens here is that a person scrutinizes others and goes along forming opinions. This is what I say of Pablín, that Pablín creates the same impression as Taso did when he was growing up. I got to know Taso when he was still in short pants, you see, as children, and he never said or did anything ill-mannered. I knew he was living with his mother, that he was a native of the barrio, and he would go here and there like all of the boys. And we knew he was a good boy, just as now many people call me and say to me, "What a fine son you have; that Pablín behaves like a grown man. That boy is going to be like Taso was when he was growing up." And with this manner of his, when he began to fall in love with me, I had no reason to reject him. There was nothing for which I could reprove him, because I knew more or less how he had been brought up, and more or less how he conducted himself with his family. And my mother always used to say, "A man who is good with his mother will be good with his woman." And I had remembered that, too. And as he had never been married, I decided to test that. I said, "Well, I am going to accept this boy to see if it is true, as my mother said, that a man good with his mother and with his family is good with his woman." And in reality it turned out to be the truth.

Your mother never scolded you for going with him?

Once. I came to the barrio [i.e. to where Taso lived, from Colonia Cuatro Hermanos where Elí was living]—and that was the only time she scolded me. But it was because he brought me back alone toward home. I had stayed in the barrio till quite late, and he came bringing me back toward home. And she came to meet me, and she saw me with him. And she didn't like it, because she saw it as something suspicious. His bringing me home—she thought people might talk. But I felt sure people would not talk, because where he was bringing me was to a place where he used to leave me to go the rest of the way alone, where no one would see me. But she realized he was courting me because she came to meet me that time. And she scolded me; indeed she did.

Not years, but months passed, and we got married. When we decided this, Taso took me to my own house. It was not that he carried me off, but rather that he came to live in my mother's house. Because here it is very different, depending on whether one is a señorita or not. But as I was not a señorita, well, Mother was glad that we might become a couple. Because he began then to visit me at home, and by then they knew already at home that we were going together with the idea of eventually getting married. Then, when we discussed marrying, he decided to move his things to my house, because I didn't want to move here to the barrio. I didn't want to move where he was because he had a bad house. He lived in a bad little room, in a house that was falling down and almost had no floor. Then I said to him, "Where I am coming when we elope is right here!" And then, well, we agreed, and Mama knew he was going to move into her house. Then they gave us a room in the house; and as I was not a señorita, there was no need to be careful to hide this from the public or anything. Because already the world knew we were in love and that he was staying here. At any hour of the day he would be visiting me in the house. And the days he wasn't working he would be at the house. The world saw him at the house; already everyone knew we were a couple. All that was lacking was that he remain in the house. And he began staying at the house, with Mother's consent. Because here they have the custom that when a youth carries off a señorita, he has to carry her far, far from her family, because he is stealing her, he is fugitive. But when it is with the consent of the parents, when the parents like the boy or however it is, with their consent, then they may be married in the house of the parents, and later move to another place. The way it is with señoritas is different. But when he took me, he took no señorita, because I had already had another spouse, one with whom I had lived eight months. So Taso didn't have to go through the business of carrying me far away; rather, he could leave me in the same house, only in a separate room.

I was quite young, quite ignorant, at that time. Let me tell you what happened only a little after we began to live together. My brother was a barber, and I stole a razor from his barber box. And my brother missed the razor, and he said, "Someone took a razor from my barber box, and I need it." And I had the razor here [she points to her blouse] and I didn't tell him I had it. I told no one. I didn't want anyone to know that I had it because I had a bad thought in my head. I was being unjustly jealous of Taso. What I thought was not true, it was a vicious jealousy, you see, a vicious thing, and I was imagining it. I thought he was with another woman; but actually he was not out with any woman. My jealousy had blinded me, I had this hallucination that I saw him with—with a woman that I was jealous of, you see. And I believed I could surprise him walking along the road and talking with her. It was when he went off to the burial of that infant of Cornelio's who had died, a little girl named Isabelita. You remember, we told you of one occasion when Cornelio beat up Nenita, his legal wife? Well, that was the child she had in her belly at the time. We told you he beat her up in the house, and when he hit her with that chair, the child leaped inside her belly—well, when that child was several years old it died.

Taso went to the funeral. And I was jealous of a particular woman; and I knew he would have to come back from the cemetery on foot. I awaited their return. I thought, they are going to come along here feeling fine, along the road, talking and falling in love, and I don't know what else. And so I hid myself under a culvert, in a drain pipe in a place they call Las Montañas,—there it was that I hid myself. And I waited. But they didn't pass by; I believe they came back in a car— I don't remember for sure, but I know I didn't see them go by. And finally I came back along the road and came home. When I got tired of prowling about with that razor because no one came, well, I returned, and I put the razor back in Mariano's barber box. The razor reappeared. And my mother knew it had been me, and my mother said to Mariano: "This razor! Hah! And if it was not Elisabeth that was going about carrying that razor with her—hah!"

Then they questioned me to see if I had had it, and I said no, that I hadn't been walking about with any razor. Because I didn't want my mother to know about it, you see. And I had this maliciousness, apart from being jealous. Taso never has been an argumentative man, but at times there would be fights in the house because of my jealousy, you see. As I wanted him to be jealous of me, then it seemed to me that if he were to go out in the street, well, already he was out with some other woman! A matter of my ignorance, because the man is not like that. Ignorant thoughts, because when I joined up with him, I was still pretty ignorant. I was quite young.

And he was quite ignorant, too; we were young, two young ones. He had as little sense as I. Any little thing I would tell him would hurt his feelings and also might make him angry. But he never became infuriated with me like some other men who beat their wives.

One time we had a—a passing thing, but it was not—it was nothing. He gave me a slapping once! And it was my fault! One time he slapped me. But I was in the wrong. It was because of that same jealousy of mine. Also a matter of my ignorance. My mother, you see, had her little business. And a girl came in the store to buy tomatoes. Taso had planted some tomato plants behind the house. And the girl, as my mother had a business and used to sell tomatoes and sweets and different things—well, the girl came and she said: "Doña Tole, do you have any tomatoes?" Then Mother said, "I have no tomatoes, they're all gone." And as Taso had those little tomato plants growing behind the house, he jumped up and said, "She has no tomatoes, but in a couple of months, I will have some, because I have some plants behind the house, more than enough." He said nothing more to the girl. The girl began to laugh when he told her he had those little plants and that she should wait. But as I was so jealous, I believed it was a love-joke that he had told her. And I got mad. I felt this rage in a second, and what I desired was to fall upon him. Because of those few words, nothing more.

Well, then, I got into this real fury, and when it was dinnertime I didn't want to eat. I left my food. And he always used to say to me that what made him angrier than anything else was when someone cast aside what his sweat had earned— that is, you see, the bread he earned with his sweat. And I— knowing that made him very angry—well, I took the plate of food, and I threw it in his face; the food with the plate together. And he became poisoned with anger. He approached me, he alarmed me; then we began to fight—he said something and I answered him. Until there came the things said in heat, and he slapped me! Well, that has been the only time, and it is now about twenty-six years that we've lived together; it was the only time he ever struck me; it was just that once.

We had a baby already, very little at the time. I remember that already Vitín had been born. I had him at the time in the corner, in a little hammock—I had him there in a hammock—and this happened in my mother's house.

We were then living in a little house close by that Mother had bought for us. Well, afterward, he went off to the house. And I remained in my mother's house, sulking. I didn't want to go to my own house. But then Mama made me go there to sleep. Mama always defended that one; my mother knew quite well what a wild one I was. Ah, I had the deepest hurt, because it seemed to me that the world turned over. He had never hit me or punched me, and when he threw that punch at me I thought the world was coming to an end. It left me with a very great hurt, and I didn't want to go to our little house. I wanted to stay at home. Actually he hadn't beaten me at all, he merely touched me—but I told my mother that I wouldn't live any longer with a man who would beat me like that. But truthfully the one who sought the beating was I. It was a mere touch, a glancing blow; yet it seemed to me like the kind of punch boxers give each other. And it made me so nervous that I began to scream, and I filled the house with my screams when he struck me. I suffer from nerves, and this nervousness came over me. I cried with the deep hurt I felt, I cried and cried and cried—I cried nearly till midnight because of it. But finally I went home. Because Mama was a grown woman, you see, and she knew best. She knew that my obligation was to go to my own house, and she advised me to go.

When I got there he was well wrapped up in the bed, snoring loudly! He was as if nothing had happened. I arrived in a rage, and I sat on the doorstep and I didn't want to go to bed, I was so poisoned with rage; I didn't even want to go to sleep. And he was snoring—snoring away when I got there. Next day, I was still not willing to eat, what with the rancor I had; I was always a bad-mannered one, you see. I keep grudges; until finally, we began talking about some trifle, and we became contented once more. Ah, but that was an anger I passed through that day, when he gave me that slap!

Taso picks up the narration once more.

In 1928 there came the hurricane of San Felipe [September 13]. At the time of that hurricane, as I told you, I had a wife already. We passed through that hurricane safely in the store of the Mora family. At that time Don José Guilbé had his store there. I went to work that morning, and at that time I was an irrigator at Colonia Destino, in the part they call Valdivieso. I went to work at dawn and started the water, and before beginning work we were standing in front of the sluice that brings the water, waiting for it to reach us. And then the irrigation foreman, Juan Morales, arrived. We talked a while because the water had not come yet, and we were already feeling some rather strong wind. And he told me we wouldn't work that day because the wind was suspicious. Then he sent me to close the pond, and we sent the irrigators home. At that time the men who were under my direction were Juan Borges, Evaristo Rivera, Ramón Borges, and several others whose names I don't recall at the moment; I know I had about seven or eight men working with me. After I closed off the sluices I came to Antolina's house, where we were living then.

And while Elisabeth was making lunch—good and early because the hurricane threatened—I went out to walk by the seashore, to gaze upon the way the sea was. And the sea was good and strong. It was around 10 A.M. and the tide was coming up and passing underneath the sea grape trees already. Afterward I came back home and ate lunch; it was already prepared. And around eleven or eleven-thirty the hurricane struck. In the middle of the squall we forced our way outside. I took Elisabeth by the arms, clasping both hands around her body, and we struggled along defending ourselves from the wind, so that we could get to Don José Guilbé's place. And Antolina and Sico also came with us, and the rest of the family. When we arrived, I left Elisabeth and

Antolina there. Then we men devoted ourselves to helping those persons who still had not been able to get to places of the greatest safety.

After that I stopped outside the store, and from there I watched the hurricane as it unfolded. I saw the first-grade school tumble to the ground, and I watched the way the houses were going down. In front of the store building there was a vegetable stand, belonging to Nico Suárez. The stand had fallen down and there was a great quantity of ripe vegetables and avocados and every kind of food around there. At that point Antolina had disappeared from the store. Elí and I looked for her among the other people, but could not find her. But we were not surprised or frightened by this. And at around five Antolina appeared; she had gone home to prepare dinner. She brought rice and beans for us, and coffee too, which she had prepared there. We ate from what she brought us, and we gave the rest to some ladies there who had little children, so they could give it to their children.

And so night came. When night arrived, then everyone found himself his place in the building. Actually a number of us had to remain standing, and others were sitting here and there, because there were a great number of people in the store. It was completely full of people who were looking for the safest place to stay. And down there in the sixth-grade school there were lots of people, too. Luckily no one had taken refuge in this hurricane in the first-grade school— though it had been one of the places of refuge before. Somehow, on this occasion no one ran to it.

The storm went along building up, and by 9 P.M. many houses here had fallen to the ground. From the steps of the Moras' store there I watched our house. It was moving backward and then swaying forward again with the force of the wind. I waited from moment to moment for it to fall to the ground, and I could see from there when all the front part, of galvanized iron, tore loose from the rest and was carried off. The house actually swayed to one side and danced to the other, but it did not fall. While the wind was blowing from this side, it leaned away from the sea. Then when the wind changed—what we call the *virazón*—then it leaned toward the forward part. But it did not fall. Absolutely nothing happened to Tole's house—I don't know, it may be the work of God, because her house was a very weak one.

While the storm was building up, it seems that there were people who valued their lives little and forced themselves out to collect iron sheeting and wood and those things scattered everywhere. And really, people who didn't have houses appeared after the storm with houses, and people who had had houses were left without any! While the storm lasted, one could not walk through the streets. Many houses lay in pieces in the road, and many zinc sheets and plenty of lumber that had been blown about now were in the road. It was perilous to walk about at night with the boards and spikes and such that were around.

But around 2 A.M. there were many, many little children crying with hunger. Food had been prepared, but with so many people it was not possible to give it to everyone. It was hard partly because there were not enough pots, and partly because it got to some and not to others. Then I asked for a flashlight from a friend of mine—if I'm not mistaken it was Inocencio. And I pushed my way outside, and got as far as where the vegetable stand had been. During the afternoon food had been blown all over, and we went and put some stems of ripe Martinique bananas in a nearby horse cart. And having borrowed the flashlight, I went along lighting my way, little by little, in the midst of the wind, and got to the cart and brought back a stem of bananas, and they were distributed among the crying children. And so we passed the night.

Around eight o'clock the next morning the wind began calming, gradually calming, and then each person started back toward his home. One would find his flat on the ground; another's would be spread about in a thousand places; and so it went. And those that found their houses flattened collected the sheeting and lumber that they could, and raised whatever and wherever they could—their house as before, or just a shack—but to begin with, anything at all. They propped up the zinc sheets, and so these makeshifts stood until one could remake one's house or shack.

About two weeks afterward I went with Elisabeth to Coamo to see her father, who was there. At that time they were beginning to distribute some food. I don't know if it was the Red Cross or who it was that was giving it away—they gave it to us in the name of "I maintain" (*"Mantengo"*). And while we were in Coamo they were distributing the food in a bus through the whole town; they went about carrying it through the streets. That afternoon we were sitting in front on the street when the bus went by. And they brought it to us too— to Elisabeth, to me, and to Elisabeth's father, and to his wife, a woman who was called Caita. They brought a tiny thing to each one of us, in a little bag—a trifle that they were giving away—but they brought a bag for each of us. We left them there because two or three days later we came back here to Jauca.

And so, when it was all over—when I came back to Jauca— I went back to work again. Then we began struggling with the cane, the cane that the wind had felled. We set to work propping up the cane that had fallen into the irrigation ditches; not in all the cane field, but just in the irrigation ditches where the cane had fallen and the water couldn't go by. We were put to work setting these up and putting earth around the stalks, because we found that the wind had so ripped them out that when we stood them up they nearly tore out of the ground. So at the same time that we set them up, we put earth around the stalks.

During that time, in the first week, there was a great abundance of vegetables here in Puerto Rico, because so many properties had been destroyed, and the owners had cut all the vegetables there were rather than lose them all, and there were great quantities available everywhere. But afterward they got so scarce that it was only after a great while that one could get them again, even such common ones as bananas and plantains, because the farms that had provided them were completely destroyed.

There had also been some deaths. I remember that during

the storm a girl who was telephone operator in Coamo—I didn't see her or know her but I read about it in the papers, and people who came from there told us—continued to give service at the phone until the office fell down, and she lost her life. And here in the part they call Boca Caballo we found a dead woman, too, whom the river had carried from the place called Borinquen, in Salinas. We found her because a wave had carried her to the beach, and she was almost completely covered by sand; there we found her. And so accordingly there were deaths in different places caused by the storm, because really that storm was something serious. I was able to appreciate that it was a strong hurricane since, as I told you, there had been storms of lesser intensity before.

Elí was already pregnant, during the hurricane of San Felipe, with our first child, who was named Victor Manuel Zayas. He was born March 23, 1929, and the midwife who attended was Comadre Lupe. At that time they didn't attend as they do now, when a woman must be a registered midwife. At that time they didn't have that. On that occasion Elí was sick almost continuously during the nine months of her pregnancy with chills and toothache, and I went repeatedly to the doctors to see if they could treat her illnesses. During the final months I sent her to Guayama, to my brother Pablo's house, so they could take her to a doctor. And she went there, and after he examined her he told her that at the end of the nine months the illness would pass, because it was a direct consequence of her stomach—what we call here "bad stomach" when a woman is pregnant. And so it happened. Still, after she gave birth, she had about two more such spells of chills, fevers, and afterward all of that passed and she was left completely well.

Before Elisabeth became pregnant, I was always waiting for the news of a child. Because it is the most desired thing. And one certainly can't count on it, since it is the work of God whether one will have a family or not. And after a year went by—I don't know if it was a whole year or not—she became pregnant. And then one feels content, because another member of the family is coming and, as we say, children brighten the home. One knows when one's wife is pregnant by the time that—that she has her periods—when she misses at least two consecutive months, well, it is certain proof that the woman is pregnant. And from there on I never lose track of the date. I count then from the first, and I know more or less the month the woman is going to give birth.

And then I—I don't know about anyone else—when the woman is pregnant, I begin to prepare as soon as possible, knowing that a woman can give birth from seven months onward. And one may be caught unprepared. In Vitín's time, I told Elisabeth that she should prepare everything she needed as soon as possible. She began with the sheets and built right up to the layette. I think you know what a layette (*canastillo*) is—the layette includes the bonnets, little shirts, and the band the women tie round the umbilicus of the child, round and round. And another thing they used in those days that they no longer use. When they were four or five months along the women prepared a bottle with rum, and they put in garlic, rue, and *anamú* [a medicinal herb], and a number of other herbs, and this stuff becomes foul smelling. The women had the belief that when pregnant they had an animal inside them and that after a woman gave birth the animal could sting her. And so she would take a draught of this drink —a foul rum. Elisabeth used that also in the beginning. Then later, when midwives had to pass examinations, and the doctors went along explaining, well, women gave up this custom. I don't know if some still may have it, but in our house we rapidly eliminated it. And, as I told you before, all this was in readiness for when the moment came. And especially, a hen was always kept ready for when the time came. Then immediately they would take it up, when the pains came to the woman, and the hen was killed. And they began to give soup to the woman, and chicken broth during the period of labor, until the woman gave birth. And after she gave birth, she also continued eating it.

And they also had the custom that they would not give women in childbirth common water from the rain barrels, but rather they would use what they call *moscada* [nutmeg], which they sell in the pharmacy. They put these to parch, and then they throw them in a jug of water, and this was the water that the women used to drink during almost the entire cuarentena. Now today they don't do that either; now women drink water from the barrel, without using this method. There were many such customs that the women used to have, but now little by little the doctors have gone along explaining to the registered midwives, and they have gone along explaining to the women, so that now they don't use these processes.

When the moment of Vitín's birth came, I was working at Colonia Valdivieso, and I was laying rails with Compadre Gueni when Salvador, Elisabeth's brother, came to find me at work. We were working that day in field No. 136 when he arrived with the message. Immediately I left my work, called the foreman, and told him to take charge of the work I was doing since I was going to look after the situation. I knew already of several cases that were a little delicate; Tomasa had died as a consequence of a delivery. And I had witnessed that. Immediately I went to Antolina's house, and when I arrived Antolina was making certain preparations, and I went rapidly to find the midwife. I brought Comadre Lupe, who would struggle with her. That would have been about two in the afternoon when this was going on. And I became very uneasy because at eight at night the woman had not yet given birth.

While the midwife was struggling in the room with her, I was in the living room going from one side to the other, expecting some grave peril—grave, you see—and I was completely upset (*impacientado*). And then around 9 P.M. the boy was born. When I heard the boy cry there in the other room, then, with the change in the situation, I felt content. And as soon as she had arranged her in the bed, and taken care of the little boy, I went in to see the boy and to see how she was. Then, well, I felt content because the woman had come out all right.

We did not plan before the birth who the godparents would be. And as for my children, I never, never gave them their names. The names of my children were always given by

Elisabeth's father or by Elisabeth, and at times Rosaura; they were always intervening in these matters. I left it to them, and the day that it came time for me to go and inscribe them in the register, then I'd say, "Well, let's see"; because sometimes there were different opinions among them, some believing one way and others believing another. Until at last they would decide on one, and then that was the name that I would go to inscribe.

When they poured water on Vitín [i.e. in unsanctioned baptism], they poured it on him in the house of Antolina. Then we spoke to Compadre Gueni and Comadre Paula; they came to Tole's house. And that was a simple thing, the pouring of water on a child. They take the water, they raise it up, the godfather or godmother holds the child, they recite the *credo* and the *padre nuestro,* and the child is ready. They pour water upon the head, and it is done. That is all there is to the ceremony when you water-baptize a child. When you pour water on a child, they don't make a fiesta. It is on the occasion of [church] baptisms that they are accustomed to do that, to make a feast and eat barbecued pig, and those things. But in the case of pouring water, no. One may make a little chocolate and serve that.

The water [for an unsanctioned baptism] one always gets at the church. I do not know how they get it at the church now, because recently I have heard that the priest will not give water for that. But I know that they always used to get it in the church. And they would keep it in bottles, in those little grape juice bottles that one can buy in the store—they would save the water in these. And, actually, if they don't have that water, they don't pour water on the child. It has to be water they bring from the church.

I'm going to describe now the life of Vitín over the course of about two and one-half years. That child was born with a live spirit; he was an agile child, a child that was never quiet. And a child to whom one could say things and he would act like a mature person. He had reason at a very young age, and one was able to say things to him and he could understand them easily and carry them out. To such an extent that when I would come from work in the afternoon he had the habit of coming to me as I reached the shoulder of the railway. I would take my pala off my shoulder, and he would pick it up by the handle and drag it along; and while I held him on the other side, we would walk together until we reached the house. He was raised together with Luis Godineaux, a boy who is here, the son of María, and they would come to the house and eat. And afterward they would go to the house of María Godineaux and there the two would eat again.

And the boy was in complete good health when sickness came upon him suddenly. I remember that it was a Saturday. Fé Mora, the sister of Cosme, passed by along the road near the house, and we were sitting playing with him. And he said, from where we were playing with him there, "Adiós," he said, "Adiós, sweetheart," to Fé. That boy had—I don't know if it was together with the other kids that he learned such things—but truly he was a boy you had to see. And the next day I went to work, and he lay down to rest completely well and hearty.

I was doing irrigation work at Texidor at the time. I left the job at Colonia Valdivieso, and I was irrigating at Texidor. And when the lunch hour came, I was awaiting my lunch and the lunch did not arrive. There was a boy who used to bring the lunches. And his absence worried me, because Elisabeth would always appear herself where I was waiting when the boy was not able to bring it. And she didn't appear. And at 2 P.M. her brother Salvador came, calling me in the field. I came out, and when I came out the news he gave me was that I should come—that the child was very ill, that he had had an attack. Then I came swiftly, leaving my pala out there in the field. And I came to the house.

When I arrived, it turned out Tole had already attended to things, and they had given two injections against those attacks. And I went to town and brought Dr. Vélez; Vélez came again and gave another injection. It must have been about 8 P.M. and they put ice bags on him, and then he underwent what seemed like an improvement. He remained thus rather quiet, and then at around 11 P.M. there came this other attack, and then it was attack, attack, until around—around 8:30 A.M. he died.

And at the moment he died I was not in the house. Because as soon as the brightness of dawn came I left the house again to go to the town to try to get the doctor. And then Salvador followed me on his bicycle and caught up to me there almost at the hill in the middle of Colonia Destino—to tell me that I should come back, that the child had died. So I didn't succeed in bringing the doctor back here. While I had gone with this aim, he reached me along the road and I turned back. Then, when I got back to the house it was terrible. The first son—and Elisabeth was having nervous attacks that were terrible. And still Elisabeth's attacks of nerves are such that I must struggle very hard with her. Then we had this struggle with her, until we were able to calm her somewhat. And at the time we were already living in the little house, and it was very uncomfortable there for the wake. Then we made the preparations and went to Antolina's house, and it was there that we kept vigil during the night. And that is where the history of Vitín ends.

We always believe in God, although some believe in one manner and others in another. And there are times when one believes in God in one manner, and a time comes when one believes in another. But as for dying we all know a time comes when one must die, and that—"Bendito, that is the fate of the child"—nothing more, and he died at that time. Now I really believed that I was dying when that happened, because he was the first child and truly I had put all my love in him as if he were the only one. Carmen Iris [the second child] was still very little, see? And then when the boy began to talk, and as he used to have that way of behaving with me as has my Tasita [his youngest daughter]—well, one has an immense affection for one's children, you see? It seemed one had lost half one's life when that happened. It is a moment that one— that I do not want to recall, you see, when a thing happens as in this case, with a child that one has raised so indulgently, treated so freely, the first child and all that. And not just the first child, because you see all the time how I am with my children, that it matters not which one, that for me Tasita, who is the last, is as if she were the first, that we raise them in this manner—this love that we give the children; so that when one dies we believe that the world has come to an end.

And so we were a long while, thinking thus. Until at last, well, the memory is gradually erased, and then with the affection toward the others, well, one goes along erasing the need for that child. At times one despairs, truly. At times one is in the midst of despair, one suffers, until one cannot speak of it, you see? I have seen different cases of a person crying for a member of the family who had died, and I have heard them say things that one would not say in his proper mind. Truly, one feels so despairing. And I know well that when this child died I felt so wretched. In the midst of the sadness one feels, at times one may say things—almost anything—far from all reason.

Afterward we began to care even more for Carmen Iris. And in the midst of this, one goes on acquiring more experience, you see? As the family grows, one gets more experienced in how to treat children, and so on. As with all things, you see, when one has one's first children, well, one really doesn't know how to care for them well. But through having more children, one grows more careful. If a child gets sick, one knows how to treat it. And so after Vitín's death, well, we took yet more care with Carmen Iris. For example, now when a child is sick, well, right away we are careful that it doesn't go out into the night air, that it comes in when it rains, and all that. And it could be that before, since one has little knowledge concerning these things—well, one doesn't worry, one is careless, and any kind of abnormal thing can happen. But when one goes along experiencing these things, one acquires experience, and one worries more about it.

Now, Carmen Iris was born in March 1931; she was born in the little house Antolina bought for us. Carmen was born in the dawn, and the one who attended her was Tole. She was the one who did everything; she was the one who looked after and cared for Elisabeth. That birth was completely easy, and Elisabeth during that pregnancy felt few symptoms and had a completely happy delivery. When Carmen Iris was born, I was cutting cane seed at Río Jueyes [part of Colonia Boca Chica]. And the same day, after Antolina looked after the tasks, fixed up the woman and the child, then I went to work.

Of Carmen I can tell you that that girl—I don't know where it came from, the kind of disposition that girl has always had ever since she was a little girl—but she has always been given to rages. I remember—I wasn't at home, but Elisabeth told me—the story of how she had a real fright one time with Carmen. She was washing the floor in the house, and the women here are accustomed to fill tubs full of water in order to proceed with the washing. And Carmen was bothering her, playing in the tub, and wouldn't let her work with the water and the broom in washing the floor. And she scolded her and told her to get out, that she didn't want her playing in the tub any more. And she picked her up by one hand and put her thus to one side; and the child ran out crying. And at that moment, Joaquín, Elisabeth's father, was standing outside. He had bought bread from a truck that came from Coamo and he was putting butter on it. And when Elisabeth took up the child and put her to one side, well, she didn't notice that the child ran off crying. And when she looked at the girl again, she discovered that in the fit of crying she was having she had almost suffocated, you see. The child wasn't able to get her breath. When she saw the child was almost unconscious she dropped the broom and took the child in her arms. And Joaquín, who had the pieces of buttered bread in his hand, put them on the ground. And while he was helping Elí with the child, a dog came by and stole the bread! Elisabeth had a great scare. She had to toss the child up in the air and throw her about until at last Carmen regained consciousness—she says the girl almost suffocated in the midst of that tantrum.

Since she was little Carmen has always had that disposition. You have seen her ways—you've seen how she orders the children around. You would think the house was falling down, the way she orders things to be done. She has been like that since she was a little girl. She has had illnesses, though not of great seriousness. When we moved her to this house, she had the measles—I brought them all here with that sickness. And chicken pox, and those kinds of illnesses. When she was very little, she also suffered from indigestion—what we call here *empachados* [colic]. She suffered from this when she was little, though she has never been sickly. But her disposition has always been that way.

But I would like now to tell you some other things. I'll tell you first what it was that led me to enter politics. In 1928 the candidate for mayor in Santa Isabel was Don Pastor Díaz. Now before, as I have told you, my family had a house, an old house and a piece of land. I don't know what it was that motivated him, but Don Pastor Díaz came one day where we were and told us that that house and that piece of land were his. My family had always lived on that plot of ground, and Mama had told us it had been a present that had been given to our father. But actually we had no deeds or anything of that kind. Afterward Don Pastor Díaz said that only the land was his. And then he put pressure on us to move the house, so that he would be left with the land. This was in 1927; I had a wife already. And as we had no deed to prove the house was ours, I went and dismantled it.

Now the following year, in the campaign of 1928, when Don Pastor Díaz was a candidate for mayor, I had the opportunity to get into political activity against him, though I wasn't even old enough to vote. But I made every possible effort to help whip him in that political campaign. And in the end we were successful. We beat him. And so it was that I had entered politics. I don't recall well, but it seems to me that at that time the Puerto Rican Alliance was fighting against the Socialist party. He was with the Alliance—their candidate for mayor. And as I told you before, in the beginning, in 1928, I didn't think about politics, but rather about the attitude of that man Pastor Díaz—it was his behavior that motivated me to get into political activity.

We surrendered the land to Don Pastor Díaz. And then after some time he rented a piece of that same land to Compadre Ceferino. And we saw a paper he gave to Ceferino, showing the amount of land he was renting him. And another part remained unrented. Years later my nephew Lalo decided to move his house and nail it up on the land Díaz had taken from us, and there he has it still. But when that happened Don Pastor Díaz was already dead. And then the lot remained like that, split in two. And the part where Lalo put his house they have not disturbed. It's a small lot but Don Pastor rented it to Ceferino as if it were his. At that time I was working at Colonia Destino as an irrigator. And the afternoon Don Pastor Díaz came with this demand, I wasn't at home. I was working, because at that time we were working half the night through, irrigating. And when Elisabeth came to bring my dinner she told me what he had said. I thought of perhaps seeing him in order to talk about it, but my older brother Pablo didn't want to go. And it was he who knew more or less how Papa had been made owner of that land. He refused to go and I, being younger and not knowing how it was, decided that I would do nothing. When he told me we would have to take the house apart, well, I accepted this, and took it down.

Now, concerning Don Pastor Díaz, there is little else I could tell you, because he was a man with whom one could scarcely talk. I do know certain of his habits. He used to charge around on a horse, and when his employees least expected it, he used to go riding around on that horse, checking on everyone. I remember that he introduced a system one time of not paying the workers for time when it rained. He said he wasn't going to pay for rain. Then the workingmen used to go home each time it rained in order to avoid fights with him in the pay line. So you can judge his behavior. He was a man who, with regard to work, was completely paltry. He had many bad customs. I told you before that sometimes when we would go at 5 P.M. to get paid he would be walking around, revising the lists, and then finally he'd tear them up, and there'd be no pay till the next day. Things such that, if they were done now, with the government we have now, he would have died of rage or suffered greatly!

His wife was a Guayama woman whom I did not know. If I'm not mistaken he had a son, and there were several suits with regard to his inheritance after Díaz died [an oblique reference to the claims of an alleged illegitimate son]. He had an old, big house in the colonia; he lived there part of the time. It was in that same house that he paid [the workers]. And there were rooms full of things he was saving. But afterward he built two houses in addition to the big one, good-sized ones; and though he built those two, he remained in the old house. And we ourselves used to ask what this could mean—with two good houses and he continuing to live in a house that is practically a barn? But after a long time he left the old house and went to live in one of the new ones, which is still the house there. And when he died everything he had remained there. Then Doña Eva, the wife of his son, and his son, who was called Ignacito, were there a while. And afterward they went to San Juan where they'd been living before. Then Ignacito also died there and she was left. And according to what I've been told—it's not anything I can vouch for —all the things were left in that house, and they say they have all disappeared from there. I have no idea in what mysterious way this might have happened, but they say everything that was there has been carried off.

I'm going to tell you another experience I had with that man. After the hurricane of San Liborio [1926] I remember that my brother-in-law Cornelio and I went for a walk along the seashore. And there was a woman here, a prostitute, and she was also walking by the seaside. And in Palo Seco we passed by her. From there, we returned once more to the barrio. But we neither looked at nor touched anything belonging to the colonia. In spite of that Don Pastor Díaz wanted to denounce us. He wanted Herminio, the first mayordomo, to swear out a complaint that we were stealing coconuts. And if it were not for Herminio arguing with him, saying that he was not able to do this, he would have denounced us, without any reason and without our having done anything at all. I don't know where this thing came from with that man, because we had not committed any misdemeanor or taken anything of his. Instead we were simply looking at the disaster of the storm and what the sea had wrought. And he was intent one way or another upon denouncing us, to such an extent that Herminio had to hide our workbooks; because he wasn't able to denounce us since we had done nothing. If he had had us taken to court we would have lost our jobs—and if he had proved it, we could have gone to jail. But he could not prove it, since really we had committed no crime. But there were cases in those days when *they* were the government, and without being guilty one could be thrown in jail by them—there were those cases, too.

People had no bias against working on Don Pastor Díaz' hacienda—because it was a question of who the mayordomos were. He didn't go riding about often—just every once in a while. He was very exacting about the jobs. For anything at all—if he saw a worker leaving half an hour early, well, he would call him instantly, and instead of taking off this half hour he would take off a quarter of a day. Then they didn't reckon by the hour—it was a quarter of a day or half a day which they used to take away, you see? A man could lose a quarter of a day's work for five or ten minutes. But other than that, he didn't often go where we were working. And with the mayordomos the workers worked quite well. He on the other hand was a bit hard. As to what people here thought, I don't know about others, but I never considered him good.

For instance, this story I'm going to tell you now. At one time in the colonia of Boca Chica, that part called Río Jueyes, they had a farm where they raised male calves that were prepared during the harvest for cane carting. And there was a *sabanero* there named Don Tito. The sabanero is in charge of caring for the animals—taking them to drink and taking them different places to eat. In the colonia there were two mayordomos, the second one being quite a friend of mine, named Torres. And about that time Torres had a baby boy who died. Torres was a man who would tell almost all his problems to the boss; and when he told him he had lost a baby, Don Pastor answered, "Well, one has to resign oneself; that is a test through which all of us must pass, eh?" And the man resigned himself. Some time passed and a machine killed an animal Torres had, and he came that time also to Don Pastor and told him: "Look, Don Pastor, a mare I had was killed by a machine." And Don Pastor answered him, "Well, then. We who have, we are the ones to lose, eh? Because those who have nothing lose nothing. As you and I are ones who have, well, we are called to lose." And the man resigned himself to that also.

Now Don Pastor Díaz had a burro there at Río Jueyes. And with the passage of time it came about that the burro died. When the sabanero Don Tito came to bring milk to the colonia, he brought the news that the burro had died, since they used to keep a record of the animals that died. And when he came, well, he told the wife she should tell Don Pastor; but she didn't dare. And he also didn't dare tell him. But then Don Tito finally asked Torres to tell him what had happened. Well, as soon as Torres told him, "Don Pastor, the sabanero has come and he says that the burro died," Don Pastor answered, "It cannot be! Under no circumstances. That burro cannot die!" So the baby of the mayordomo could die, and his mare—but Don Pastor's burro wasn't allowed to!

Now to go back to my story. When Don Pastor demanded the house, and Elí told me that, I felt quite uncomfortable. It was our only sure refuge; once we departed from there, we would have to keep moving. So I felt angry and upset. At the same time, I was angry with my brother because he ought to have helped me straighten it out. But as he refused I left it as it was. He should have known something about it, but he obliged me to remain silent. At that time Pablo was here in Jauca working at cutting cane for seed. He did little enough of it; he didn't care much for working in the cane. Now, I don't know if Pablo thought we were in the right or whether he thought we no longer had rights to the land. What I can tell you is that Mama always told us that that piece of land had been given as a present to our father. Had Pablo gone with me to Don Pastor Díaz and explained his position, if he had said something like this: "Friend (*fulano*), it was a gift to my papa, in such and such a time"—well, we might have been able to do something. Although perhaps not—because Don Pastor was quite a rude man. But at least we might have done something. But Pablo didn't want to.

Does it seem to you that in those days people knew less about their rights?

Yes. And I'll tell you a little more. In that time, it was hard to get to see these people in order to explain one's point of view. I recall those very elections, in 1928. I myself had no vote, as I told you before; but they had a terrible system they used on voters they knew were Socialists. They would make up some falsehood, some lie, to implicate a man. He would come home from work in the afternoon and the police would be there waiting to take him to jail. Then the man would have to sleep in jail. And that was enough to make him lose his vote in that election. They'd hold a hearing in which this person would end up guilty. And if they put him in jail for only a day, that was enough to make him lose his vote in the election. So they used to have control over these matters.

I remember that Francisco Aguirre, Tole's husband, had this experience. We went to take dinner to him the evening that he was a prisoner in Santa Isabel; and to Felix Godineaux, who was also a prisoner there. A fellow who is employed now in the Santa Isabel hospital accused Sico Aguirre, claiming that Sico was a charcoal-maker in the place they call the Wells of Río Jueyes and had no right to vote in Santa Isabel, but rather should have been eligible in Salinas. Imagine—a charcoal-burner—and Francisco Aguirre didn't even know how to build a bonfire! That was the sort of trap they used to keep votes away from the Socialist party. I remember that Doña Herminia Torme, the lawyer in Juana Díaz, used

5. Sugar cane in bloom

6. The sugar cane farms of Santa Isabel

7. The harvest

8. Workers' houses, Colonia Destino

9. Workers' houses, Jauca Beach

10. A sugar mill

11. Foremen during the harvest

to defend them in those days. But it was hardly ever possible; almost always they came out with one day in jail. Few were absolved. In the case of Francisco Aguirre the witness against him was the selfsame Sico's brother-in-law!—he didn't dare declare against Sico. And so they were not able to throw Sico into jail for that full day.

They could tell who was a Socialist. One always shows what one is. Few people keep their points of view secret. That kind of attitude one would see mostly among those who lived on the colonias. But almost always those who lived independently around here, well, they used to express how they felt. And, in '28, '32, and '36—things were practically the same throughout—the person who lived on a colonia and was a Socialist could not say he was a Socialist. Because if he said he was a Socialist, well, automatically he was finished on the job. And they would come and put an oxcart alongside his house and carry out the bed and his other things, and he'd have to leave the colonia. If he didn't want to, well, then he'd have to humiliate himself by giving his vote to them. That was the way they used to do things. And we who didn't live on a colonia, we who lived apart in the barrio, outside —as soon as they knew one didn't belong to their party they left him without work. And you would be without work all that time. And after election time passed, you would continue without work a long time. Until finally they would come around to giving you work again. So it was something they wanted, no matter what—that you vote with them and always give them the reins of government. Now in that regard we have gained a good bit of ground. I don't know if you have noticed that when we've walked through Colonia Destino you could see the flag of the Popular party everywhere. In that time—*Díos Libre!* imagine showing it with a flag!—they could not even express it in words! Today it is otherwise.

Yet in spite of everything, well, people would go on. The time it happened to me in Colonia Texidor—they threw me out of work even though I wasn't living on the colonia. I suffered terribly long because of that. But in spite of it I went on being a Socialist; and if the Popular party had not appeared in 1940 God knows if I would not have continued being a Socialist.

Now I would like to return to the jobs I have had. One that I used to do a lot when I started living with Elisabeth was carter (*carretero*). Helping to drive the oxcarts was work I used to do as a child—but when I was already fairly grown up, not a very little boy. The smaller child works as a cuartero, with two yokes of oxen, taking the carts out of the fields. And at times, while the carters are filling the carts and there's nothing for him to do, he helps them and so he learns how to fill the carts, and afterward he becomes a carter himself. At the time, I was carting cane at Colonia Bomba, the property of Don Clotilde Santiago. The mayordomo was Don Rafael Gracia. There they would load cane by the ton, at various rates per ton. Sometimes they loaded at 14 cents, and other times at 15 cents, and at 16 cents; those were the wages per ton for loading cane on oxcarts.

In dead time the carters were put to work carrying gravel from the river bed at Paso Seco to be used for repairing the pathways in the cane, to prepare them for harvest time. We would put gravel in the places that used to get bad when it rained, and at the same time we would take advantage of the opportunity to train the bull calves, the oxen that had never worked as yet. That work was a little dangerous. They still wouldn't know how to draw the carts, and sometimes it would be a lot of work even to yoke them to the carts. And when they were finally yoked, they'd be running and bucking, and many times the carts would even upset—dangerous work, that. The purpose was to prepare the animals so that when the harvest came they would be more docile and could be used for carrying the cane. I spent a lot of time with Don Rafael there, not a matter of years, but quite a lot of time. Later on I got a little tired of the dawns—one had to get up early to go from here to Colonia Bomba.

Then I stayed on here at the colonia of Don Pastor Díaz. I stayed with the idea of working in irrigation, because there was a system established on the basis of piecework rates at the time. They'd done it that way formerly, but they had given it up; and then they returned to a piecework basis. And as I had considerable experience in irrigation work by the piece, I knew that one could make more money that way, and I decided to stay on there in order to get work with my brother-in-law, who had already offered me work.

Later on I had still another job, laying rails. You know already what that is like. That was when Central Aguirre [the biggest corporation in the area] took up this colonia here belonging to Don Lucas Pérez Valdivieso. And Don José Godineaux, the father of Compadre Gueni, was the foreman of the little wagons. Compadre Gueni and I used to take charge of preparing the pathways for the wagon-loaders. At Destino they already did that. Now when they brought this method to Colonia Valdivieso, it was new. Don Lucas Pérez Valdivieso had used oxcarts up till then.

Compadre Gueni and I did that work by the day. There were times when we used to earn $2, $2.10, and so on a day, with the wages for the job fluctuating somewhat. And that, too, was where I learned to load the little wagons that were brought into the cane on portable rails. But as we were doing the same kind of work, I learned to load the little wagons there, and later on I came to be a *vagonero* [loader of the wagons on portable rails] too. Before I got to be a vagonero I first loaded the big *fulgones* [standard railway cars on Puerto Rico's narrow-gauge railway]. That same year I worked at the siding here at Valdivieso. I worked part of the time laying rails and toward the end, in the last weeks of the harvest, I wasn't working on the rails and they sent me to fill the railway cars. The harvest was almost finished. At the time they were paying 12 cents a ton for cane loaded onto the railway cars there at the siding. I worked there until the end of the harvest.

And the following year I took up this work again when the harvest started. From the first day of the harvest I loaded railway cars, and I continued to do it for some years. That was the kind of work in which I told you once I squandered my youth, because that work is really a little rough. A man would be loading at least 24, 25, and up to 28 tons of cane a day, by hand. There were also days when one loaded only 18 tons—it depended on the amount of activity there was in the cane. The tonnage was paid at 9, 10, up to 12 cents; that was the wage range. I worked at that for several years. And I also filled railway cars from little wagons—that is, emptied little wagons into the big cars. But I also used to fill the railway cars from cane dumped on the ground. They would bring it in oxcarts, put it on the ground, and then the railway cars would be filled from there. I was there for many years working at that.

At that time there were no winches. I remember that the first winch I saw was here at Colonia Usera. You could see them in a few other colonias, but not like now. Now all the sidings have their winches, but not then. Then they used to bring the cane to the siding, and we filled the railway cars by hand. The cart would be backed up close to the railway car. The oxen would turn about and they would put the cart end-to-end with the railway car, the part in back meeting with the railway car. This cart had what they call a hinge (*gozne*); they would unfasten the hinge and the back part of the cart could be lowered and the cane would fall to the ground. They would haul off the oxen, the cart would be drawn away empty, and the cane remained. Then we used to gather it by hand from there and put it inside the railway car, picking up two, three, four, six canes at once and throwing them inside the railway car. You have seen how the railway cars have vertical side posts. Well, one would begin to fill the cars by collecting the cane and pushing it between the side posts. When it got somewhat piled up, then one would throw bundles of cane on top. That used to be easier. There was something they used to do to make the railway cars hold more cane. When he'd throw in a quantity of cane, the *fulgonero* [railway car loader] would take a machete and get inside the car. There he'd chop up the cane a little so it would fit better. Then he'd fill a little more and afterward go back in to chop some more.

I liked this work a lot, in spite of its being heavy, because one could earn a little more money. And one only rarely had to move from the place where he was working; he could always stay in the same place. That was the part that agreed with me. It was not like being a carter always going back and forth from the corral to the cane field. Rather, in the morning, one used to arrive at that place and not have to move until the afternoon to go back home again. In this sense it was one of the jobs I most liked to do in the cane, hard as it was. When I was doing that work, I had a woman already; I was already living with Elisabeth. I can't remember ever having filled cars during my childhood. I did that after I began living with Elisabeth. I believe a boy would hardly dare confront one of those railway cars. I was a young man—young. I was rather strong; I used to attack that work with gusto. And I did it for a good long while.

And after I finished with that I worked on the railroad. One doesn't learn that work until one gets to do it, because one can look, and looking, still not learn. One can more or less get the idea. But if one doesn't try it out, it is hard to learn. Because one can go to the railway with the crew, and if one doesn't concern oneself with learning how to do the work, well, one doesn't learn how. That really must be learned. When I went to do that work, I didn't know anything at all about it. But I learned. At the time, the crew foreman was Inocencio Torres, and I remember that the first day that I worked—it was at the siding at Colonia Florida, or rather at the branch track at Florida. We were making an elevation. Those are in the places where the rails have sunk, and then you put gravel on each side, and later the rails are lifted with jacks and the gravel is put in under the rail itself, with the aim of lifting the road up.

I got the job in the following way. During dead time the railroad always used to take on more people in order to speed up the work. And when the harvest would come, then they would take off those people and the regular brigade would be left with the work. And as in those times nearly everybody was unemployed, there were plenty of people.

And then Inocencio Torres made me the proposition that if I
wanted to go to work I could, and so I went to work with
him. He was from here. We knew each other from here.
And a number of times when the brigades were working
around here I had stopped to watch them working. So we
knew each other, and they always had the habit—or he used
to, when he had this job—of going to seek out people to work.
The foreman always busied himself looking for personnel
that he thought would be the best. And that's how I got the
work. And when the harvest started then they terminated
our work and were left with the regular brigade. That was a
system they'd had a long time. And in that work they were
paying 65 cents a day, 80 cents when the harvest came. The
dead time would come, and 65 cents; come the harvest, and
the increase, 80 cents. As soon as the harvest ended it would
go down to 65 cents. That was their system.

Now I'm going to tell you about pala work. I have told you
how I learned the work of the pala, going with my sister
Tomasa to bring Cornelio his lunch and helping him. Now
I came to do it on my own account, earning money. I recall
that the first time I undertook it was at Colonia Alomar. I
went there to work and worked several weeks. And then from
there I changed over to work at Destino here. I worked three
weeks here in Valdivieso during a heavy rain, ditching to
drain. And I continued; I went on until I'd made myself a
palero for real. Then we took charge of the pala work
here in Destino: Compadre Marcial, Conrado Davíd, Tomás
Torres, Tomás Famanía—who also would do ditching at that
time, but was not a regular palero—Santiago Alicea, and another man who lives at Mil Cuerdas, called Pedro Moreno;
we used to take charge of pala work. Bernaldo Echavarría
also used to work at it. So when there was need they would
put on a few more, and when the work was scarce there
always remained Conrado Davíd, Compadre Marcial, Tomás
Torres, and I. And Santiago Alicea. That was the number of
paleros that used to stay with the colonia.

They had not yet established the system of making maclaines with palas. The system before had been that maclaines were made by oxen. That is, they would make the ditches that were used for watering the cane with oxen and a plow. Don Rafael Gracia established the system of making the maclaines by pala. Don Rafael began by using lots of paleros, almost all the paleros there were. The work at the time was not well organized—there were many problems (*rompeca-bezas*) because we ourselves still didn't have a clear idea about the work. But we learned how he wanted it, and then he took all the paleros off the maclaine work, and left only Conrado Davíd, Compadre Marcial, and me exclusively in that work. And we were the ones who used to make the maclaines every year in the *primavera* [spring-planted cane] during the harvest and in the *gran cultura* [late-planted cane] during the month of August. We were doing that up to the time they brought in this system of irrigation which is called today "oil-line"; and then they went along eliminating the maclaine work, until finally this work disappeared entirely. The ditch work we did they now do with machines. It is rare today to encounter a palero making a ditch, because they now make the selfsame maclaine for irrigation with a machine and what we call a bombo attached to open the ditches.

Before, the palero always used to have his work in dead time. The ditches collect weeds and get clogged with dirt, and the paleros were always busy in dead time reopening the ditches, digging them, and cleaning them. Now that is all eliminated because they pick the weeds with a machine. The pala work has almost disappeared completely. They only use it in certain special cases or where the machines have trouble in entering; that's where they use the paleros. That was the way, at any rate, that I learned how to do the pala work. And in those jobs I earned a good bit of money. Because the palero is rather shrewd and always looks for ways to make more money. In spite of the [low] regular wages one used to be able to earn $18, $20, and $25 [a week]—it depended—especially in digging cane holes (*hoyados*).

I've never told you about the work of hoyados. This work was in preparation for planting cane, and the palero would come to make the cane holes in the field. They used to use a measure for the distance from hole to hole. The palero used to use the measure while the mayordomo was around; and when the mayordomo wasn't around, the palero would throw the measure ahead of him, and he would know his measure more or less by using his stride for where the hole should come. It was awkward and also cost time to use the measure. And that was the procedure: he would take the pala, and throw the measure a little ahead, and continue digging the hole. And when he got to where he estimated the hoyado would end he would come back and clean out the forward part.

I did palero work for many years. Although, you see, I am telling about years of work, and it's actually this way: during the harvest, if there was no shovel work, we would employ ourselves in other jobs. But as soon as there was shovel work we used to go back to it. When the harvest would begin there was no pala work and we used to load wagons. As soon as pala work opened up we would leave the wagons behind, and they would send us to work with the pala. So there were times in a single year when we would work a good while with the little wagons and another stretch with the pala; but we always worked at these jobs.

The work of *hoyado de resiembro* [digging holes for replanting cane which had not taken hold] was also a piecework job. I've done that at various wages. I've done it at 35 cents a hundred, at 50 cents, at 55 cents, and more, according to the way wages were, going up a little as they would at times. In digging cane holes, one used to be able to dig 500 holes, or 600 holes; that would depend on the nature of the soil, the palero, the skill that he had, and so on. For example, a palero who digs 500 holes a day at 75 cents per 100 holes —that's $3.75. And that per day, if one worked a whole week, came to $15 or $18; because one could also see the instance where one could come to a place, a cane field, where you could take up and dig 500 holes early. Now there could be the morrow when you meet up with a bad soil—tough—and you are left with 250. If you were to go on working in a good soil, you'd have a good week. That depended on the terrain and on the condition of the palero. That depended on these things, and one used to be able to earn his $18 or $20 or even more.

I can tell you a story concerning those years, which also concerns Don Rafael Gracia, the mayordomo. What I am going to tell about now happened in a harvest when we paleros had to go fill wagons since, when the harvest is beginning, the work of the pala runs out. And wagon-loading was a job that very many people resorted to, since even boys could do it, and an excessive number of wagon-loaders had turned up. And sometimes we had to go at four in the morning, and we would be there until five in the afternoon and fill only two cars of cane, or three, and truly we used to make hardly anything. For that they would pay us at 17 cents a ton; and there were times when in two cars we were able to load five tons and a half, or six; and in three, we could load seven, seven and a half, or so, at a price of 17 cents a ton. And a group of wagon-loaders agreed to speak with Don Rafael Gracia, who was then mayordomo at Destino, to see if he could find some way in which we could earn more money, or if he could reduce the number of wagon-loaders and use those people in other jobs, so that those who were left might earn more money.

And that morning we went to him. All of us wagon-loaders came to an agreement and then we withdrew to a road where they had picked up the portable rails—where they had already collected the cane—and we were seated there, waiting for Don Rafael to get to the field. And the field where we were lay very close to the colonia, and from the place where we were sitting we could take cognizance of all of the activity on the colonia. There we sat and ate our breakfast; and when it was time for Don Rafael to come down from his house to get a horse and come to the cane field, almost all the wagon-loaders were there together with us at that moment.

But then suddenly they went off to pile up the cane to fill the wagons—and what was left was a matter of six or seven of us wagon-loaders, waiting for Don Rafael to arrive. I do not know the attitude of those who went off, what it was in this regard—I am not going to say they were afraid—but at least they acted as if they were.

But we waited for Don Rafael there, and we explained the situation—that we were losing time, that what we were earning was a pittance, and that we had to be there too many hours even though most of the time we were not working. There were times when one would load one wagon in the morning, and then another in the afternoon, and leave in the evening with credit for two wagons of cane. Then he told us he could withdraw a few loaders, but there were times on Saturdays when there would be less people, and then he would have a problem. So then he decided to leave that considerable number of loaders, and he sent us once again to work with the shovel. He allotted us shovel work, starting up with the spring cane planting. We had enough work then, but during those days he was always looking for one way or another in which we might earn a little more than we were earning, and not have to work the hours which we were working. And we—well, we were very content going back to the shovel, because I used to like shovel work the best, and the same for Compadre Marcial.

Then we left wagon-loading. The others went on struggling with those wagons. And Don Rafael was right, because there were times on Saturdays when lots of people would go off, and then he had trouble getting people to fill the wagons which they had to fill every day. This was the view he had put before us, and it was a logical position. We could not have made a commitment for the whole wagon-loading task because we would not have been able to give him results. We were only about six men; we could not accomplish a job that 25 or 30 could accomplish. Now if we had been magicians we might have made ourselves responsible for that, but it was impossible. Then he sought that other way, and took us from the loading work and left it to them. And we were better off with the pala work.

The first time I got to know Don Rafael Gracia was at Cuatro Hermanos. When he was at that colonia they used to tell me he was a hard man, that he was a little hard as a mayordomo. But I had luck with him in the time I worked there; no kind of difficulty occurred to me with him. One time something happened to me with him and I came out all right; and after that, I left off working there with him and returned to work at Destino. Then they moved him—I don't know what kind of negotiation they made with that colonia—and they brought him here to work at Destino, and then I worked again with him here. And many people used to say he was a hard man. Now, I don't know, because during the time that he was so tough, the same ones who used to say so lamented at the time of his departure; and I could say that when Don Rafael was at Destino he was a completely good person with me and I have no complaints concerning him. And as I just said, there were people who lamented his going when he left Destino. I don't know what the explanation would be—the one who came after him was a little drastic, perhaps, and then they missed him. But many people noted his absence.

You told me once that the paleros of old used to suffer from hernias as a result of pala labor. Can you tell me more about that?

When we used to be together—Compadre Marcial, and Conrado, and other paleros, those of now—sometimes we would talk of this matter of the paleros of olden times. And it would come to our minds that it might have been this determination of theirs in piecework, trying to earn more money, to such an extent that they looked less well after their health and might have gotten ruptured from it. For example, by a bad dig with the shovel a person might suffer this sickness. I believe so—I'm not sure, but it seems so to me. The palero must use his feet and at times push with the foot that presses on the shovel—hard. Well, in a swampy section or in times of rain, when he presses hard with that foot, he can slip, and I believe a man can easily incapacitate himself that way. And in the same way in the swamps, where ditches are cut, each time the palero struggles to take up a mass of mud, lift it out of the ditch, and throw it to one side, it is a great quantity of earth that he lifts because the earth is wet. And when he lifts it up, he lifts what we used to call a *cospe* [a mass]—heavy—I attribute it also to this. If this same palero is not standing the right way when lifting this great lump of earth he also can easily get a rupture from that. What's more, they used to gamble and compete in these jobs, because each one didn't want the other to do more work than he. And if he were making cane holes, he would be anxious that the other not cut more than he. And they always used to have this kind of fight, see?

These are things that we ourselves used to wonder about sometimes when we used to get together. Because today not so many of these cases occur. You may see one, but it's not like then, when almost all paleros ended up useless from this sickness. I have in mind many persons who were incapacitated and were paleros—for example I remember Don Venturo Antonetti; Don Juan Toro, the father of Compadre Marcial; Valentín Alicea; Celestino Santiago; all of these men were paleros, and all were useless (*inútiles*). So all this had to be a consequence of something, because one didn't see so many useless people on the other jobs. I believe that it must have come from something they did. It could be from the excess of work, or not looking after themselves in time, or from the way they handled the shovel, as I explained before.

But today's palero isn't maimed like this. In spite of that pain I told you about before, well, that trouble of mine was not a rupture like the others had. Rather, I felt only this pain, and I had had it before I became a palero. I felt this pain, but I didn't know at the moment it occurred if it were from some badly placed dig with the shovel or what. Finally, thank God, it has disappeared, and I have not felt it any more.

Something else I ought to tell you about. I once spoke of a strike they had here. At the time of that strike I was a boy [1917]. I only took part because as they were coming along the road and shouting *vivas* and so on—well, I joined up with the group and walked a while shouting too, but I didn't know even what they were shouting for! Yet I can remember when they used to have strikes here, and the way they used to bring those who came to break the strikes [1920–1922]. They would go and bring trucks full of people from the west, from Yauco, Guanica, and those places over that way—they would bring them from there to break strikes that were started here. They would bring those people and stick them in the colonias. And the colonias also had a great number of people living on them. Then it was the ones living here in the barrio who used to suffer the worst. Because while the strike was going on, the people of the barrio, those who lived here in this outside part, would remain on strike while those who were living within the colonia used to go on working, in addition to those brought from other towns. And that is what made it a little hard for the strikers to control the situation. The colonias had many different points of entrance—gateways—but when the strike would start, right away they used to lock the gates— they'd put on a lock. And then some employee would come to guard and to care for these gates so that no striker could enter. And so the workers that were brought here would remain inside the colonias until after the strike was over. They would never come out to the barrio. After the strike was over was when they would begin to come out. It was rare that you would see one of them coming to the barrio otherwise so that the strikers would have a chance for some exchange of opinions with them concerning their supporting or joining up with the movement.

I never worked during a strike period. First, because at times my necessity was not so great, and other times because it seems a little hard to me that a person should be called a strikebreaker. To me that word is a little strong. So I always have abstained from work during strikes. And when strikes came along and I had to stop working, well, I always had my credit. And my credit would always carry me a part of the time that they were on strike. One restricts oneself to eating less when one is not working; and those periods of strikes passed that way. But there are people whom necessity compels to work. They have big families and often no credit, and necessity obliges them to succumb.

There was a lad here, a friend of ours, who sometimes worked during a strike. And I sympathized with him because he had a big family. In one strike when they distributed a little food they brought here, I fought for their giving him a part of what they were distributing, even though he wasn't a union member, so that he might hold back a few days without working; because in reality necessity obliged him to work. He had so many little children. I myself took out a part of what there was and gave it to him.

But I never, never in my life have worked during the period of a strike. One learns. They can teach one, because indeed you know that you are doing something that is bad; you know that there are many fathers of families here in the street whose sons are not eating because they are in this movement. Well, those people cannot be in a good humor, and if you work, you run that risk. I believe it is a lesson that does not have to be taught; one learns it alone, for himself.

I would have credit at our little stores in the barrio. I am not able to tell you if the company stores gave credit during the strikes because I never bought much from them; I never liked this business of a company store. First, tickets were needed to buy in the company store. Then one had to be at the heels of the timekeeper, and if the timekeeper wouldn't punch the ticket, well, one could not buy at the company store. It was a system I didn't like, always waiting for the timekeeper to come to punch the ticket in order then to be able to go to buy at the store. They had another system I disliked. Those stores formerly were closed off in the front. There were several little windows through which one had to make purchases, so the customer didn't see how they were weighing goods or anything. I didn't care for those things.

I always preferred credit at local stores to the American stores, thinking of the week when I might not be working. The American store would not give me credit, while with credit here, if I don't have work one week or two, well, the local stores give me the food for my children; and when I return to work I can pay off the account little by little. I don't know if the American stores would give credit in the period of a strike to the people they used to sell to. I know that they do ordinarily, because recently when Clemente was living there in Destino many people traded there and they got credit there, and even used to owe accounts there during the harvest, which they paid off little by little. Now during a strike—I doubt it. It seems to me the company would be the first to correct that and not trust them, in order thereby to obligate them to go to work.

Let me turn now to the year 1932. When Elí was pregnant with Pablín in the first months, Compadre José Espada, who came every week from the highlands to this barrio to work, made me the proposition that I send Elisabeth there so she could recuperate a little from an illness of the pregnancy. And I told him I was going to send her. But after about two weeks, I was left without work, and then he invited all of us to go there for as long as a month. I accepted, and the two of us went, with Carmen Iris, who was just a baby. They brought us a donkey, and we went by animal as far as Santa Catalina [a rural barrio of Coamo] because at that time it was difficult to go there by car. The roads were no good. They were merely paths, quite difficult for car travel. And we were there about two or two and a half months. There was Compadre José, and Comadre Dulfa, and a girl they called Luz. And they were bringing up a little boy about the size of Roberto [Taso's eight-year-old son]. And Carmen Iris, always given to yelling loudly, used to spend the whole day screaming, and the little boy would tell her, "Shut up, fire whistle!" And we enjoyed the fights between those two, she for not shutting up, and he for making her.

I got quite used to it up there; but only during the day. And the same happened with Elisabeth. During the day it

is a lovely highland. But when night came I couldn't get used
to it. And we were up there for that period of time, during
which Elisabeth recuperated somewhat—though it was really
a foolish matter, since it was a consequence of her pregnancy.
But at least in the time she was there she rested. And I rested
too, although I helped Compadre there with whatever he had
to do in the house. Elisabeth used to go out walking with
Comadre Dulfa, but as she was not working she had an easier
time.

At night, however, the highland country is a little sad,
different from what it is here, what we are accustomed to on
the coast, in terms of moving around, friendships, conversing at night, and so on. There it is very different. The houses
are remote from each other, set back from each other, and the
roads rather bad. If one arrives there at night and without a
light, one can't move around because there are ravines and
dangerous places. And for one to walk about without a light
is impossible, and a person who doesn't know those places,
well, he really can't leave the house. So when night would
come, the only diversion was to seat ourselves in the front door
and talk, Compadre José and I. During the day Compadre José
didn't drink. But when night arrived he would take a bottle and
put it in the doorway and light up a cigar, and there he would
be until he finished the bottle and smoked two or three
cigars; and we would converse there a while, and then to bed.
And I never got very accustomed to that atmosphere, for I
was a little uncomfortable at night. Although in the daytime
I liked it a lot because we entertained ourselves, Compadre
José and I, walking through the farms and helping with the
things they were doing there, minor crops that they were
cultivating, and with Comadre Dulfa and Luz, picking coffee
and singing in the coffee groves. And really I liked the days
a lot. But when night came it was as if it were a cemetery.

When we left I invited Compadre José's mother to come
here, and she said no, she was afraid! The highlanders fear the
people of color of the coast because they believe all the people of color are witches, and that they are able to bewitch

them, and that is the fear they have of the people of color. So they don't want to come down to the coast.

One day in 1932 at a time when I badly needed a house Adolfo Davíd came to me. He is a friend to whom I will be grateful for the whole of my life. He told me, "Go where my mother is; tell her to give you a house plot; and I'm going to help see that she gives you a lot." I was a little timid about it, for at that time people didn't want to rent lots to anyone— but I decided to do it, for necessity decided me—and I came to talk with her. Then she put many obstacles before me. She told me she had problems with her mother, that her mother had started a lawsuit against her. But then Adolfo got into the discussion and said, "No, Mother, let him; you know what he's like, we know him." Then she said, "Well, take the spot you want."

Then, when I got back home I was very pleased. Elisabeth's father was a carpenter. And he came to put up the house in Comadre Antonia's lot. And when he began to put the house together with the material I had we found we were short one wall; we were left open to the street. Then he recommended to me a man who was living here, to see if he would lend me money. Wood at that time was very cheap, and I went and got money. I remember it as if it were now; I got $14. With this $14 I bought wood for the wall and I bought the doors I needed, in short, I finished the nine-by-sixteen house. And then I had this account with him. I settled it with a few animals I had, raising them on shares, and with surplus from my earnings. At that time one would work from six in the morning until six at night—a day and a quarter—and they paid one dollar. We used to earn $5.80 per week, for on Saturday there was no quarter day.

After we paid the money then we no longer had the problem of a house. At that time we already had two children. We had—better said—we had had three, and the oldest had died—we had Pablín and Carmen Iris. Rather, Pablín was born when we moved to the new house.

Concerning Pablín's birth, I am going to tell you something that you brought to mind with a question. It was in the time of the 1932 political campaign. At that time I was working at Colonia Texidor, and they threw me off the job. You could say I was then in no position to help Elisabeth to prepare for the new baby. It was a terrible situation. At that time I was not able to make twenty-five cents available for her needs. It was the year in which I think I suffered the most. And I can tell you that for that child, Elisabeth had to take her good dress to make shirts for Pablín. That was how things were. I had bought that dress for Elisabeth and it had cost me $9; I had bought it from Don Cayetano, and I had bought it on time. And that was the situation and that was what Elisabeth had to do when the time of Pablín's birth came. So I was badly off at the time. And after he was born I had to make great sacrifices in order to give something to the midwife. And Comadre Antonia used to come by to lend us a hand and to do something for us. And Antolina, who was not in very good condition herself at that time—she also helped us with whatever she had. But at that time I really suffered enough; and after he was born I had about six or seven months wholly without work.

Afterward they gave us work on the road. And I went to work. I never had worked for the government and I believed I had gotten a great job—that I might be working some fifteen days. And after I worked the first day the boss on the road came and told us each one was going to work just two days because the work had to be divided among all those that needed work. It was a humane thing, but really my situation was a little serious and I needed to work more. Yet I had to make the best of it. And I went so far as to do something that was not good—there were times when I had work as much as four days, and then would put down two days to another's credit in order to cover me for the four days. The name of Salvador, Elisabeth's brother, would be put down and he would get the money and give it to me, so that I would have something more to live on. And after that campaign was over

I was still a considerable time without work, keeping going
with God's help.

At the time they threw me out of work it was a few months
before the elections of 1932. What happened was that they
sent me to repair a canal which the water had broken through.
They sent me to close it off with some cement. And I was
closing it off with another person who was working at Colonia
Texidor, a man who was always close to the mayordomos; and
he was against my political position. And while we were
working there, the mayordomo came by. We were not discussing politics at the moment, but when the mayordomo, Don
Benigno Patiño, arrived the other began to show off his
politics. And I, never being one to hide his ideals from anyone—I always thought this way—we undertook to discuss
politics, he defending his party and I speaking about mine.
I was a little partisan about my party; I already had much
love for it. Well, the mayordomo did not mix in the conversation. And I remained at work the rest of the day and came
home, and when I went to work the next day, they told me
there was no work. And the next day there was no work; and
finally work ended for me. So I believe this was the origin
of my being suspended from work—the conversation right in
front of the mayordomo, and then the mayordomo doing
things in this way. I was what you could call a long while
without work.

Here is Eli's description of Taso's blacklisting.

Well, Taso went off to work and came back because they
gave him no work. According to what he said, it was an
arrogance of that mayordomo Patiño, done to him because
of politics. We were Socialists at the time and they wanted
to punish Taso because he was in politics. They retaliated by
not giving him work, and that was when we really began to
suffer. He would go out looking for work at all of the colonias
and wouldn't find it. And Mama would help us out "with
a plate," as we say. If it were but water she was boiling at
home, she would send some to me. Many times you would

see the plate of food she sent being shared between us two and a small child we had then—it seems to me it was Carmen Iris, because that was when I was pregnant with Pablín. Carmen was already weaned. And we spent a long time that way. And that was the period when, if we came to have a quarter, or 8 or 10 cents, we always used to buy cornmeal, because you got the most for your money. And the way to make it so it gave the most was to boil it soft. I used to take that cornmeal and put it in a pot of water to boil, and that cornmeal would buzz around in that pot! I was trying to get the most out of that cornmeal; and the cornmeal painted the kitchen wall yellow. When the meal began to boil it would begin to shoot out bits and paint the wall, and many times I had to leave the pot by itself because it used to paint me too! And as it was hot it would burn me, and I'd have to run out of the kitchen till it stopped spitting. Because it was like a tornado, it was as if it were shooting off bullets, and those little balls would fall upon one everywhere.

We were in that situation for some time, living like that. And during that time I was pregnant with Pablín, and we were in the worst possible condition. I had not been able to prepare even a rag. And there came the time when the only good dress I had was in the trunk; it was of a cloth they call *claro de luna*. And when the moment came that I had to make the little shirts for when the child would be born, there was no way of doing it. Some neighbor women helped me with some clothes, some old worn-out things from infants they had. I don't remember who those neighbors were, but I know they helped in that regard. And then it came my turn. I took the dress—which I had for an emergency, you see, if it should happen that I had to go to the hospital—I took my new dress and I put it to the scissors and I made, it seems to me, three or four little shirts from the skirt, which was full. And for bonnets, I made several from the top part. I made little bonnets, and those were the bonnets I used on Pablín when he was born. I don't remember if he had shoes or not. It seems to me I didn't get shoes, and if I did they were old ones given to us. I know I didn't have anything to buy them with. And then near us there was living a neighbor lady they called Doña Candida, and when I bore Pablín that lady used to come and take the diapers and wash them; and you could say she was the one who attended me, who helped me in the necessities of the house.

That mayordomo made me angry, see? I said he was a man without a heart, see, that he was a man who didn't think of the sufferings of others—he didn't think about how a man's family could go hungry. That man was heartless; or else he didn't think of his own family, he didn't think that perhaps some day the same thing might happen to him, to suffer hunger with his children; that was what I always thought. I didn't discuss it with anyone, you know, because I don't like to comment about these things with neighbors. We suffered whatever we suffered, but we suffered in the love of God and silently, at home. Very few people knew what we were experiencing apart from the nearest neighbors, like Comadre Antonia David, the owner of the neighboring lot, who would appear many mornings at our door with a pot of coffee for us. She would call me or Taso and give us coffee in the morning; only the nearest neighbors knew of our circumstances.

Taso continues his story.

At the time that I was blacklisted, I was sergeant-at-arms of the Committee of the Red Card (*Carta Roja*) which functioned within the Socialist party. We members of the Red Card were the people who would be candidates for possible jobs in the municipality if the party should win. At that time we had to pay dues. I don't remember how much they were. If I recall correctly, it was something like a dollar every three months; a small matter, but we had to pay it. My work was to summon all the members each time there was a meeting and maintain order during the meetings. And I came to the Socialist party in those elections with much enthusiasm, since they had a good program and they told us the laws that they proposed to put in force. I remember some of them, such as the 500-acre law, and the distribution of land, and an infinity of laws that exist today but that were already in the program of the Socialist party. That was what made me come to the Socialist party and fight for some time on its side.

When the days of the elections came around I worked in a voting place on the Calle Guayama in Santa Isabel. It was a two-room house and those rooms were the voting places. I worked that day as secretary for the Socialist party. During the morning a man who has since died, named Francisco Robledo, came to work for the Liberal party and for the Republican party one named Julio. And during the course of the election the functionaries of the Liberal party were changed many times, because of the many arguments that developed in the voting place in those campaigns. They would go and leave their posts, and then other officials would have to come to carry out the work until the end of the day.

The last one we worked with that day—that is, with whom I worked that day—was Don Rafael Gracia. It was already around nine at night and we were still struggling with the election returns, and he was the one representing the Liberals at the time. He was the mayordomo at Colonia Destino, and there he was, working alongside me in the polling station. In the other station, on the other side, was Don Benigno Patiño, the mayordomo of Colonia Texidor, who threw me out of work and blacklisted me. They used this system so that when the voters came from their colonias to vote, they were confronted with the mayordomos sitting there. And then you could see the fear. Then they would vote for *their* party for fear that when they went back home they would be thrown out, or some such thing—whatever oppression the mayordomo would think of—and so the voters would vote with them.

They had a system that almost always told them how one voted. They'd know. Because I've also worked at the table, and when I was interested in knowing how a person voted, I've investigated. The voting booths were made of thick paper, and the paper would wrinkle and tear. And the functionaries of the polling station had the privilege of standing around. And they walked about while the voter was marking his ballot, and they usually could get to know how he voted. And one has his little methods for investigating—something else.

In the elections of 1932, the Socialist party leaders instructed us that the voter who came with a little yellow ticket hidden under his shirt front was a voter who really didn't have a vote—who was coming to vote in place of some other. And so we Socialist party committeemen were to let this one go by, because he was going to vote with our party.

See how it was? That was in 1932, and in 1936 the same things were going on. We had that procedure, and they also must have had the same; but we didn't understand their code. Now when such a person came, we would secretly identify him by the yellow ticket that he had here in the front of his shirt. And we gave him his chance to vote, unless the others opposed him, because we knew that this was a voter who would vote with us. If they knew the person and they opposed him, then it was for the judges at the table there to decide. There would be a discussion and it would be clarified, and if he wasn't able to vote, he didn't vote; and if they had any doubts, they didn't let him vote. And that was the way things were carried out. In that election we won—or rather, the Coalition won, we Socialists alone did not.

The Socialist party leaders had made me a promise that I would have work—that if they shared in winning the elections, they would help me in one way or another. But after the elections were over, I went to them different times with the end that they afford me what they had offered me. And they never gave me a chance. Some of those who had worked in the voting place with me were given up to $10. I don't know— I was the one with bad luck because they never gave me even a penny. I was there the next day, celebrating the triumph in the Municipal Hall, and they did give us food; but they never gave me a penny. And I know they had money because they got help from different places, and they collected money with our help. But never, never did they give me anything, or meet the promise they made me, that they would give me some little job—that, too, they failed to give me.

There was for instance the mayordomo of the hospital—the one who looks after the hospital. Or the janitor's job. In the Municipal Hall there is always a janitor, and in the schools there are also janitors; and there are different jobs in the town, so if they had wanted to help one, they could have. It could be that there were others in the town who were nearer than I, and they gave the chance to them, since I was farther away; but in any case they gave me nothing they promised me.

And the treasurer and school director was a relative of mine. And I troubled him one time for some medicine for one of my kids who was sick and he refused me the help. He told me he couldn't help me, and he put a great many obstacles in my way and so I gave that up. And then Carlos Curet met me in the street, and he asked me my situation and I told him, and then he went with me to the pharmacy and authorized my getting the medicine. And Saturday when I went to pay for it, he didn't want me to pay for it, saying that he would. In those days they had given him a little job working in weights and measures, and he made himself responsible for those pennies for medicine. But honestly, the one to whom I'd gone to get help—and I knew that he really could give it to me—and he refused it to me—well, that was the pay I got for the service I had rendered.

When all that happened, I then told them the same as I am telling you—that I would work no more in those committees, and they could give my post as sergeant-at-arms of the Red Card to anyone else, and that I would not work in the voting places either. And actually after what I had gone through there, I didn't feel like working any more in the voting places; it was a tremendous struggle. In Santa Isabel, I believe the whole town voted in just eight voting places. And it wasn't like now when, if I am not mistaken, there are 150 voters to each voting place. In that time a great number of voters used to vote in a voting place, and sometimes we would still be struggling at midnight with the returns. One went through a lot in that 1932 period that we're referring to—one suffered hunger and thirst in those voting places. One could not stop work for a moment to go out of the polling places, and if one were to go out, afterward they wouldn't let him go in again. It was excessively fierce politics in that period. And I decided after looking at the way things were and the way they behaved that I would struggle no more with those matters.

Now I always continued looking to my party—that is, not my party, but rather to the [political] obligations that I had. And in the campaign of 1936 I had no political activities at all—Elisabeth and I simply went and voted. Elí also voted. She also voted in the same polling place as I. Elisabeth was one of those Socialists who used to like to get dressed up in a red dress, with red stockings, and she would go there to vote—a veritable torch. She always voted for the same party as I. And we came back to the barrio to await the results of the election that they would bring there to the barrio—something I had always awaited before in the town. That time, well, as soon as I voted, I went and came back to my house. I decided to fight no more in political matters.

I ought to mention the hurricane of San Cipriano [Sept. 26, 1932]. Here on this coast it was no great thing; but we always have to prepare for the worst. I had come from the Moras' house, which was the only place in the barrio that had a radio. It had been a little hard to understand the news they were giving on the radio at the time. The radios were not so modern, and since the electric lines are so near here they operated with terrible static; and a great number of people were eagerly awaiting the news they were giving. We were listening to the news, listening to what they were saying in San Juan. There had been a very strong wind here already. It was not a question of danger, but rather that one took notice of that wind; it was not an ordinary wind. It was much stronger, causing a great movement of the trees and the cane. And I remember I was there listening to the news until they announced in San Juan that one of the station towers had fallen. And that ended the transmission and we could hear no more. Then the night passed, but here in this area there were no grave consequences.

It's a custom here that always when they announce hurricanes one goes to the place of greatest safety, and if the hurricane passes somewhere else, well, it goes. But particularly when night comes one wants to have refuge in the safest place, because if it comes this way during the night that is a little dangerous. And one always takes these precautionary measures and seeks to do them during the day. And the night passed and another day came, and actually nothing happened in this region. But then we were able to read about it in the papers; they reported afterward what had happened there on the north coast.

I had a problem in the hurricane of San Cipriano because at that time Rosa and Lalo were living on the north coast in Aguadilla. I wrote to find out how they were but I didn't get any answer from them. That made me anxious because I read in a paper what had happened in that area. In the place where they were living there was a ravine, and a family of eleven persons had been carried off and drowned there. And when I read of such things, it had my mind in a turmoil. I didn't know how the family was. Then I decided to make a trip to where they were, but I had no money. I wasn't working then either, because the work we got in those days, as I've told you, was scarce. And we continued suffering the scarcity of money when this storm came. So I decided to go to where my brother Pablo was—to Guayama. My brother always used to make out all right there—he always managed with his $40 or $50. I got to where he was and explained my situation and what my aim was. And I remember that he gave me $3. He wasn't doing too well, but out of what he had he gave me $3. I made that trip to Guayama on foot, because I had no money. Then I took a public car back here. I got home, and from what I brought I told Elisabeth to make dinner, because we were really badly off at that time.

I took the rest of the money to make my trip. In the morning I got a car—the one that was carrying the newspapers around at that time. The driver was taking the papers as far as Mayagüez—it was only during the hurricane period that he did that. I'd thought that it would be a trip only as far as Ponce, but when we got there, he told me he was going to Mayagüez. I continued with him to Mayagüez, and there he charged me $1.50. I was carrying with me $2 and change. In Mayagüez, I caught a bus and the bus cost me 50 cents to Aguadilla. And when I got to Aguadilla I was out of money, but I was already pretty near to where they were.

Then I continued on foot. It wasn't very far but it was pretty rough because there is a terrific hill. I wasn't happy about walking there in that rough country but I climbed up to the place, and when I got to their house it was getting dark. That section was really completely torn up. The cane plantations there looked as if a fiery wind had passed over them. I saw houses that were completely overturned, with the top parts underneath and the bottoms up in the air. And along the road that led to their barrio, I saw families living on the shoulder of the road, sitting and cooking without hope there. When I got to my brother-in-law Cornelio's house, one of my feet was badly cut and had swollen up from the walk I'd taken. I stayed there two weeks. The mayordomo there was disposed to put me to work. I didn't want to, because my foot was bad, but he wanted me to do anything that I wanted there, so I went to work for a week. They put us to work removing the waste that the ravine waters had dragged along and cast about in the cane. I worked there those days. Afterward I came back home.

No harm had come to the family; they were completely safe. They told me of the things that had happened to them because they were living in such a perilous place. I could appreciate it because their house was situated where a great deal of water used to concentrate. During the hurricane there was a heavy rain. And the entrance to the ravine nearby got plugged up and the water was passing underneath the house. And it backed up at a place called La Charca and began to rise, and then the overflow began to reach the house. They told me that the water reached to the house floor; I could appreciate all this because there was more rain while I was there, and some cartloads of cane at the side of the house were covered over by the water. I can well imagine that the night of the hurricane they must have been a little worried in that house! During San Cipriano there were great problems there, great suffering. They told me about a family who had left their house seeking refuge. Their house remained perfectly safe but all of them lost their lives. Afterward I returned home here and went back to work.

Later on, in 1934, Elí endured an illness which was terrible. I suffered greatly, greatly with this illness of Elisabeth's. The woman was failing, failing, failing. And she was pregnant—it was with a boy we had who died, whom we called Güiso; he was named Luis. And I sent her to be examined in various hospitals here and as far away as Aguirre. Nowhere did they discover the embryo, and the woman simply got sicker and still sicker. Then I sent her one day to the District Hospital in Ponce. There the doctor examined her and took some X-rays. And then they told her exactly. She was pregnant—and they even told her the number of months she had. When she returned home we began to treat her illness. She had become terribly weak. Then we began to treat her.

Well, the woman improved. But in that period of her sickness, I came one day from work and told Antolina to take her to Ponce to Dr. Om so he could examine her and prescribe for her. And when they came back in the afternoon, she showed me the prescription and I realized that Elí was seriously ill. I had been paid $5.10 that day. At that time I was working on the railway and that was my weekly earnings: $5.10. And because her condition was so bad, I took the prescription that Tole brought and went immediately to seek the medicine. I went to Salinas and could not find it; I went on to Guayama but they did not have it there; then I came back toward Ponce. I borrowed money in Salinas from our boss on my way through, and went on to Ponce. And in the new pharmacy there I got the medicine. I tied it up in a little sack—that is, in a handkerchief.

It had been about 8:30 P.M. when I passed through here en route to Ponce. I didn't stop to say anything to people in the house because it was a matter of haste. I left no word at all, and went on swiftly. After I got the medicine I waited on the Calle de Comercio in Ponce for a public passenger car, but it was impossible to get one. I had to start home on foot, with the hope that some car would overtake me. And at the end of the Calle de Comercio in Ponce I got on a bus that came as far as the Mercedes sugar mill. And in Mercedes I got off and continued walking as far as the causeway when a driver I knew came by; I waved to him and he stopped. He was named Fernández. I told him that if he would bring me home, I would pay him well—though I didn't have much money on me, Antolina would be able to give me a couple of dollars to pay him. Well, he told me he couldn't do it because he had to take the relief workers to Boca Chica mill—it was harvest time. Then I got in the car and he let me out at the very entrance to Boca Chica. There I spoke with the gate-keeper who puts the chains across the railway crossing on the road. I spoke with him, and he told me, "If you can wait till morning the trucks that leave here go to carry sugar to the Caribe mill and there—" But I told him that wasn't my problem, that by morning I would have to be here, that I was in a great hurry; and I continued walking.

Before I had reached Pastillo village a truck reached me— one of those carrying sugar. I had seen this same truck stopped in the Calle de Comercio in Ponce when I left. The driver later told me that he recognized me, that he had thought I was going to some place near Ponce. When I signaled him he stopped. I got on and he asked me what had happened, and I explained my situation. Then he gave me some advice. He said, "Look, if this should ever happen to you again, never come to this place, because I only stopped here for you because I recognized you from when you passed by on Calle de Comercio carrying that little sack in your hand." Actually, I knew it was a tough spot. But necessity had obliged me to come, even though I was on foot, because I had left my woman in grave danger. So it was that in this truck I finally got to Jauca.

When I got to Tole's house the door was ajar, because one who goes to Salinas to seek medicine for a sick person and at midnight still has not appeared—they believed that something else had happened. But, thank God, when I arrived I had the medicine and we gave it to the woman and she improved. And she convalesced. But when the time of delivery came she was terribly sick. When she gave birth to the child Elisabeth suffered a relapse—she went four days without knowing anyone. And the first day I went in a hurry and got Dr. Vélez. And Dr. Vélez told me I could do nothing because she was dying already. I told him to prescribe for her—that while there was life, I would make the necessary efforts to help her. And he answered me like this: "Well, if you wish, give her serum. That is the only thing that may help her endure a little."

Afterward he prescribed three bottles of serum daily, one in the morning, one at noon, and one at night. The one at night was given hot. The bottle was wrapped in a towel put first in hot water to heat it. So for four nights we kept vigil over her, giving coffee and crackers to the people who came, and watching a movement we could see here [he points to the base of his throat]. And on the fourth night, between 1 and 2 A.M., she opened her eyes and looked at us.

And Antolina and I, who were always near her bed, rejoiced greatly. And Lola Lebrón, in whose house I had formerly lived, was there at that moment; and Epifanio also had come to know how she was. Then on the next day I went and I told Dr. Vélez that the woman had improved, and he came and saw her. When he saw her he marvelled. He did not believe he would find her alive. Then he began to change the medicines, until the woman gained strength, convalesced, and finally arose from this sickness. After she got over this illness, then the situation got bad, bad, bad. Work was what you could call completely scarce. And I had to buy milk for that boy, Güiso, who later died.

At that time, as I've told you, my brother-in-law, the father of Lalo and Rosa, was living in Aguadilla. He was working there as a mayordomo for a boss named Don Rafael H. López. And there, well, he had certain comforts—he had his own cows and he had some he had let out on shares besides. He had written me to ask if I wanted to go there for a while. I thought about it and I decided to go. But there I had to struggle with different problems. For one part, it was good; for another, it did not suit me. In his house I was fine; he had many things there. But then I went to live apart—you see, I brought my family there. I brought my wife and the children I had. Cornelio himself helped me out, helped me find a house, and I went to live there.

But at that time things were even worse there than here—a man used to earn 50 cents a day. That was the wage they were paying for agricultural work, irrigation, cane cutting, and all. Then when I went to live in that little house, the greatest problem developed. With the 50 cents they were paying I was not able to pay the rental of a house and maintain my family. Now, for the people who lived there it was easier, because they had their cultivated plots, and almost everyone had his cow. But I—everything I wanted to consume at home I had to go and buy. So our situation was aggravated. These people I am telling you about had little plots of land and with that 50 cents they used to buy their seasonings. But they already had their chick-peas and sweet potatoes and every kind of green vegetable; they had these but I did not. I had to buy them. My brother-in-law helped me a lot: he gave me milk for the children and many things, but my problem was serious. I needed more money to resolve my situation.

While I was in Aguadilla I received a letter from Guayama. The wife of my brother in Guayama had died and he was seriously ill. My brother-in-law then gave me money so that I might visit Guayama. I took the money and went. Then I began to struggle with that problem besides. But my brother recuperated soon. While I went to look after my brother my family stayed behind in Aguadilla. I returned there, and then we started living in the house I'm telling you about, and we lived there a brief period. But I saw my situation as excessively bad, and at last I decided to return once more to Jauca. Then I spoke with my brother-in-law. And he didn't want me to go. But I explained my position. Compadre Obdulio, who was first mayordomo, committed himself to pay for my house so that I would not go. But I refused; I said, "No, I'm going."

When I first went there Obdulio had baptized our youngest child, whom we carried there. We became compadres there. And he didn't want me to leave under any circumstances. He saw I was a worker, that I was quite efficient in the work they did there, and he didn't want us to leave; he had come to appreciate Elí and me. But I wasn't able to stay; the situation was too difficult. I spoke with him and resolved to come back here. Then I sold many of the things I took from here, and I returned.

My house here was then stacked up as lumber in Comadre Antonia's house and had to be rebuilt. Elisabeth came back and got sick again. Antolina was selling knickknacks in the cane and it was hard for her to watch over Elisabeth at the same time. Then Antolina suggested that I move my house from Comadre Antonia's lot to her lot so she could look after Elisabeth. I began working again on the railway; and when I would come back in the afternoon I would work on the house, lowering it from the house posts in order to move it. And I moved Elisabeth to Antolina's house and then I moved the house itself. I was thus three days moving and putting it up there. Then we began living there and Antolina looked after Elisabeth.

Now Luis—whom we always called Güiso—was born in 1934 before we went to Aguadilla. And it was in that period that Elisabeth had that very bad sickness when I had to run all over during the pregnancy to different places seeking information because the doctors had told me that she wasn't pregnant; until at last they made those examinations in the District Hospital in Ponce and established that she was pregnant. Then when she gave birth she had that serious illness. Comadre Jesusa assisted at that birth. This woman came from the barrio of Paso Seco to live here at the time. And she was the person easiest at hand when Elí was in labor.

Here I'm going to tell you something that happened to me at that time. When Elisabeth gave birth to Güiso, I had come home from work sick with influenza and during the night Elisabeth was complaining because she was sick, and I was also what you could call completely ill with influenza. And when morning came she told me to get up and make her tea. I got up, sick as I was, and lit the light and made ginger tea and brought it to her. As soon as I gave her the tea I went and lay down once more, and it was a matter of a moment—she lay back and in a minute the boy was born. I was frightened—I hadn't expected anything so sudden. I got up right away and put on my pants and ran out of the house and brought Comadre Jesusa who lived nearby. She came and took care of everything, arranged the child and fixed her. Then I went to Herminio's store where I traded, and bought four or five beers—the malt beers we used to give to women after a delivery—and opened one and poured it out in a glass. And when Elisabeth took it a great dizziness overcame her, and then she had this great collapse. It was a terrible thing, and she knew nothing more of the world for four days. That was when I had to walk hard and fast to bring the doctor and to struggle with her, Tole and I, the two of us struggling with her.

Later on Moisé was born [1935], and Comadre Jesusa also attended for Moisé. Moisé's birth was very easy for Elisabeth and during the pregnancy she had few difficulties. I went to seek Comadre Jesusa, who lived in Paso Seco at the time, and when I returned, the child had already been born. All she had to do was take up the child and cut the umbilical cord. Elisabeth was already in bed when she arrived. And after that José Miguel was born, in 1937. If I don't remember incorrectly, it was May 9. On this occasion, I don't recall that Elisabeth had any difficulties or illnesses during the pregnancy. And Comadre Jesusa attended on this occasion too.

On October 27, 1939, Blanca was born. Elisabeth already had her favorite among the midwives and it was Comadre Jesusa. And though there were midwives nearer, I had to go that night to Paso Seco, though it was late at night. I went in the railway handcar (*terecina*) up to the Santa Isabel station, and went to the house and called her. And when I called her they told me she was in Cortada. Then I came back and passed by home and in the same handcar went as far as Vaquería [a nearby upland farm] where Comadre Sandalia was living and called her. I brought her back and she was the one who attended the birth of Blanca.

Now of the deaths of Luis and of Moisé. In Luis' birth Elisabeth had her grave illness. That was the birth in which she was in danger for a period lasting four days, as I explained. And after a period of some months we moved to Aguadilla, and later we returned from Aguadilla and came back here to the barrio. Luis had two sicknesses that were very serious. First, he had an attack of pneumonia, and that time Dr. Vélez treated him and was able to cure the sickness. Later on he got those attacks of perniciosa, from one of which he died [October 27, 1937]. Long before that, Moisé was born. That child was born completely robust (*grueso*) and fat while Luis, when he was born, was quite weak, surely as a consequence of Elisabeth's illness. But Moisé was quite otherwise; Moisé was born a very robust child. And he was a white, white child, completely, like Elisabeth. He had blue eyes. And that child died, you could say, in health—it was very sudden. When he began to get those vomiting attacks, he was completely well. And suddenly the vomiting began. And in the midst of the vomiting, diarrhea. And Elisabeth and I took him to different places treating him. We carried him to Salinas; and to Santa Isabel where Dr. Vélez was. And it was not possible to stop either the vomiting or the diarrhea, until at last these killed him—weakened him so that at last he died. And that birth had been one of the easiest that Elisabeth had had. As I told you before, Elisabeth had already given birth to that child when Comadre Jesusa arrived. She came only to cut the cord, to take him up and fix him, and to care for Elisabeth. It was one of the best deliveries Elisabeth has had. Later on Blanca was born. With Blanca, too, Elisabeth had a very easy time.

It seems that Elí had Pablín, Luis, and Moisé in three successive years. That would mean you had sexual relations al-

most continuously during a period of three years; is that right?

What happens is that at times the woman turns out to be pregnant sooner. Because as I told you before, one has a time when one leaves the woman alone. But after this time is past, the woman can become pregnant again. It can be soon, or it may be later, as in the cases of the others, who took more time. I don't know if it was a consequence of her having taken so many medicines in the course of her illness with Luis, or other things that would have inclined her to have those children more rapidly. It's a little difficult to understand, but this is my opinion, because one always leaves the woman alone during the cuarentena—it is the custom.

You never used birth control techniques?

No. My opinion is that I don't like those treatments. Now, there have been many cases here, cases I know, where a woman went on her own account and got these things. Other times it may have been because the husband wanted her to get them. But there were also cases where there were certain troubles between spouses on account of that. I didn't like the idea. And one has little knowledge of what is involved, you see? And they have different kinds of things; but in truth I never gave much thought to it. And lately also they began using other things, operations and things, and that I liked even less. They put a woman's life in peril, you see—that even less. I never gave it any thought.

And no one suggested that many births could have an effect on the life of the woman? No one suggested you should wait more than the forty days?

Well, the doctors never talked to me about it.

And birth control devices?

Well, when we were kids, there were those who used different things for that, and I never—I saw them, and I thought

they were [he shows disgust and laughs uncomfortably]—
The handling of such things [he laughs with distaste]—

*And when one has many children—for instance, you never
thought it might be a good idea—*
Well, I never thought about that, see? But there are those
who took those treatments, and when not, their women went
and got them. But I never thought about it.

Nor Eli either?
Neither of us.

She never complained about having too many children?
Never. Elisabeth, she sometimes says, "So many children!"
[he laughs]—and the children keep coming. And truly, as I
have said other times, in spite of my poverty and everything
I always earned the bread for my children; when there were
two, when there were three, when there were seven and eight
—I always earned my children's bread, and really it has been
a satisfaction in itself that I could supply those things. But
as far as that goes—well, for that part I will tell you that
always thanks to God, in one way or another, I managed to
provide bread for my sons. There might be some people who
stopped having children because of their economic situation.

*So it seemed to you that those were disagreeable things. It
never occurred to you that using them might be considered
a sin?*
At that time I had no knowledge of that. Now it seems to
me I have some knowledge of that.

*Can you tell me if your distaste was associated with the
fact that one uses such things with prostitutes?*
Yes. Particularly those things that men used much here in
the time of the prostitutes. Then there was a spread of disease,
a series of great sicknesses of those women, and the men
sought means of protecting themselves from them. And then
the thought of using one with one's woman [he shows dis-
taste]—

You told me it was never possible that the children might be able to see the sex act itself?
No. I am sure that never happened. No.

Till when do the babies sleep in the bed?
When they begin noticing things we move them out. Or else Elisabeth sleeps with them and I sleep alone.

About what age would the child be then?
Like Tasita, see? [Tasita is five years old.] She is still sleeping with Elisabeth and I sleep on the cot. Now within a year I will leave my cot and we will give it to her.

There was never a time when one of your children three or four years old was sleeping with you at the time of a sexual act?
The little children? No. We—there are times when the child is—here in—at such a time, well, we either have a small cot or something else. Now I don't have it because I dismantled it, they damaged it—good springs, too—well, we had that and we put two or three little children to sleep there in that separate bed.

And it has never happened that the sex act occurred with one of them in the same bed?
[Long pause.] It may be that one of the little ones may have been, at the time when they were very little, but when the children already have a—when one knows that they wake up for anything, one doesn't do it. One seeks some other way, but not [he laughs uncomfortably]— Those are special occasions which depend on the opportunity one has, see; one must seek every way possible to avoid their seeing.

Taso here turned to another subject.
I would like to mention something further here of illnesses I have had. I told you before that I first felt the pain of hernia when I was still a child. Much, much later—though it bothered me occasionally in the meantime—it got so bad that I was put in the hospital in Santa Isabel. There a doctor and

a head nurse examined me. He was telling her what he discovered, probing thus with his fingers, and they had me there for observation, and I believed they were going to operate. They gave me a treatment with ice packs and some applications of black ointment, until the inflammation went away six days after they admitted me, and then they didn't operate. I don't remember the date of that, but I had a woman already—it was Elisabeth who took me to the hospital. I was at home about four or five days using some local remedies, but in view of the fact that the pain continued and it became difficult for me even to raise myself from the bed to use the chamber pot, well, she decided to take me to the town.

About that time I also suffered an infection in my hand, which was the result of the prick of a fish spine. At the time Tole had a little store—it is larger now—and when I had nothing to do I would help her in the store. And that day Elisabeth was ironing, and they came by selling fish and we bought some for the house. And as Elisabeth was ironing, I set about cleaning the fish. It happened that as I passed the knife to scale them a spine pricked my finger. I thought it would be a trivial thing, and I only undertook to squeeze a few drops of blood out of the finger and left it that way. And later on I went again to serve in the store, and I attribute what happened to putting my hand in a barrel of salt pork (*tocino*). It formerly came in barrels, with water and everything. And I believe I got the infection from that. When night came, well, the hand hurt and during the night it bothered me a lot. The next day it bothered me even more, and more, until after two or three days, well, I had no life with the pain I had. Elisabeth stayed up all night struggling with me.

And now there comes to mind a story of what also happened to me in connection with that. Christmas Eve was approaching at the time, and they roasted a pig at Tole's house and made a liver stew. I didn't have the least desire to eat. But to humor them I ate a little stew, chittlings (*asadura*), and so on, and a bit of roast pork (*lechón*), and when I went to go to sleep that night I couldn't sleep, and I was insane with pain. At that time Tole was selling *pitorro* [illegal rum] and she kept it hidden in the house, and as I was crazy with pain, I sent Elisabeth to bring me a quart of grape juice and I mixed it with a quart of rum. I could never drink rum straight. I mixed them and made a half bottle, and with two gulps—with two drinks—I drank that bottle, because I was insane. And when that too failed to help, I took the rum straight. I drank and drank, in quantity, and when morning came I was far from the world.

When I awoke in the morning—Elisabeth was sleeping separately—I smelled the foulness of my own drunkenness [he laughs nervously]; I had vomited everything up. And it was something terrible. And when I awoke I was terribly weak and I called Elisabeth to ask her to clean me up. I was filled with loathing. Getting into such a condition was a consequence of that pain, you see, which had me so crazy I would do anything.

Then the pain returned, and since it was the pain which had caused me to think to drink liquor and all that, I resolved to go quickly to the hospital in Santa Isabel. They did not want to operate on me because the infection was not yet mature (*estaba verde*)—it was not yet ready for operation. But I insisted, because I was very tormented. I said they should cut off the finger or whatever, but I was not returning home that way. Then the clinician [male nurse; *practicante*] told me there was no anesthetic. I sent Elisabeth to buy it, and when she arrived with it they had already operated on me with anesthesia. They did have it at the hospital, but they didn't want to operate because they saw it was not yet time for operating. But actually, when they operated and I came home, I slept completely well, what with the night's sleep I had lost. I felt relief and slept well. I felt better. But after two or three days the infection was then moving into the palm of the hand, and then I spent some three or four days treating myself at home with hot water to see if I could avoid having to have another operation.

But in view of the fact that it wasn't possible, I decided to go to Salinas. Then Ramón, Elisabeth's brother, and Elisabeth took me to the doctor, and the doctor gave me some pastilles to dissolve in hot water, in which to put my hand, and he told me to wait three days. As soon as we got back here, Elisabeth prepared the water and I began immersing my hand in the hot water, as hot as possible, and with that it matured rapidly from one day to the next. And on the following day I had no life with it. The hand was completely black and swollen and the fingers could not be bent. I got Elisabeth and Ramón and went to Salinas again with them; and when I showed the hand to the doctor he was amazed. He told me that if I had waited any longer I would have got gangrene in the hand. I told him, "It was you who told me to wait three days, but I could not stand it and came now."

Then he ordered a nurse there to perform the operation immediately. She covered the hand with iodine and performed the operation, which was something terrible with the state that hand was in. And I was suffering from that hand something like seven months afterward. It simply would not form a scar over the wound, and afterward also the higher part swelled up again, so that was the cost of forming a scar on the operation they performed on me.

I had about seven months of sickness with that. They put thirty-three stitches in my hand at that time. I remember that at first it was a barbarity that I suffered. At the beginning they used gauze drains, and it was a terrible thing because they put them in with clamps, and those clamps at times would break off and swell up in the flesh and with that one suffered very much. And later on they put in drains of rubber, and with rubber drains one didn't feel it, since they put the rubber over the wound and push them in easily; but those gauze drains are a terrible thing. It was one of the illnesses that caused me great suffering.

The preceding interviews cover the period from 1927 to 1939 in Taso's account. Considerable additional material—on illnesses, jobs, and other matters—has been omitted. Viewed sequentially, the major events seem to have been the following: the loss of the house plot to Don Pastor Díaz, and Taso's decision to enter politics because of it; the birth and death of Victor (1929–31); the birth of Carmen Iris (1931); Pablín's birth and the acquisition of a house plot at Comadre Antonia's (1933); Taso's blacklisting and his subsequent political disillusionment (1932–33); the brief stay in Aguadilla (1934); the births and deaths of Luis (1934–37) and Moisé (1935–36). Then follow the births of José Miguel (1937) and Blanca (1939).

Much of the material which Taso and Elí provide in these narrations does not fall neatly into chronological form. Elí's jealousy of her husband, for instance, was a continuous aspect of their relationship, and did not cease to affect them both seriously until after many years of living together.

Rather more of Taso's personality and intellect are revealed by these narrations than in the material on earlier years. One notes his angry reaction to Don Pastor Díaz's high-handedness; he goes into politics at first not to fight *for* something but to fight against a man who he felt had abused him. Díaz himself appears as a prototype of the old-time hacendado—eccentric, imperious, selfish, and cruel. Other Jauqueños told me of Pastor Díaz, however, and did not paint his character quite so blackly. He would invite local working people to serenade him and his wife on the terrace of the house; at Christmas, he might distribute pennies or small gifts of food and sweets. Whether behaving kindly or cruelly, Díaz seems to be a symbol of an earlier era in Puerto Rican life, when the relationships between workers and their employers were as between superior and inferior, the powerful and the weak, and often, as between arbitrary father and fearful and dependent son.

Taso's radical spirit is revealed in the story of his blacklisting. By the 1930's most of the land on the south coast was in the hands of a few corporations, most of them North American. The political situation was very dark, and workers were forced to vote in line with their employers' interests to keep their homes and jobs. The distinction between *agregados*— resident laborers—and *independizados*—those who did not live on hacienda land—is important here. The agregado was even more under the thumb of the corporation than his independizado co-worker. The agregado lived in a company house, traded at a company store, and was locked on the plantation during strikes, when he was compelled to work as a strikebreaker. The independizado was also at the mercy of the corporations, but not so completely. When Taso lost his job because of his political beliefs (that this was the cause is not proved, but seems certain) he was apparently blacklisted at all the colonias of the area, for he walked the roads for miles in search of work on any farm and was always turned down when he gave his name.

His political attitudes are worthy of reflection, since they seem to be a blending of high principle and self-interest, both freely admitted. He would not conceal or surrender his political beliefs even when he knew that they threatened his economic security. When he describes how he sat in the polling stations with his own mayordomos, who represented opposing political parties, he mentions that workers would come in to vote, that they would see the mayordomos—"And then you could see the fear." He says this without contempt; it is the objective judgment of a brave man who feels sorry for the coward because he knows how hard it is to be brave. At the same time Taso was concerned with more than ideology in his politics. He wanted a better-paying, easier job—a political job—and he was disappointed when he did not get one. His disillusionment with the Socialist party when it failed to "protect" him, as he puts it, led him away from politics (though he later returned, only to undergo a similar experience). Taso's sympathy for a frightened voter is like his concern for men who broke strikes because their situation compelled them to do so. He points out that he never broke a strike, partly out of principle and partly out of fear of violence.

Elí's jealousy and Taso's ramblings on women, love, and sex, are not sufficiently clear to permit distinguishing between the true and the imagined or supposed with certainty. It seems clear that Elí's jealousy was possibly inappropriate and certainly excessive. It also is likely that all the relevant facts are not reported. In any case, in the early years of their life together, Taso and Elí were in conflict much of the time, and Taso's alleged interest in other women was at the root of their trouble. As so often occurs in Jauca life, the theme of sexual love lies close to the theme of violence. Elí can describe laughingly how she lay in wait to slash Taso and his supposed girl friend with a razor. But the laughter lies in the retrospect. The edge of violence is also revealed when Taso tells how Elí threatened to kill the mother of a girl in whom he was allegedly interested, and how a relative of the girl threatened publicly to attack him in turn. What the interviews do not reveal in this connection is an aspect of Taso's character which seems to be important for what develops later in his life history: a growing sense of guilt.

The narrative reveals something of Taso's restlessness, both physical and intellectual. His descriptions of work are precise and detailed. He talks with spirit and interest about the strikes, the changes in work routine, the hurricanes, his visit to the highlands, and other matters. These were very hard years: political repression and frequent unemployment, the lack of a secure home for his family, illnesses and injury, the deaths of three children—the picture Taso provides is harsh and gloomy. The rare touches of humor, as in Elí's description of the boiling cornmeal, only add poignancy.

Certain features of Jauca culture are pointed up. The constant moving about and the search for a home are aspects of a cultural norm described earlier—the expectation that a man will be able to provide his wife and children with an independent residence. This problem plagued Taso through much of his married life and was only resolved permanently in later years. Another side of Jauca culture—or rather lowland culture—is exposed when Taso tells about their stay in Aguadilla and the visit he and Elí made to the highlands in 1932. The highlands are set apart from the lowlands in Puerto Rican life. The lowlands have good transportation, more electrification, more contact with the towns. They are the areas in which the majority of Puerto Ricans of Negroid phenotype are concentrated. The people of the highlands speak of the "witches of the coast." When the coastal town of Guayama had a baseball team, the team was officially called *Los Brujos* (The Witches). Highlanders are not as used to large-scale mechanized agriculture as are lowlanders. They are not as familiar with working for wages and buying their daily food needs; and they are considered backward and unsophisticated by lowlanders. The paternalism which typified rural economic relationships in all of Puerto Rico in the nineteenth century persists in greater strength in the highlands to this day.

Taso makes clear that he prefers lowland life. His visit to Aguadilla was brief; he never found conditions there wholly satisfactory, and he returned to Jauca with his family after less than a year. He was at a disadvantage ¹nce he lacked the subsistence plots and livestock of his highland neighbors. His description of his visit with Elí to Santa Catalina in the Coamo highlands also suggests that he missed the evening social events and the relatively greater bustle of lowland life. Correspondingly, he talks humorously of the fear the highlanders have of the people of the coast. The lowlanders are Negroes; they are witches; they cannot be trusted. There is a remote analogy with the way city dwellers and country folk feel about each other in other countries. Of course, Jauqueños are considered country folk by the town dwellers; but the Jauqueño quite accurately recognizes that he is as much like the townsman as he is like the rural highlander. He would represent some sort of midpoint if one were to view the differences along a continuum. In his experience with wage labor, union organization and political activity, store buying, mechanized agriculture, and similar things, he is close to being urbanized.

In the years between 1927 and 1939 changes of great importance occurred in Jauca culture as well as in Taso's personal life. Standpipes providing pure water along the village road replaced the surface springs of Palo Seco. Radios were first introduced into the barrio. Cars became more common and the roads were surfaced. Midwives were required to take out licenses and to meet official tests of knowledge and competence. Greater knowledge of birth control and contraceptive devices was acquired by some Jauqueños. Home medical remedies, such as the rum-garlic-rue-anamú mixture used by women *post partum,* began to be discarded.

Even greater changes occurred in the sphere of work. Taso describes the job of the fulgonero—who would load up to 28 tons of cane a day into railroad cars *by hand*—and how mechanical winches replaced the fulgoneros. The palero was gradually eliminated by the introduction of new machines and new ditching arrangements. With the virtual disappearance of the palero's craft, the last vestiges of artisan skill were removed from the cultivation of sugar cane. Work became increasingly standardized in this period. The rematistas and encabezados, labor bosses who earlier set the price for work in consultation with the mayordomos, were replaced by regular employee-foremen, and the prices for work became fixed either by piece or day rate. In the first years after the United States Occupation the new owners could not accurately estimate the maximum amount of work they could exact for the lowest cost, and the labor bosses unconsciously assisted them in achieving rate standardization. The standardization of work and the elimination of special skills meant that almost any worker could learn to do any job, and workers hence became highly interchangeable, like standard parts in a complex machine.

This change was accompanied by another. As more and more land was cleared and became irrigable, cane cultivation spread into sections which had served other purposes before. In the plots where workers had previously kept their livestock or gathered their tinder or animal fodder or building materials, cane now came to be grown. The value of such land before had been little and the local hacendados had afforded their workers the use of such land as part payment for labor. The employment of idle land of this kind for sugar cane cultivation drove local workers toward greater cash expenditures, changed their consumption needs and preferences, and made their cash incomes the real measure of their labor worth.

The extension of corporate control over vast south coast areas signaled the removal from the zone of the hacendados —the men of Don Pastor Díaz's stripe, who had previously played so important a part in the lives of local working people. Taso has already pointed out that formerly many of the holdings on which he had worked had belonged to particular landowners—Don Clotilde Santiago, Don Lucas Pérez Valdivieso, Don Pastor Díaz, and so on, always with the honorific "Don" attached to their names. The lands of these men were gradually absorbed by long-term lease or sale and consolidated within corporation holdings. The owners themselves moved away, persisting only as memories for the older workers. Their former holdings sometimes bear their names— Valdivieso, Descartes, Alomar, Texidor—but nothing else of them remains.

These changes taken together mean that the people of Barrio Jauca in, say, 1940, were very different in their style of life from their parents or grandparents. A man like Taso was living through the period when the changes were in most intense flux. A man in middle years who worked on a Jauca hacienda in 1900 might have certain special skills which helped to set him apart from his fellow Jauqueños. He might own a cow and several pigs, which he could quarter on hacienda land and feed and care for in part out of the hacienda resources. His cash income would be very small indeed, but he could eke out an existence by subsidiary activities, such as fishing and raising livestock, and by availing himself of whatever perquisites the hacienda provided. He would not be able easily to measure the cash or purchasing value of his labor, because so much of what he earned would be given him in the form of services and privileges of use. He would buy little for cash and be exposed to little expectation that there were other worthwhile things to be bought besides those known to him in his limited experience. His cash dealings would be mainly with itinerant peddlers or with the small barrio stores which stocked only the daily necessities. He would know little or nothing of politics and unions. His sense of security would flow from the personal relations, based on deference and favor, which he formed with his mayordomos and the hacendados, and from the friendship and kinship relations he had with his neighbors. His inclination to appeal to authority higher than that represented by the local landowners would be slight—such a possibility might not even occur to him.

A man like Taso, in his middle years in 1940, must have seen the world differently. Artisan skills had lost most of their special value, and they disappeared almost completely thereafter. The encroachment of the cane upon lands formerly used by working people meant the surrender of many traditional noncontractual services and the gradual loss of secondary sources of noncash income. The standardization of work meant the need to concentrate all one's energies in the direction of increasing productivity by wage labor and using such productivity as the prime measure of one's economic worth. The personal relationships with mayordomos and hacendados lost force—the mayordomos' power diminished as they too became interchangeable employees of the corporation, and the hacendados moved away, never to return. The now almost entire dependence on cash earnings meant the acquisition of a more precise picture of one's "worth" measured in dollars and cents. The company stores came to exercise control over men's use of their time and earnings, and incidentally exposed workers to a greater variety of attainable commodities. The men's feelings of security that came from their personal relationships with superiors diminished, and some other source of emotional (as well as economic) support had to be substituted. Jauqueños came to think more about the right to vote, the right to form unions, the right to be educated, and the value of impersonal institutions, such as unions and political parties and courts, in securing prerogatives formerly obtained through personal loyalty and service or, in some cases, previously unknown.

These many changes had the effect in part of "proletarianizing" the people of Jauca. They were made more alike, so to speak, by what was happening around them. At the same time, however, these same changes had the effect of making individuals more aware of their own separateness of identity—Jauqueños were becoming more "individualized" simultaneously as they became more proletarianized. This is no paradox. The effects of the United States Occupation, particularly in economic terms, were to make individuals see themselves as isolates rather than as members of a coherent hacienda community. On the one hand, they came to feel more sharply their identity with many workers throughout the sugar corporation zones. On the other, each became increasingly aware that his fate depended quite precisely on his own performance, especially at work. It was impossible to curry personal favor with something called *la compañía.* It was not easy to coax special dispensations out of a mayordomo whose quotas of work and disposable funds were set more and more by agricultural scientists working in an office fifty miles away.

Certainly Jauqueños tried—probably quite unconsciously—to maintain the traditional patterns of relationship. But mayordomos grew less and less willing to become godparents to workers' children. Fewer and fewer personal services could be claimed on the basis of faithful effort or long-time residence. The impersonal institutions of the larger society, such as political parties and labor unions, had to become more important at the same time that each worker inclined more and more to perceive himself as separate and alone in his economic struggles.

In 1940 the Popular party (*Partido Popular Democrático*) came into being. It marked a turning point in Puerto Rican history, and in certain ways it was a turning point as well in Taso's life.

CHAPTER 6

Manhood: The Later Years (1940–49)

I HAVE YET to give you a description of the way Elisabeth helped me from the time we first lived together. In the beginning she helped me by taking in washing and ironing. Later on she gave that up and started selling *pasteles* [cakes made of mashed plantain and meat, wrapped in banana leaves and boiled]. She used to make the pasteles on Saturdays and go to sell them at Colonia Texidor. She had that business for about two years. But one Saturday after she had made the pasteles and prepared to sell them, she got a fever and wasn't able to go. At that time, I was loading cane on the railroad cars at Colonia Valdivieso. When I came home in the afternoon I found her sick with fever. We divided up the pasteles among the neighbors and sold some to people in the houses nearby.

Elí had a different kind of *pastel* business before that, too. She had it a long time, and it was a business that paid well. She used to make $15 to $20 weekly. It was a business that she herself invented. She would make a quantity of pasteles on order. When she set about making them, she already had orders for 80, 90, or 100 pasteles. Any that were left over she'd sell at the pay line. In the house of Don Rafael Gracia, the mayordomo, she would sell around $1.50 worth, and in the house of Don Dolores Suro, who was second mayordomo, she used to sell a dollar's worth. The bookkeeper and all of them used to buy, and here in the barrio she would sell a great quantity.

But then Elí gave up the pastel business. I was out of work, and then they started some ditching work at Colonia Boca Chica. That was when the colonia was first being rented.

And Elí set up a stand with bread, coffee, salt-fish salad, and other things. She went to sell there to a number of the paleros and to the seeders who were working during the time of the late summer cane. That was how she spent the rest of that dead time. In the harvest a regular peddler customarily did that work, and so Elí gave it up and the other one began again. After that there was about a year that she wasn't working.

Then sometime after 1935 she established a beverage business here in this colonia, Destino, in the first years that the corporation had it. She began with that business in Colonia Valdivieso with hardly anything at all—she used to sell ten, twelve bottles there. Later on, the next year, she no longer went to Valdivieso but transferred to Destino, where there was more activity. At that time a great number of people worked on the carts; they use a lot of people in that work. Or rather, they used to use them; now they're all eliminated. Anyway, she used to sell up to twenty dollars' worth a week in her business.

One Sunday when she went to buy ice for the drinks from the bus that brought it from Ponce, she leaned against the side of the bus, and a sixty-pound block of ice on the scales came loose, fell on her foot, and crushed two of her toes. I had to put her on my shoulder—because she was quite unable to walk—and take her to the hospital. The nurses cut the nails off, and I had to carry her back on my shoulder to the town plaza, and I got a car there and brought her home. For a while she wasn't able to move from the bed.

At that time I had Rosa living in the house. Rosa said she would take over the business. So I hired a boy, one from the highlands—he happens to be living in the barrio again right now—and I gave him lunch and dinner here, and about $1.50 a week, to take the cart to the cane fields for Rosa. There in the fields Rosa would sell the refreshments and keep the accounts in the notebook. She went along keeping up the business until Elisabeth finally recovered from the accident.

Later on, around '42 or '43, the corporation had people plant a great number of beans here because of the war.

When they went to harvest them she wanted to go too. All the time she had lived with me she had never done that kind of work, but something got into her to go. And I let her go. She worked at it until they harvested almost all the beans they'd planted that year. They planted a whole lot of beans, and it happened that they lost a lot of them because there were heavy rains. But they also saved a lot to advantage, and she worked hard at that. And after that, when the bean harvest was over, she felt she wanted to continue working.

Then Don Rafael Gracia put her to work collecting the cane that used to fall in front of the siding where they loaded the cars. She used to gather the canes that would fall in front of La Quinta [a company barracks nearby]. She worked at that, in the cane, for a year during the harvest periods. And about then she became pregnant with Lilian [1943] and she got a "bad stomach," as we call it—fevers and bad vomiting— such that she had to give up working. And I wouldn't let her go back to work under any condition. After she recovered she wanted to work more, because Elisabeth is a strong woman. But I didn't let her work any more.

From then on, she hasn't had any work of a business sort. Though she always has helped me with the domestic tasks, looking after her family as the family has grown larger—at this point we are so numerous that often there is insufficient time for her simply to look after her very own family. The tasks are many and it's hard for her—now at times we ourselves must send the clothes out to be washed. As the family is big and we are many, if we all change our clothes at once there are enough dirty clothes for a laundress. So she has been a woman who has worked a lot with me, has helped me, and on the occasions when I've been sick she has always worked hard to scrape up the money we needed. Thank God, we haven't suffered, because she is a woman well prepared to help. These are the ways in which she has helped me. When I haven't been able, she has put her hands to the situation and has resolved it.

There remains Elí's most important business in which she handled a good deal of money. When the *bolita* game business appeared here she decided to sell tickets. And really she had a lot of luck in that. She won many times and she also sold lots of prize-winning tickets. There were times when for four or five weeks in a row she made the money in the house, sometimes because she sold the prize-winning tickets [on commission], other times because we won ourselves.

I remember one time when I was having some dental work done. I'd made a promise in town to pay something down and the rest weekly, whatever I could manage. One night the *bolitero* [illegal-lottery salesman] came to the house and offered us some tickets, and Elí bought a piece of a ticket. In the morning before I left for the clinic, I walked down the road along here, and they were chanting the bola [giving the winning numbers over the radio] in Don José's house, and they sang out a number for first prize. I heard it, and I went back home and said to Elisabeth, "Elisabeth, that piece of a ticket you bought last night—wasn't it such-and-such a number?" And she told me, "Yes, it was 885." I remember it as if it were now. I thought that she had only taken a piece, and I said to her, "How much did you win, $20?" And she said, "No, $80—I took four pieces." That was on 885. And with that, I began to pay part of this work.

And our house—I can say that more than half of the money invested in it we got out of bolita. I made the most of it—I used it in buying wood and I repaired the house. And Elisabeth handled a great deal of money in this. This bolita business came to such extremes here at one point that tickets were being sold like bread, in the streets—children and everyone were selling. There were some drawings that were called *La Mucara* [the owl] because they used to have them at night; it was a lottery conducted in Cuba, and the same numbers announced as winners over the Cuban radio won here too. They used to have to sell those during the day, and they'd collect the money the same day; we also won on that a number of times. I remember that with 163 I once won $100, and Elí took out $100 the same night—the two of us hit at the same time. So that it was a business in which Elisabeth handled lots of money. All the same it's a bad business; I know that it's bad, because many must sacrifice in order that one benefit. I recognize this; but he who has the business has a great advantage.

Why did Elí give up the business?
The way she gave it up was as follows. She used to go out to collect what she had sold during the week at Destino. And in 1948 a bill was before the Governor [to punish sellers and buyers by jail sentences]. I remember that that afternoon I was watchfully waiting for the least movement in the capital. The bill was signed into law, and when she came back from Destino I said to her, "Well, this is the last you are going to sell." And so she liquidated her business. Since then I've thought—suppose by chance they had caught her? She would have had to go to jail, and then with fines I wouldn't know how to pay and having to stay home attending this mass of family, it would be something terrible! It is better that she look after the kids and I work.

Could you reconstruct the attitude you had when we formerly discussed the bolita, before you changed your mind about it?
Yes. We were discussing at that time why people preferred to play bolita [rather than the government-sponsored lottery]. And I told you that it was easier for them, and they felt they won more easily playing this game. Because when they used to want to buy a favorite number, they could get it more easily than if it were in the legal lottery, see? They would say, "I want to play such and such a particular number," and they could buy it easily. In the legal lottery this is difficult to do.

Another thing: in a bolita series composed of a thousand numbers, those thousand numbers are almost entirely sold here in the barrio. It's a rarity when the winner doesn't turn up here in the barrio. You understand? And if, for example, there are four, five, eight, or ten series that are being cast, it's remarkable if a Sunday should pass without people winning prizes. In the legal lottery it's rather more difficult, even though there are more prizes in it. This is why people much prefer to play the bola. Because they're playing within a thousand numbers, and in the government lottery they have to play among many thousands. And one way or another, among the thousand, the prize always turns up here. And then there comes this enthusiasm—"If that one wins this week, next time it's my turn." This enthusiasm that the people have is the result. They are always living with this hope—"If the other hits today, tomorrow I'm going to hit." And so it goes.

I've always admitted that the bolita game is bad for those who play, you see; I know it's bad for those who play it. Now those who have the business of selling—they benefit a great deal. For the player this is a bad game. Say you have three numbers among a thousand—you really have 997 numbers to lose with, and only three to win with. Now the sellers—one can say that for them all the numbers are opportunities to win. That's the difference. He who has the selling business has a good business indeed. But of course now it's a little dangerous.

Can you tell me your moral or religious attitude about this matter?

That is something else—though I had given up bolita already, we also don't play now for religious reasons. We're not able to play. That is part of our doctrine: we can't do that. Now before, as I told you, when we were selling, we used to receive great benefits. And looking back on it, it may have appeared to me at the time that the people who played also got great benefits from it. But even after selling a whole series of numbers—when you sell all of them—you see clearly that although you are handling the prizes, still the game favors the bankers the most. After the tickets are sold, *they* never lose. Now, when I gave up selling—or rather, when Elí gave up selling—then I found myself in the position of those to whom we sold. And then there would be time and time again when I used to gamble $2 and $3, and a long time would go by when I wouldn't win a single dollar back, see? So little by little I came to say, "Well, this—we have to give it up." And many people here who have won money in the past don't want you even to mention the bolita to them now—they have given it up. It may be that what's happened to them is what happened to me—in the first few years they won and the game looked good to them. But afterward when they got taken by the numbers, well, they saw the game wasn't so good. It can be that what changed me changed them too.

Long ago I told you that there are many houses here built with money from bolita. Now see how it works. A person plays the game for several dollars' worth a week and doesn't win for a year. Then at the end of the year he wins. And then suppose he wins as much as $300. Then he's able to build a modest house or do something to improve the house he has. Now my opinion is this: yes—he took out $300—but he was playing a year without taking out anything. Now, one must compare the money that he played in a year with the amount he won.

I can give you an actual example. Someone was saying, while we were talking on the railroad this week, that his house cost more than $1,000, and that he had won $600 in the bola. But then he himself admitted that he had already lost more than $1,000 when he won the $600. At the time he was working—he was doing all right—and yet he himself says that he would have kept on until he was without a pair of work pants playing the bola—you see? If, after a long time, they come out winning $500 or $600 they go and build a house or make repairs. Sure, one can enumerate the houses here that people got through the bola and those repaired from bola winnings. But one must compare this with what they have lost—that is to say, with those dollars each week which are left over and which they do not save but gamble, because they believe that from a few dollars a week, three or four hundred are never going to appear otherwise. And they continue gambling. It can be two, three years, perhaps, and they never win. But over the years, at some point they win. And that is when they realize the gain. They do what they want, whether it be building a house or anything else, with the money. But I believe that if it were worked out with a pencil, they'd still be losing.

Now for myself, what I won used to vary—it might be $8

or $10, $15, $18, and it could be $20 too. I remember that
there was one number that I played up to $2,000 [i.e. the
biggest prize, if he had won] and as luck would have it, I
played it seven years, and in seven years it paid off $140.
That was 231. With the money we got from that I made part
of the front porch of the house—which forms part of the room,
the half porch. And part of the back of the house used for
sleeping—what we call *colgadizo*—that too was built with
that money. And some oak boards that are set up as part of
the walls and part of the zinc sheeting for the roof were
bought with that money. It went for many such things.

But I stopped playing long before I entered the Church.
As we say here, "He who plays always loses and he who
drinks gets drunk." But, one thing—we Puerto Ricans believe
that saving money, we'd never get to have very much. And
that puts the people to playing. I believe that if they would
devote themselves to saving the money, they would save it.
But the way they do it today, if they don't invest it in one
thing they invest it in another. They don't want to save when
they think that dollar by dollar, they're never going to get to a
hundred. If they hold the dollar in their pockets, well, they
throw it out on some other vice. They never seem to have
that something to believe that $1 today, $2 tomorrow. That's
my belief; I don't know about others.

*And since you've given up bolita, have you ever saved up
little by little for something?*

When I made this floor, I had a bunch of dollars I pulled
together that way. When I'd get my pay I'd meet my obligations, and what was left over I gave to Elisabeth to take care
of. I should also include a little pig that I sold for money;
and with that, I did the job. That is how we do it now
when we have a debt—for example, an obligation with a
peddler—we already know what part of the money must be
set aside to pay. And if I tell Elisabeth we're going to save
for this or that, then she tries to help. Each week I'll give her
something to hold—$2 or $3 or $1—and at week's end if it's

nothing, then nothing. But that's how we do it, until we have saved what we need.

Now I would like to go back to the year 1940. When the elections were coming, when the 1940 campaign was approaching, then there arose this business of the Popular party. I had no knowledge of it then, although there were already some people who were fighting for that party in some towns of the island. And one day I was in a local store when Cosme Mora arrived with petitions to get the party on the ballot. I filled out a petition for the party. But it did not pass through my mind at the time that I was going to be a Popular. I was still a Socialist. When I filled out the Popular party petition, I did it with the end in mind of cooperating with them, so that they might register their party; but I continued being a Socialist. And through my conversations with some of their leaders who came here to the barrio, and because of the program they used to advance when they held their meetings, and the laws they said they would pass—all this information they put before the people—well, then I decided to leave the Socialist party and enter the Popular party. I was losing my interest in the Socialist party, because some years had gone by and they had fulfilled none of the promises they had made, you see. Because of the coalition between the Socialists and Republicans, the Socialists were unable to put their program into action. They were completely obstructed and they could not realize the program they had.

And then the Socialist party began to lose force and we members began to lose our love of the party, since we saw that it could not achieve the program offered us. And I went along finding the program of the Popular party more and more attractive. They told us that if they won and did not fulfill in that year what they had promised, we should vote against them the next time. This promise meant that one would not have to wait so very long, just the period of one term—and then if disappointed, vote against them. The Popular party made up its program before it went into the elections. And they would tell us: "You want these laws in this country. So give us your vote once. If we don't put through the laws, then in the next election vote against us." And so we—that is, I—saw that the laws were very favorable, and I decided to vote with the Popular party in 1940.

There had been political campaigns before in which I had worked hard—campaigns in which I can say that I wasted my time. Afterward, I worked hard in the others, but I obtained some benefits, although not directly—but indirectly, see? In the previous ones, fighting in the Socialist party, I got none at all. Then I decided to work in the campaign of 1940 for the Popular party. And while I can't truthfully tell you that I've received the greatest help directly, indirectly the Popular party has helped me a lot. It isn't perfect; it has its errors, but it has lifted the workers up a little. Think about this. When Lalo was still a youngster we used to work at hoeing there at Colonia Destino. And there were times when we were working that we used to earn $4.50, the two of us, for the week—and that was what you called *work*. There was this system that if you agreed to do two cuerdas of weeding for $3 and it took you the whole week, that was what you earned. At that time there was no minimum wage law.

Now, after the minimum wage law came in, it didn't matter if the mayordomo were to say to me while I was digging irrigation ditches, "This cuerda of ditch is worth 75 cents." This wouldn't matter because after I worked seven hours, he would have to pay me what the law stipulated. Now, if I could earn something more beyond this, I would earn it— but my minimum wage always had to be paid. In such ways, the Popular party has come to alleviate the situation. I recognize their errors. But they have made it possible for us to live a little less afflicted economically.

Now I'll tell you something else too. Here we have a thing—it's like with religion. There are people who say that they continue being Republicans because they must be grateful to some old leader for such and such a thing. And many vote out of gratitude to one or another leader this way. Do you see how it is? We have a lady here with whom you still can't touch on this matter of the Republicans. She says that Don Rafael Martínez Nadal did a great favor for a son of hers and that she can't stop being a Republican even though Martínez is long dead. And they go along this way—"My papa was a Republican, and I can't change"— "My father was this and that, and I am the same." As they say, "I must honor his bones."

Now as I told you before, the Popular party forecast the laws they would put into operation. They explained to people what was happening, what the government in power was like. They talked to the people in a way that was easy to understand. Before, at political meetings the leaders would hold forth, and it was truly eloquent oratory, truly lovely. But what we heard we did not understand—orations about the mists, the seas, the fishes, and great things. Then, when Muñoz Marín came, he didn't come speaking that way. He came speaking of the rural worker, of the cane, and of things that were easier to understand. And the people could go along with him, understanding and changing. And so they learned to trade the mists and the sea for the plantain trees and for the land they were going to get if they gave the Popular party their votes.

The first time I heard Don Luis Muñoz Marín speak was in the barrio they call Coquí, in Salinas. That night there came before us the heavy artillery of the Popular party; I knew some of them. Many of them had been with us in the Socialist party. But then they left to found the new party. I remember that that night Don Benigno Fernández García spoke there, and many others that had gone over to the Popular party. Of course, now many who were with us have moved on and others remain. That night Don Luis was explaining to the people thus: "In this election you give me your vote, and I promise you the following things. And if I don't keep my promise, then vote against me in the next election." It was an easy thing to understand; the people understood. And one saw a great enthusiasm among the people because the party was just beginning, and everywhere they had meetings there were lots of people.

Now, when I registered in the Popular party, I did it with doubts. We had been fooled many times. I was going to try it out. If they had not given us those same laws which they offered us, I probably would have voted against them the next time. Or I would have given up politics, which had been my idea. I had pretty much lost interest already. I saw that the situation of the workers never changed. It was always the same. In the barrios, we always had the same conditions; they never changed. Even if something good were done in the towns, things in the barrios were always the same.

Now, I can tell you that when we began with Popular party affairs here in Jauca, there was hardly any campaign. In the first meetings of the Popular party here, the people here flooded into the Popular party.

If I'm not mistaken, we had a tie in the House of Representatives in 1940, while the Liberal party got one representative. When that representative joined his vote to ours then we used to have the majority in the House. That one representative used to be very important, because however he voted, there was the majority.

At that time I did not know most, or even any, of the local leaders of the Popular party. Their board of directors made the nominations of candidates for mayor and for the municipal assembly of the town. Afterward they would come to the barrios and hold meetings and explain the results of the directors' meetings they had had, and the candidate who had been nominated, and the assemblymen who had been nominated. They explained it and we accepted it.

In that election the candidate for mayor was a gentleman named Luna. Although we had enough votes to win that election, we lost it because he was a rather inactive candidate. Moreover, voters from the country didn't understand things— many didn't know where the polling places were and lost their votes. In town the campaign was badly organized. It's not like now, when they name people who don't have a vote to serve as escorts to bring voters to the right voting places. Then there was none of that prepared and, though we had the votes to win, we lost. Although we lost in the municipality, in the Legislature we made a beginning—there we could realize something in our favor immediately. And in that period of time, the Popular party did a number of quite good things which I believe contributed to their continuing to win. And we went along getting more confidence in the party and in the leaders.

Now another thing happened, you know. Before, we all used to go and deposit our votes and we thought no more about it. So Don Pedro Juan Serralles [a member of one of Puerto Rico's wealthiest families], for instance, there in the Senate, could do whatever crossed his mind, and we here— well, we were far away from whatever he was doing. Little knowledge on our part about matters of government, and little interest, too, at the same time. Today, from the time the Legislature reconvenes, people are watchfully observing what one legislator does and what the other one does. Now it reaches such an extreme that at times when the Legislature has finished its business, there are those who say, "Oh, Fulano in the Legislature, he hasn't done a thing." In those times, well, the Legislature would come and go, and no one knew when it started and when it stopped. No longer today—because today the people are watching to see what each leader they voted for will do. The people have been waking up, see? The leaders have been preaching, and orienting, and interesting people in things, and interest has been awakened.

Well, we continued fighting for the party and then came the 1944 campaign. The party was picking up more steam and we won more and more people to us. You could say that the people were becoming more convinced, because the party put through new laws and went along keeping its promises. And I continued working in the party. Of course, at times the leaders say things before they win, and after they win it's not as they had said. But at least the laws themselves brought some benefit and were good.

Anyway, I was never intent upon the question of municipal employment or anything of that kind, see. When I used to have some need, I'd go to the mayor or someone else, because during the election periods I would help them. I was working with them, and it was only fair that if I had some need I should go where they were to ask help. But I wasn't interested in any political posts—rather I always used to hope that help would reach me through means of the laws the government would pass.

In the elections of 1944 I came to know Pancho [Francisco Robledo, who became Popular party mayor of Santa Isabel in 1944]. A number of us here then undertook to direct the party's barrio committee—Compadre Gueni, Compadre Marcial, Compadre Berto, Daniel Torres, Julián Texidor, and I. There was a fight among three party mayoral candidates at the time. There was Francisco Robledo, whom I came to know little by little. And we had Norberto Bernacet and Ventura Rodríguez. These three had a great struggle trying to line up delegates. I don't know if this has been explained to you. This matter of delegates is why they have meetings in the barrios, and one reason why they need the barrio committees. They allow a delegate for a certain number of party members—one for each 100 members, it seems to me. Sometimes Barrio Jauca has three delegates, sometimes four; and so it goes in each of the barrios. The delegates are nominated here in the barrio and the delegates from the different barrios and the town party committee name the candidates for mayor and the municipal Assembly.

And these three candidates were trying to get control of the delegates, each one of them, because the delegates were divided, and each candidate wanted to win control of the number of delegates necessary to come out on top in his candidacy. Two of the candidates knew they didn't have enough delegates to be nominated, but they agreed to continue working until the day of the election.

I was not a delegate the day they had the local convention, but Compadre Gueni was. I was in the back observing the assembly when the meeting began. Then Don Ventura Rodríguez withdrew his candidacy and ceded the votes that belonged to him to Bernacet. The election itself is secret— they use little slips of paper. Then the delegates voted, and it was a tie between Francisco Robledo and Norberto Bernacet. Then they had to have a new election. Now when they counted the votes, one was blank. And Compadre Gueni approached a boy who was at his side whom he knew had turned in a blank ballot. Compadre Gueni coaxed him to give his vote to Francisco Robledo, and the boy did.

When the new election was tallied Robledo came out with a one-vote majority. Then there was a great hubbub in the assembly. Bernacet threw himself out of there in a fury and said he was going to found a new party. And at that time he had a lot of people who followed him, from that part of Cortada called Descalabrado [in the western barrios of Santa Isabel] and those places. He went out in the street very angry, saying that they had robbed him, and there was a lot of talk about how he would not knuckle under, and that he was going to register a new party. But he didn't. His support came from his having been fighting for the union, the CGT. And although a large number of people withdrew their confidence in him, there were a lot who still followed him; but finally he lost the trust they had in him. Now, I noted that many times in the newspaper *El Batey* [the official Popular party paper], they would show him as a cane cutter, and he would be suggested for election to the House of Representatives. They used to give him prominence in such a way that one had to recognize something special about him.

But I want to return to where we were a little while ago. Bernacet continued protesting, but in the end he had to align himself once more with the party. I don't know where the pressure came from, but he realigned himself again with the party and accepted what had happened at the convention. Then he went on working, although not as strongly as before, with the Popular party. After that he got a government job; he was employed in the tick bath program. He remained working there and it seems to me he is still in that job. We won the 1944 election locally, and then the party here could develop its program better. Robledo had a somewhat difficult administration that first period, however.

In 1944, Lilian was born. Lilian was a tiny baby. She was such a little thing that you could hardly see her on the bed. And when she was about two and a half or three years old—when she was already walking—she had a fever so severe that afterward she had to learn to walk again. I didn't know even what kind of fever it was, what it was we were treating. The doctor didn't tell us. They gave her medicine, she recovered, and afterward she came to walk again. But one may see that she walks with one leg turned out sideways. Perhaps you have noticed; I believe that is a consequence of the fever.

After the 1944 campaign I decided I had to move my house from Tole's lot, where it then was, and find a place to live where I could really consider myself independent. By that time I had worked for Robledo, who was then mayor. I had helped him a lot. And the previous administration had bought an acre of land in Jauca to be divided among local people who had no place for their houses. I pestered Robledo and he agreed to help me get a lot. But it happened that another person went and solicited the lot at the same time I did. And because there was no more than one lot available, an assemblyman was sent here to look over the situation and they brought me to town. They asked me whether I believed this lot could be divided between the two. I told them that my only aim was to have a place to put my house. If the other person would accept half, so would I. So it was decided, and we divided the lot.

Didn't you tell me that your compadre Don Berto helped you in regard to this lot?

Yes. Compadre had the idea of building a house. He had a bicycle he could sell and he was putting together some other money. He began to fight for a lot, and most had already been assigned. But one was still unassigned. It was on the edge of the road. That lot led to vicious gossip (*chismes*) here because there were very many persons who wanted it. But they assigned it to Compadre, and it was in his name there at the Municipal Building. But during that period Elio Burgos, who is the owner of the house where Berto now lives,

12. Close-up of *palero* digging *hoyados*

13. Distributing seed cane

14. Planting seed cane

15. Weighing produce in a local store

thought of leaving there to go live at the land grants at Arenal in Salinas. Then he told Compadre that he was going to sell his house. Compadre Berto had little money, but he had sold the bicycle I told you of before, and he had some more money that he had saved by economizing. And Don José Guilbé lent him a part for the purchase of that house.

So when Elio offered to sell him the house and he decided to buy it, he came right away to my house and told me what was going on. He told me to go directly to town to raise the matter of the lot he would not need now, lest some other person go before me. But it happened then that the very one who sold the house to him also had notified someone else that he was going to sell it. And that person also went to the town and spoke for the lot. So we two met with the problem almost simultaneously. Then when Berto bought the house, there were already those two petitions for the lot there. I accepted the idea of dividing the lot on seeing that the other was also a poor man and needed it.

In 1944 the CGT began its activities in Barrio Jauca. At the time I was still living on Antolina's lot. They came one night and asked permission to hold a meeting in front of the house. The leaders of the movement came and began to speak and explain their aims. The workers needed a union which would represent them, they said, because the employers were abusing the workers. And the workers had to unite in order to defend themselves against the employers. They explained a great many things there, of the way they would do it, and they asked the consent of the workers. If we were willing to accept what they were doing, then they proposed to nominate a committee that would function here in the barrio. Then the workers said yes—they agreed to unite themselves in a union, to unionize themselves. Then they answered some questions that some of the workers asked as to how the union would function. They explained that they would provide a rule book for each of the members, a set of regulations so that each would know how the union was going to work, the obligations of members to the union and of the officials to the members. Then they proceeded to nominate a committee from local people here in the barrio.

They had no good knowledge of us at that time. But they directed the local people to choose the ones who would be able to carry out the work. Then the workers here began to pick from among themselves. And so it was that I became a member of that committee. We began to take the names of the persons who were going to join the union on that same night. I'm not sure, but if I am not mistaken the president they elected was a man named Dionisio. The secretary was Compadre Lorenzo. I was treasurer. And it seems to me that Compadre Gueni took part in that committee; I don't recall if he was the vice-president or what, but it seems to me he participated; and also Compadre Marcial. That was the committee they elected. And we began to work.

The people came to join and I kept the membership rolls. We began immediately—the very next day. As soon as they came to us we made them members. As people came to join the union, I had to list them and give them credentials that the officials had left with us. On that night they didn't leave the bylaws, but they left credentials—that is, membership cards. I would fill out the information required on the card, then each paid his dues and took the card with him. The local president remained president only briefly. Then it seems to me that the one who became president was Compadre Gueni.

We continued working, and at the time there was considerable enthusiasm here. I didn't have time to live; whatever free moment I had was spent struggling with the union. I felt good and contented at the time though, because I saw the love of the people who came to join the cause. I saw the cooperation everybody gave. The moment came when it was not necessary for us to go anywhere to propagandize. People came on their own account and expressed their desire to join the union.

Afterward the CGT signed a contract which stipulated that a union member had to go to the pay lines to sign the checks when they were given out. The checks had to be signed by a representative of the union as well as by a representative of the company. They named me to carry out that job. So I had to go every Saturday to the pay window. The company prepared a big table, and as the checks were distributed at the table I had to sign them. They were also signed by the mayordomo of irrigation, or by Don Pedro Aldebol, or Don Rafael if he was there.

But when I would return home, then there was the big job. The house would already be full of people waiting to pay their dues and of others waiting to join. There were times when I would still be struggling with it at eleven at night. And sometimes on Sunday before I got up there would already be people in the yard waiting for me. I had prepared a little table in the corner, and I would seat myself at it as soon as I was up. Sometimes Elisabeth would bring me my coffee at the table and there I would be until four in the afternoon. Then at four, or at three or three-thirty, I would take the money and count it, and then I would go to town. I'd go and deliver the money there, and then they'd give me a receipt for the money that I carried. I would also keep track of the number of new members who had joined so they could enter them in the general book there.

There were times when I came back from town to find that Elisabeth had $15 or $20 more from people who had arrived and signed up during the time I was in town. Then I'd have to return again to struggling with that until I put everything in order. We were coping with a growing thing—with great enthusiasm. And too, we saw that things were moving ahead well. And the people, especially those in town who knew the president, Bernacet, were very active. There was a great enthusiasm for him.

But afterward we got into a fight with him and differences began to arise. The assembly was supposed to be sovereign over everyone, but sometimes at the meetings we would order certain things to be done and the president would not carry them out. For instance, the president frequently had to go considerable distances within the colonias. In order to avoid the expenses of a car, which could not be borne, we ordered that the president buy a horse. We wanted him to take union funds and buy a horse for those services instead of using a public car. He would hire a car and report $10 expenses each time; and he would have to take that car two or three times a day. It was a terribly expensive thing. Cases could arise in different colonias where the members were, and there would be a tremendous expense. Then we presented this idea and the assembly approved it. And time passed and many meetings, and nothing at all happened. And it came up again, and again nothing. And with different kinds of proposals it always remained the same. And we here were aware of those things.

We had other funds in the same union. We set up a separate fund by unanimous agreement, with the end in mind of not exhausting the regular funds of the union. We agreed in a meeting that whenever a member of the union died, each member would contribute a quarter from his pocket. With the number of members we had, it came to a large amount of money. Our proposition was as follows. From this money they would take $100. With that $100 they would buy a coffin, and they would pay the costs of the velorio. And the money that remained would be given to the widow. And if there were no widow, they would give it to the mother, or to whatever person had been a dependent of the deceased. We decided this at a meeting at Descalabrado, and we contributed our quarters. Everybody gave. I was in charge of collecting here, and we sent the money to town. Now, we didn't know how it was handled; we simply complied by paying our obligation.

But then one of the union members here died. All the members came and made their contributions of a quarter each. And I sent to town to get the coffin. I ordered it, and I spoke with the president telling him what had happened. We ordered the coffin and if I am not mistaken, we requested $10 for the expenses of the velorio. They sent the coffin from there and the money for the velorio. And I assumed that the central committee would not wait for the moment when we made a formal claim—since they knew already that it was an approved procedure—the rest of the $100 had to be brought to the dependents. And I believed they had done so.

But then time passed, and time passed, and we didn't know

what was going on. The wife of the deceased called and told me that the money had not come. She knew what the procedure was; probably her dead husband had told her before how it was. It struck me as strange that the president had not carried out the directive. I called the president's attention to this situation. I went next Sunday, taking the money we had collected. By then the money we collected was less—the enthusiasm of the people was not so great. They were not paying a year in advance as they had been, so the collections weren't so large. Before, people had been saying, "Well, I want to pay that now, during the harvest, so not to have to worry about it in dead time."

Well, I went and carried in the collection that I had made that Sunday and then I asked for the money for the widow. And then the president told me that it wasn't like that. He told me a union member had died in Cortada and they had not done it. Then I fell into an argument with him. I told him that if they had not done it in Cortada it was because the committee in Cortada didn't know its rights, but that that was what *we* had agreed, and I was not leaving until he gave me the money for that. We had words, and then finally they gave me the check. If I don't remember incorrectly, they gave me $70, something like that. They bought a coffin for $30 and they sent $10 for the velorio, and some $70 that remained they gave to me.

But those sorts of things went along piling up. We were becoming aware of the things that were going on; many workers were coming in with complaints. Our responsibility was to take them to the president, and there were times that the president would pay little attention. One noted less interest then, and there was a lot of gossip about the president and the company. We here watched that situation and we resolved to take a stand. We were disposed—the committee here decided—to ask for the president's resignation. And then we had a big fight in a meeting. But he had great support from the western barrios, and we were beaten. When we asked his resignation they were almost ready to beat us up. And then we withdrew from all of that. When we saw that it was impossible, that we were unable to shake the president's support, we decided to keep ourselves apart. Afterward we attempted to start up an independent union.

That idea began with those of us who formed the subcommittee we had here in Jauca. We decided that we could establish a union. We saw how things were, and we saw it was necessary that we have a union. Then we spoke with Robledo, the mayor, and he said, "Well, let's start it." We held a meeting one night here in front of the house and named a committee. Another committee was named for the town. The workers themselves decided the dues they were going to pay, and it was agreed to set up subcommittees and organize the workers who would want to be in an independent union in all the different barrios. On that occasion they named Pancho Robledo as president. We struggled to organize the workers; but many workers had had bad things happen to them in the other union. And with those who remained in the other union, the same things were continuing to happen.

Then there arose a sort of contrariness among the workers. They themselves formed bad opinions of unions, and with good reason. Because when one enters a situation with good faith and sees so much quarrelling, when one needs something and is not helped, then people lose their interest. Many did join the union but many didn't wish to. And many said the same thing was going to happen with this union that had happened with the earlier one. But in spite of this we came to have quite a lot of members.

It was at that time that something happened to Compadre Marcial at Colonia Destino. He was there one Saturday, and as he was a member of the new union committee, he was telling people that it was necessary to establish a union, and that if they wanted they could join the union. And then a certain lad spoke up, saying that I had built my house with money belonging to CGT. And then Compadre Marcial, who knew how I worked with the union and what I had done, he socked the boy. Now, I was far from the crowd—I was at home, I didn't know about it. But Marcial, on returning from Destino, before going to his house came and entered my house and told me what had happened. And truly there rose up in me an anger—I said, "Good, I am going there to see him face to face, to see if he is able to prove that I built my house with union money."

For when the CGT came to Jauca I already had my house. As a matter of fact, they wanted to pay my electric light bill for electricity used during the meetings, and I never wanted that. And there was one time when they wanted to pay me something for my work; and I didn't want that either. What I did was best—because if I had accepted some salary, even if it were the slightest thing, something more serious might have happened to me. But actually all I did was sacrifice my time in the work.

Then, about two nights later if I remember right, we went to Destino, still struggling with the matter of the independent union. And while they were talking there trying to organize the workers, I went to that youth's house with the receipts I had for the money that I had delivered to the CGT. When I delivered that money, even if it were only 10 cents I was delivering, I made them give me a receipt. And when the boy's mother saw me arriving she fell upon me, calling my attention to what had happened with Compadre Marcial. And I told her that if I wanted, I could sue her son, because I had proof that I had not built my house with CGT money; I had receipts for all the money I had taken in for the CGT, and furthermore I had the records in my house.

And then this woman whom I had known for many years asked me to excuse him, claiming that these were things he said while drunk—that Compadre Marcial also had had his drinks, and so on. I told her not to worry, that I was not going to do anything, but that he should be careful when he talked, because in matters concerning my reputation, I was willing to go to any lengths—that if I had to take it to court, I would do it. Then the boy arrived and he asked me to excuse him. He said that it was a matter between Compadre Marcial and him, and that it had come up suddenly. And I said, "Well, it's all right."

While many of the workers joined the new union, many

said no, because of what had happened before, and that is why it too came to fail. A few were left who stayed in the union for a short while, but then they too did not want to continue. And so the union failed. Meanwhile, the people in town finally came to understand the situation and the things that had been happening in the CGT local. They got out from under—they threw out the president and named another. And then they stumbled along with one president after another until at last it destroyed the union.

In Puerto Rico, as long as the worker struggles the way he is struggling now, he will always fail. They start one union over here and another over there, and that's the way it always goes. Last year, if I'm not mistaken, there were elections here because one union claimed privileges here and another claimed them in the same place. And I believe that as long as that goes on, the worker in Puerto Rico will always fail. That's where the corporations win their objective, when the worker is like that—confused, not knowing where to go, to one side or the other.

And if it were up to me to make the nominations, I would never pick people mixed up already in politics. I would always keep the two apart. That's my position—I don't know about others, understand. They should pick men who are free, free of politics, who are not mixed up in that. The politician often has the idea of capturing a portion of the people for his own political benefit, and he is not thinking of the workers' interests. You understand what I mean? It may be that he is a candidate, and he presents himself as a labor leader though he isn't a labor leader at all, but just needs the workers' support for the moment. Now if there is a man in government and one can see that he cooperates with the labor movement, then in an election it's proper to give him your vote, understand? A man who cooperates with the movement and makes efforts for the workers, well, it's right; but it seems to me he ought not to be a union executive.

In 1946 I got the job I have now, on the railroad. At the time I was working with the pala. We had finished the work in the big cane, digging the maclaines and the irrigation ditches and the like, up to the point of planting. After finishing that we were left *chiripeando* [doing odd jobs]—digging little pieces of ditch here, there, and everywhere. And that day they had sent me to make a ditch through a stretch of grass, this American grass that they grow back of the Destino storehouse. A heavy rain had fallen, and there was a lot of water still around and it was rotting the grass seeds, and they sent me to cut a drain.

This grass was for the horses. It was on new land that had been pasture, and they had left it for cultivating this grass. The soil was really bad—the kind of earth that sticks to the pala—one would lift it with the pala and then have to use a stick to get the earth off. I worked there two days—two completely bad days—fighting with that muck. And that afternoon I came home late, and after I had my coffee I sat for a while in the house. Then I walked out to get a can of water at the standpipe. And when I went out Cosme [the railway crew foreman] asked me if I wanted to work for him. And as the work I had been doing was pretty bad, I told him yes. Then he told me, "If you're disposed to work, you can begin tomorrow." And then I began working with him. I remember that it was a date a little earlier than this month, because the fiesta of Santa Isabel had already been given at the time, and the year was 1946 [June or early July]. And the first day I went to work we went to the siding at Colonia Florida. So I returned—and I have remained to the present day.

When I started in 1946 they had about five men in the brigade. The company told the foreman to take on two more men, and Cosme got me and another. Then we were seven, and we worked the whole winter. When the harvest began they told him to discharge two. Then the two they had to let go were the last two who had come on—namely, Ruperto Vásquez and me. But it happened that at that time the railway union had required us to become members ourselves in order to work. So I felt I had certain rights; it seemed to me that if I was a member of the union, I had a right to work too. Ruperto quit and went to work in the cane. But I didn't want to do it; I didn't want to do it. I made my claim to the union; and they told me they were going to see what they could do. But then Compadre Berto and I made an agreement with the others on the brigade. It had to do with the number of hours that they gave us to work. I don't recall if it was twenty-one hours each week that they allowed us. But we resolved to divide the hours available among those of us that then remained on the brigade.

That is the way we arranged it. Sometimes this one lost a day, sometimes another, but we shared the total time among all. And since then I've continued. It is a job where your rice and beans are a sure thing even in dead time, while in the cane in dead time things get a little hard, a little hard. Now they've been telling me that the people who work in the cane during harvest period are earning a tremendous sum of money, especially cutting cane in which the trash has been burned off first. I'm not going to affirm this, because I didn't see it, but I've been told that there were cane cutters this harvest who earned up to $40 a week, working piecework and the like. But I prefer my work, with less money, if it provides for me in dead time too.

As for cane cutting, I never did that more than once, and only for a little while, nothing more. I don't know how that idea came to me, but once I bought a machete and went to cut cane. I began in the morning, and at about ten-thirty they needed a fulgonero at the siding. They sent me to do it, and I finished with cane cutting—I never went back! I don't like that work because it's a little dangerous. I am really afraid of it. Especially when they're cutting cane heavy with trash, a machete can easily get tangled in the straw and incapacitate a man, what with so many people cutting at the same time. So I've always been a little afraid of it. And actually it is a little rough, that job. I never found it agreeable!

I would like to tell you now of the 1948 campaign. Before the election I was made a barrio delegate, and they sent us to attend the island convention of the Popular party in San Juan. We left here around three in the morning, and they had organized us as follows. We got into the cars in Santa Isabel, and when the delegation from Ponce arrived then the delegation from Santa Isabel was to set out for San Juan. And when we arrived in Salinas, the Salinas delegation was to set out before us. Each delegation had its hour of departure.

We were on a truck in Santa Isabel that was already full of people. Something funny happened to me with that truck. When we left here Pancho Robledo forgot to give those on the truck in which I was going the credentials we needed to be able to enter the convention stadium. When we got to the military highway outside Cayey, we stopped to wait for Pancho. He had lost us in the terrific traffic and we had not been able to locate him. And when we stopped for a moment, there came a truck from Santa Isabel full of people, out of gas, and without money. I had to "pay for the broken glass," as we say—I had to pay $5 there so that they could put gasoline in the truck; I had to pay my passage. Then Pancho reached us there and gave us our credentials so we could enter the stadium.

It was a terrible day we spent there. The crowd was tremendous. They were selling water—one had to buy it to drink it. And the soft drinks that they'd throw through the windows to one cost 20 cents or a quarter. But at least we had the trip and we saw that convention, which was a very special thing. And we enjoyed ourselves that day even though we suffered much too, because the heat was terrible and we didn't get back home until it was almost midnight.

And later on when the campaign came there were no problems. That was the greatest triumph of all. During it I worked in no voting place. Instead I was working at getting together the voters of the barrio and sending them to town, until there were no more left here. Then I went to town myself to deposit my vote. Elisabeth had gone on ahead. I sent her ahead because she had given birth recently [Tasita, their eleventh child]. And when I went it was almost the hour of closing. I entered, identified myself, and voted. I did not have to go out to work any place else.

In that voting place we had fun because there are almost

always people there known here in the barrio—Epifanio
Torres voted there, Compadre Berto, Elisabeth—you could
say people of the family. And I took a ballot to show some
voters who were seeking information about voting—there, inside, I began to show them. And Epifanio, who was a member of the Socialist party, came and took the ballot from
me. I gave in right away because I knew it was out of order!
But we celebrated a completely tranquil election that day.
Except for some minor incidents with some Independentists
who were there—I don't know, but it seems they had had
some drinks—and they tried to interfere. But it was nothing,
and a completely tranquil election was celebrated in that voting place.

After that, well, I lost a little of my enthusiasm for politics
—I am not going to say for my party—but rather the way
people act at times, when in reality they do not give a person
what he deserves. It was in the elections of '48 that Pancho's
candidacy was imperiled. And Herminio and Pedro gave him
tremendous cooperation. I figured that at least they would
give those boys some job—some fairly regular job—because
they had earned it. And apart from that, they were good
Populares. But with all of that, as we Puerto Ricans say,
they passed the buck in the case of those youths, and the
two boys were left in the end with only a tiny reward. I
don't know if they felt the boys didn't earn more, though I
believed they did. I am sure they earned it. Whatever work,
however important, they did it. And in spite of that, they
didn't make it; and still they have gone on in their party as
always. What they did with those boys was not right.

I heard how they held a meeting on appointments, the
way they went about it, after the campaign. The town committee wanted to stop the mouths of the barrio committees
—a thing that ought not to be, because if we have rights in
everything else, if we cooperate in all the needs of the party,
then when we are victorious we should have the same rights.
It is not right that they then should put muzzles on the mouths
of the barrio chairmen. Those are the things that make one
lose interest. It is not politics, but rather the particular members who manipulate the affairs of the municipality.

Of the party itself I cannot complain. But in Santa Isabel we have always had to put up with that, for lack of people who have the necessary education to carry out the various jobs. Now with regard to the party, no—I go on always being a Popular. If I see that they abandon a fundamental part of the program, it seems to me I will vote no more. Because if the party were to break up, and another were to come—I don't know, but it seems to me I would struggle no more with politics.

In 1949 I resigned my job on the barrio committee. That was over something I needed. I needed to make a latrine here and it was difficult to get an oil drum I required to build it. Pancho [the mayor] promised me, when they were making the road to the beach, that he was going to get me one there. But they finished the road to the beach and the drum never appeared.

And when Carmen Iris—if they had wanted to help me in one way or another, well—there were different jobs at which she would have been able to work. There were times when they were appointing people for things here in the barrio and they never gave her an opportunity. There were times when they would come and they would give the jobs to women who had only come to live here a little before; they would give them opportunities to work. They never offered her an opportunity.

If they were expecting something of me now, they would not get it. I am not the kind of man who always bothers someone about some need of mine. I think that if one works at those things, helping them, and they have some interest in helping one, well, it's not necessary to be on top of them all the time with one's problems, right? That is my opinion. And they never gave me anything, and the drum—I was left waiting for it and it never arrived.

After that Colo gave me a new drum, and I got hold of another used one. I kept the one Colo gave me with the idea of keeping rainwater in it. But as I didn't get another used one, I decided to put that one in. Then I changed it with one Compadre Gueni had. I gave it to him because it was a new drum, a good one. I gave it to Compadre Gueni and Compadre Gueni gave me an old one that had no bottom. Then with those two old ones I constructed the latrine.

Taso was thirty-two years old in 1940, married, the father of four children (three others having died in infancy), a palero by trade, a man with about forty compadres, honored and respected in his native barrio. The year 1940 probably did not differ significantly for Taso from the years immediately preceding and following it. Life was just as hard, wages almost as low. His troubles with Elí's jealousy continued, and he was still searching for a secure place to establish his own house permanently.

Yet in retrospect 1940 was some kind of turning point. It was the year that the Popular party first ran candidates in the island elections. Labor troubles had begun anew in the cane fields, and a relatively powerful island union would emerge from them. Minimum wage laws had recently been introduced in the cane, and the economic situation was slowly improving. Though the following years reveal certain serious disillusionments in Taso's life and a crystallization of personal conflict in full maturity, his life broadens and enters upon a new and less pessimistic phase.

The major events of this period which directly affected Taso were the first campaign of the Popular party (1940); the birth of Raúl (1941); the birth of Lilian (1944); the beginning of Taso's official participation in union affairs (1944); the move, at last, to his own house, on inalienable land (1945); the birth of Roberto (1945); Taso's acquisition of a permanent job on the railway crew (1946); his personal disillusionment in the political campaign of 1948; and the birth of Tasita (1948).

For the people of Jauca, as for those of scores of similar communities on the south coast, the years 1940–49 were part of a new period in their society. The industrial agricultural system that the United States Occupation had introduced to Puerto Rico had already consolidated itself. No independent small-scale haciendas were left in the municipality of Santa Isabel, and they were practically eliminated in all the neighboring municipalities east and west along the coast. By this time their owners—the agrarian upper class of the region—had become completely detached from local life, having moved to the cities, or to the United States or Europe, after selling or leasing their lands. All jobs in the cane were now standardized, with stipulated minimum wages, and piece-work survived only in particular jobs—such as cane cutting —where the decision to work by wage or by incentive was up to the workers themselves. Nearly all perquisites provided to workers in place of cash had been eliminated. Child labor laws were in force. Mechanical devices were by this time essential in the fields, and the value of all special manual skills had declined, reappearing only on a very reduced scale in such activities as driving trucks and operating winches. Cash income was rising, partly in replacement of the noncash services that had been discontinued, partly because of political pressure and the improving economic situation. The decision-making function of mayordomos and foremen was sharply reduced, and their authority correspondingly declined (a process the workers themselves were only dimly aware of at first).

The maturation of a rural proletariat—landless, wage-earning, store-buying, and economically homogeneous—was complete. Individual workers were members of an island-wide occupational group and came to think of themselves in this way—and to exercise their political power accordingly. They lost their feelings of identity with particular haciendas or communities and particular bosses or hacendados, and began to think of themselves as members of a national class. They also were made increasingly aware of their separateness and individuality since many of the devices by which they had formerly allied themselves with particular patrons and power figures were no longer effective.

Taso was subject to these processes in the same manner as all of his neighbors and fellow workers. But his particular perceptions of the changes, their special effects on him, were to some extent unique. He readily gave up his palero craft to become a railway worker, where other skills are needed and "where your rice and beans are a sure thing even in dead time." He early and vigorously involved himself in the growth and success of the Popular party, though he indicates that he joined at first with doubts, since "we had been fooled many times." In his description of political and union activities, it is apparent that Taso has certain qualities which made him stand out. He was elected to the post of treasurer of the barrio union local, and he became a member of the Popular party barrio political committee. In these posts he continued to serve, as he had years before on the Red Card committee of the Socialist party. He was usually aligned in these jobs with some of his compadres, those ritualized friends who give him a feeling of security and belonging in his community.

While Taso's descriptions of his activities provide a picture of the big changes that were going on in those years, they also reveal something special about the man himself. Along with his fellow committeemen, he played a part in pushing the union local toward a more democratic and useful program—though in the end their efforts were frustrated. Again, in describing the political machinations of Popular party officials on the local level, Taso emerges as a critical and energetic participant.

It was not until 1940 that he could feel his political activity might lead to tangible results. The Popular party gave men like Taso their best opportunity to learn the meaning of political democracy and to exercise their talents as political leaders and organizers. For Taso 1940 opened a new, optimistic period of political action; he was also active in 1944 and 1948. But he reveals his disillusionment after the 1948 campaign. The cause of this disillusionment was partly personal, though Taso protests that he never sought or expected direct personal rewards for his activity. It is clear that the man was not motivated solely or mainly by the hope of direct personal gain. He continued to honor his party for the rewards Puerto Rican working-class people as a whole had won. Though he recounts many disputes in discussing politics and unions, rather than being merely contentious, Taso raises what seem to be real issues: the union president should obey the mandate of the membership; the town political committee ought not attempt to muzzle the committees of the rural areas.

His personal hurt is revealed when he discusses his disappointment at not being given an oil drum with which to construct a new latrine, and when no job is ever offered his daughter. Though he phrases his discouragement with local politics first in terms of the failure of the party to reward two other loyal Populares, it then becomes plain that he feels his lack of personal reward keenly; the final paragraphs of this narration almost border on the pathetic. Taso suffered what must have been serious disappointments in two important areas of activity—politics and unions. He withdrew from these things; but one senses that this physically and intellectually energetic man will have to replace his old interests with new activities.

Taso says little here about what was happening to him at home in these years, except for his descriptions of how Elí helped him. He mentioned earlier that Elí's jealousy of him had not diminished, but he does not indicate whether her feelings were in any way based on reality. His children were growing bigger and more were born, but he doesn't talk about them much (largely, I believe, because I could see him with them daily, and there must have seemed no need for him to describe to me his relationships with them).

My friendship with Taso, which ripened during and after the 1948 political campaign, may have gained strength partly because he felt rejected by the party leaders. During the last months of 1948 and until August 1949, while I was in Jauca, Taso and I spent a great deal of time together. I thought I knew him well by the time I left Jauca; I did, but not well enough. One of the most important events in his entire life was yet to come, a matter of his own doing. And in those months of 1949 when I thought I knew him so well, I had not the slightest glimmering of its coming.

CHAPTER 7

The Conversion

Now we will talk about when I entered the church. When you were here in 1949 we once stopped in front of a Pentecostal service. At the time I didn't know what was in the Scriptures [Taso here refers somewhat ashamedly to the occasion when he ridiculed the Pentecostal services we were watching]. But I have listened to them preach the Gospel since I was a little boy. At that time the Evangelical Church was preaching here in Jauca; there were no revivalist churches such as the Pentecostal Church. They preach the same Gospel, but not as we Pentecostals preach it. The evangelical churches do not receive the blessing of the Holy Ghost; in the Pentecostal churches, the blessing is received. When a person receives the blessing he fulfills the prophecy of the prophet Joel by speaking in tongues; that is when one receives the blessing. In the dead churches it is not permitted, but in the living churches this is why the people shout so much and why they are called living churches—and we attest to it, unlike the dead churches.

Before, I had no knowledge of any of that. But I had heard preachers of the Gospel from the time I was a little boy. And although Mama and the rest of the family were Catholic in their religion—and so was I, though without any knowledge— I liked the Gospel very much because it was preached so clearly; it was easy to understand. Now, some time after you left Jauca, they held an evangelization campaign in Ponce [early in 1950]. A preacher named Brother Osborne came there, and a campaign was held. I don't remember how long it lasted, but the first of those at home who went to see that campaign was Carmen Iris. And when she came back she told us of the things she had seen happening there in Ponce. I was a little dubious. I asked her some questions, and she affirmed what she had said. And she told me, "Well, if you want to see for yourself, go see."

And afterward, Elisabeth wanted to go. Then Elisabeth went also, and when she came from there, she too told me the things that were happening there. She knew I was suffering from a sickness [inguinal pain] and she pressed me to go myself. It was she who persisted in saying that I should go. I decided one day that I would go. At times I had had the idea of getting an operation, but I always thought that I might end up a useless [disabled] man and then perhaps I would not be able to earn my family's food. That was what made me hold back and not have an operation. And at this point Elisabeth insisted that I go to the meeting in Ponce.

It happened that when I decided to go, I had no money. But Filiberto, Elisabeth's cousin, was leaving with a carload of people from here with the same objective, to go to Ponce to the evangelization campaign. And then Elisabeth went and spoke with Filiberto, and he told her yes, he would take me. I went with Filiberto, and that night the service was being held in the Morel Campos athletic grounds. They had moved it from the Paquito Montañer Park, where it seems to me they had been giving it on previous nights.

When we arrived there was an immense crowd. It was hard work to get to the platform (*templete*) where the ministers were directing the meeting. I got up close to the platform and listened there to the whole service. In the moment when Brother Osborne began to pray for the sick, my own case came immediately to my mind. When he began to pray, he spoke in this way: "All those who have sickness in any part —put your hands on the affected place, whoever has different illnesses." And I lifted my hand to the spot where I really felt my pain. And while that brother prayed, I felt something in my body, a thing—an extraordinary thing— while he was praying for the sick. And later, after he finished that prayer, I felt an ecstasy—something strange—and then it went away. Later on they made an invitation to those per-

sons who might want to accept the Gospel. But I went out
of there; I made no profession of faith.

I came back to my house. And afterward I did not feel that
pain that I had been feeling in those days, though I had been
especially sick with it. And up to the present, thank God,
I have never felt that pain again. That was a pain that every
two or three months would lay me up for a week at least.
And in the period of time since then I have never felt that
pain again. After I came home, we still had no idea of joining the church. But we did talk about the things that had
happened in Ponce. It was a great campaign. And we read
some books they distributed here later, tracts they gave away.

Then one day Elisabeth said to me, "Tonight I'm going to
go watch the service that they're having here" [in Jauca].
I told her to go ahead [said with carelessness]. While she
was at the service, I stayed behind burning some trash in
back of the house. And when she came home she told me, "I
was converted to the Gospel." I said to her, "Well, if you
have really accepted the Gospel, well done" [again said
carelessly]. But it had not been so; it was a joke on her part.

The next week she went to the service again, and I was
doing the same thing that night. Then when she came from
there she told me, "I was converted to the Gospel tonight."
And I said to her, "But like the other night?" And she said:
"No. Tonight it was for real."

Then she swore that this is what happened: She said that
the service had ended. She had sat down in the front part,
by the store steps—that is, where the church is—and the
service had ended. She says that Brother Juan, the pastor,
made his call, and that she remained seated where she was.
She says that while Brother Juan was ending the service, he
was making his appeal. And when he said, "Come, Elí, there
is still time," she was still sitting there, holding the baby in
her lap. And then, she says, something lifted her from the
seat and carried her to the altar. She says she did not realize
what was going on until afterward, when the congregation
prayed for her. It was when she went outside that she asked

herself, "What have I done?" You see—it was as if a—as if
something had carried her to the altar.

Well—when she came and told me, none of it seemed bad
to me. I knew that the Gospel was a good thing, and as for
the doctrines of this particular church, the majority of the
people know them. If you ask any of those people you see at
the services what the doctrines are, they know them—what
we do, and what we may not do. Actually, for the next few
days, Elisabeth didn't dare attend any service. Though they
were giving the services near here, it had cost her dearly to
become converted, and afterward she was a little timid about
going out and attending a service.

But then they gave another service right nearby and she
went. She had said that she was not going to attend services
at any far-off places, to walk here and there. And this night
they were going to give a service in the house of Santiago
Alicea, who is himself a member. And I went with her. That
night I made a profession of faith there, but I did it only in
order to test something. I wanted to find out if the blessing
of the Holy Ghost, which they say comes in the midst of the
demonstration (*movimiento*) they make, was real.

I made a profession of faith that night. And I enjoyed the
service, hearing them speak, though I said nothing. I didn't
understand any of it yet, but I enjoyed listening to them
testify and sing the beautiful hymns and so on. And the next
week, they announced a service to be held in Varsovia [a
small colonia about eight miles away]. We went to Varsovia
that night. At the time we didn't even know what a vigil
(*vigilia*) was. We went to that vigil; and during that vigil,
Elisabeth swiftly received the blessing. And a few—few days
later, then I received it [his voice is soft and low].

So I had made my confession of faith so that I might remain no longer in doubt about the demonstration they make
—those things of which I was really ignorant before. Afterward, I continued testing it. The Scriptures say it—the Scriptures speak of it. It is a promise. As I told you earlier, though
there are churches that do not accept it and do not seek it—

it is a reality. We know that it is in the Bible and that it is true. People may ignore it, and we find that right here there are those who ridicule it. But for us it is a matter of indifference if anyone wishes to mock it, or to say it is a lie, or not to accept it. We know it is logical, we passed through the test, and for us there remains no place for doubt. And we have gone along the road since then. When one feels that, receives that, then one has more awe (*temor*). Then you know you have a thing which you didn't have before. One feels more awe, and one goes along learning the teachings of the church. One gets surer footing on the road.

And since that we have had further proof. Not in every case, of course, because the same Scriptures say, "According to your faith you have done it." At times we have arrived at a place where someone is sick and we have prayed for the sick one—it is a gift of God, He gives that to certain persons who consecrate themselves to Him—we have prayed for the sick one and the sick one has gotten up, has improved. But other times no, because, as I told you, the Scriptures say, "According to your faith you have done it." But we have proof that the Gospel is a sacred thing and that it is a good thing [all of this said in rhythmic, rather repetitive tones, with an air of great certainty and almost a peculiar tiredness, as if said very, very often—almost a recited sermon].

Now, there is another thing I ought to explain about this. When I made a profession of faith, what I said to Brother Juan was as follows: "I am going to be converted to this"— that was how I spoke—"but I am going to tell you something. I am not going to go off to faraway services the way you do." And he said to me, "Don't get excited. Go only when it seems proper to you."

Now I am able to affirm that it is born in one after one is in the church. That desire to go to services everywhere, to be walking about from here to there—that is a thing that grows in one after one is within the church. Before, one sees such a thing as tremendous, difficult—but it's nothing. When you come to try it out, then you feel that desire—to the extent that there were times when Elisabeth and I would go alone, with one sister more, to far-off services. That is a thing that grows in one, and one feels that responsibility.

And from there to here, well, we have gone along struggling. We who were far away were ourselves converted. And that is why those who are far away now may also be converted.

What did you know of revivalist churches and the Gospel before Elí went the first time to Ponce?

When they went to Ponce and came back and told me what was happening there, it passed through my mind that I had heard many of those same things before, from the preachers of the Gospel—that all those things could be, that they could happen. I used to hear them preaching different things about how if one were sick he could be cured. You see, not that they would cure one, but rather that God Himself could cure one. So I already knew many of the parts of that doctrine from having heard them preach before. Well, when they came from Ponce, they recounted to me the things they had seen there. And then it was that I decided to go, to see for myself. What they told me were things I had heard preached in different places, sometimes on the radio and sometimes in different places around here, such as when they would hold campaigns in the barrio. As I had some knowledge of that already, when they were telling me I knew it must be a part of the Scriptures that was being fulfilled there. And that was what led me to make sure of it by going myself.

Then you went to Ponce with Filiberto—
Yes.

And got to the park where the meeting was and got close —to the platform.
Now can you tell me the most you can remember of how you were feeling at the time the pastor said that the sick should put their hands on the place that was paining or was sick? What passed through your mind?

Since they had been explaining to me what was happening in Ponce, I went with the faith that I would be able to be cured. Then, when he told me to put my—when he told the sick to place their hands where they were sick, I put my hands on the affected spot. I had faith that I too would be made well. Now, eh—while he was preaching—the message he was preaching there—in truth at times one feels, eh—guilty (*culpable*) of many things. When one does not live a life as one really ought to live it, then at times while they preach, one's very conscience accuses one. They preach that one is sometimes far from God, even while believing one is near. At times one is mistaken about the way one lives, and what they say moves one to recognize—uh—one's situation. What I was seeking was to make sure of something that I had heard said: "One must pass through that experience for oneself."

And as I came to understand, then I felt guilty about many things. For example, they preach and advise one, "Thou shalt love thy neighbor as thyself." They present it in such a beautiful way. And other things they tell us—things that one is far removed from. And these things move one's heart, they change the attitude one has. And as the Scripture says, one feels a little—one is convicted (*uno se corta*) when they preach in that fashion, if one really does not live as one should. At times one doesn't have love appropriate for one's fellow beings, eh—has a quarrel with one's wife or with one's family. And then they counsel one that if one is in Christ, eh—all of those things must be changed. I believe this is the most important change a person can make.

These are the things that moved me to change all of my attitudes, to change their form, so as to be nearer to Christ and to have a more tranquil life. And in that regard, I find myself very contented. Though in the last few years Elisabeth and I weren't having any great battles, still we had not given up having them—and in the time that has passed since, it has ended. Especially as I told you before—the jealousy and the fights that Elisabeth used to have—well, now she feels a little more restraint. Now she knows that if she behaves that way, it is contrary to the Scriptures. Because the word of God says that the jealous are not godly. And it is the same with many other things that one has to go along giving up. Now, whatever happens to one, one seeks the most efficacious means of resolving it. Before, one tried to resolve it through violence, or in some other bad way; now one seeks to resolve it in a different manner. So that we have been made over new again [he chuckles].

When you put your hands on the affected part, at that moment, did you feel guilty?

I am not referring to being guilty for the sickness. I say "guilty," you see, because the preacher explains things this way: "You find yourself sad because you are so far from God." You see? One says, "Well, if I find myself sad it is because in truth I am far from God," according to what he says. Now, one must seek the way out, as they advise. "When you seek God, then you are made a new creature and then you have peace in your home, then you have contentment." Those are the ways in which they go along enlightening one.

Now, in that moment that I felt—eh—eh—guilty, it was because I used to do many of the things they prohibit. That is the guilty part of what I was feeling. Before, as I said, Elisabeth and I used to have our differences and we used to quarrel, and such things. And when they explain these things, then one feels guilty. I felt guilty, and she must have too. Surely it was the same for her; it came her turn too. The same thing happens now when we preach. After all, we don't know what anyone does, but there are times when what we preach really wounds someone else.

I'm going to give you an example so that you can understand a little better. Suppose there's someone who drinks liquor. And suppose he stops in front of the church. One does not know him, one does not know if he drinks liquor or leaves it alone. But the pastor there in the pulpit may say that the drunkards have no place in the Kingdom of Heaven. Well, as we say, right away that person feels himself convicted, because the words get to where he is. That is the situation when we say, "Fulano was convicted by that message, by the words that were preached."

This is how the words reach a person, you see. One knows

nothing of him; when one preaches, one doesn't know what
one person does or what another does. But when a message
reaches someone, what he does is to argue with himself:
"My conscience—it is I who am doing that; that message
touches me." And another part touches another. See? So that
each gets the part which affects him.

You told me that you felt an ecstasy. Can you describe it?
Well—they tell one to close one's eyes. One is in complete communion while they pray; and the ecstasy is as if one
were seasick; what I felt that night was something like that.
I didn't see anything. I felt as if they had put something
before my eyes, as if I had left the world. Even when he
said, "Open your eyes," I still felt something big in my head
—it was as if one were in a faint. But you know that when
you faint you are about to fall, while I had my feet firmly
planted. Elisabeth says she saw stars and things. I saw nothing like that [he laughs slightly]. Rather, I felt this big thing
in my head, this ecstasy. Now, when he told me to open my
eyes, I opened my eyes but I still felt something like an
ecstasy. Then I didn't feel anything—anything more. I only
felt that thing in my body, that ectasy in my whole body.
Now, I know there was something in me. Because before I
had never had that sensation, never until that moment; and
then afterward the sensation went away. Something was in
me at that moment.

And you can't tell me more about what happened?
[No response.]

There is no way to tell me—?
[He laughs a little helplessly.] Well—it is a little difficult,
because I don't know how. What I do know is that up to the
present [emphatically], thank God, I have never felt that
pain again. And anyone here you ask can tell you—every
two or three months I would have to go to bed—and for a
week at least. I used to get better and then three or four
months would pass, and then to bed again. Now—already

three years and a half have gone by in which I have felt nothing!

Eli was the first of the family to receive the blessing?
Yes. The night Elisabeth received it, it was in Varsovia at that vigil. We were both there. When she received the blessing, it was during a vigil—an all-night service. It is a service divided into two parts. It begins at dusk, and they have what we call the devotional part and then a part for testimony when brothers testify. And they sing special hymns until twelve, or twelve-thirty or one. Then at that hour they end the first part of the vigil. Then one goes out and drinks coffee, and if there are crackers one eats those too. And later on, the second part of the vigil begins and it goes on until the morning.

And that night when we were at that vigil, which was when Elisabeth received the blessing, there was a great outpouring of the Spirit (*bendición*) in the church. There were many brothers who were dancing in the church. And Elisabeth was seated on a bench, and she kneeled to pray and right there where she was kneeling, praying, she received the blessing. She got up from a tier of benches where she had been sitting, and she was kneeling in the aisle they have in the middle.

Now while a brother is receiving the blessing, different movements occur in his body—at times he moves just his head, and perhaps there will be a movement in the body too. With Elisabeth it was especially a movement of the head. She twisted her head violently and her hair shook loose and came down and covered her face as she remained kneeling in that blessing; until at last she received the tongues there. Then they raised her up from there, one taking her by one arm and another by the other, and she was talking perfectly in tongues.

How did you feel at that moment?
Well, I felt content because I knew—I had seen others who were baptized with the blessing, and I knew that uh—I was no longer able to remain in doubt regarding it; because

Elisabeth is a serious woman and she could not work a deception. That—that satisfied me.

And you wanted at that moment to have the same kind of blessing?

Surely—that is one's desire. But it is not a matter of when one wants it [he laughs]. It is the desire of many. I know a—we have a brother in the church—they call him Pedro, of the Coamo church—who has fought tremendously to receive the blessing. And in spite of that he has not received it. He says to me: "I fast, I cry, I have done so many things, and still I have not received it." And I say, "Well, Brother, there must still be something that you must do. Or it may be that you are doing something that still prevents you, so that you have not received it." No, it is not when one wants it [he chuckles].

But what happens when one wants and is not able—for example you wanted to receive it that night and—

Exactly. One prays: "O Lord—eh—bless me and baptize me"—but if it is not there—well, one gets up [he laughs] if one doesn't have it. All of the members of the church always await it, all of those who are not baptized always await that, because from one moment to the next they may receive it.

And when you received the blessing—that occurred much later?

It was—a short period of time passed—a matter of one week or two, something like that. The night I received it, it was in this church here. Yes. In that place here; there it was. That night they told us to pray and we were praying. And while one is praying one feels as if something comes and fills one—a thing that comes and fills one. And then I received a blessing, and I was moving myself about, and as it happened here on my knees—since it was concrete—I skinned my knees while we were praying. That was the night I received the blessing, over there. And at the same time one receives the tongues. And when one is baptized with the Spirit

—well, as I told you before, then one holds more tightly to the Gospel. One knows that in one regard that—that—that one has a thing one did not have before, you see? And by that night, well, I was able to substantiate it by Elisabeth's experience and those of all the others.

And how did you feel during the time you were receiving the blessing?

One feels most content, one feels full of that. Truly, when one receives the blessing that way, when a person thus receives the blessing of the Holy Ghost, it is a great joy that a Christian feels. And frequently you can arrive at a Pentecostal church and hear a brother who has just received the blessing talking in tongues from moment to moment. Now see, afterward, the brother gets to control himself better. For when one is converted, when one thus receives the blessing, one's desire is to be in communion always, and one is always seeking it.

And then as time goes by, then the Christian who has passed through that experience does not talk so much, because he is not so much in communion as he was at the beginning. You see—it is like when one begins to fall in love. One is always awaiting the girl and so on. And then afterward they get married and then that diminishes—and so it happens in this case. After the brother—uh—learns more, and then after the blessing, well, it does not have—he does not seek it so much as in the beginning, as when he received the blessing. In the beginning brothers come to the church, feel that desire, and want to be baptized immediately with the Spirit. You see? And so it happens, you see, that they receive it. And time passes. And then, as it is then a common thing to them, time passes, and then they get used to it. But in the beginning, one is exceedingly happy, having that thing that one did not have before.

Can you remember the moment when you were speaking in tongues?

Of course [with some surprise]. One does it when one is in a normal state. Now the Scriptures say that he who speaks

in tongues speaks and reveals mysteries, and no one will
understand, because God speaks through him who speaks in
unknown tongues.

*When one talks in tongues, are there words one under-
stands?*

It can be—I have heard some brothers speak sometimes
in such a way that you can understand them. Yes, at times
one can understand some. We have heard some brothers in
the course of the blessing order the church to pray. And
some things you understand, although others you do not. As
the Scriptures say, in tongues one speaks mysteries that no
one will understand. But many times one understands.

You can remember the sounds you made?

The people sitting close by on the benches sometimes put
their ears close to you to see if they can understand something, you see?

But you don't remember what you were saying?

Eh—eh—I don't remember understanding anything I myself was saying, you see? Now I have understood many other
brothers. Eh—Sister Teresa; once I heard her during a blessing she received in Varsovia. She was speaking very clearly
in tongues, and I understood when she told the brothers to
pray—when she said that the congregation required more
prayer. And sometimes a brother speaks and speaks and one
understands it. When a brother speaks and speaks, the pastor
or someone else takes him and helps him kneel, leaves him
kneeling there, and lets him speak what he will; and then the
service continues.

*So we can suppose that a brother has no control of the
words he speaks?*

Eh—in the beginning when a brother receives the blessing, no—he usually doesn't have that control. Afterward he
begins controlling himself. The pastor disciplines him, the
pastor sees him, and goes along exhorting him. There are

certain parts of the Scriptures concerning the control of a Christian, and so on. Because a part of the Scriptures says that if an ignorant person enters and sees him that way, he will say that the people there are crazy [he laughs].

Can you recall the first sensation you felt when you received the blessing?
Well, that was what I told you before. You feel a thing—as if you have—some say they feel something that enters through their feet and fills them; now, I felt as if a thing came through my head and filled me. There are those who feel it through—through different parts of the body. The body trembles, you see, and one always has a continuous movement while one feels this.

You were feeling no pain?
No. To the contrary. One feels no pain at all. We were kneeling and praying. They ordered us to kneel, and we were praying. Then one receives the Spirit, you see; that comes and fills one, and you have that demonstration; then it is during the demonstration that one receives the blessing.

The only sensation you recall is that of being filled—?
Yes, something comes and fills one. From there on one feels nothing more. One feels this thing that filled one, one feels *full* [emphatically].

That was the only time you were speaking in tongues?
No, that happened different times in the church, see—

But to you yourself?
Yes, to the same person on different occasions. You don't always speak in tongues in the church—but there are services —as we call them, services of great outpouring, and different brothers speak in tongues. That depends on—the communion that a Christian has in the church as well, the communion he has, and how the service goes.

The speaking of tongues always begins in the same manner?

When one receives a blessing? No, afterward it is a thing that comes at times when you are not expecting it. The tongues start up—and there are times that one person with this carries it to another one, and one becomes filled and speaks—one says he is in communion with his eyes closed. This comes over one and the tongues rush forth. And it passes and one opens one's eyes, and one is as one was, as we are talking now.

One knows one is speaking in tongues. One gets knowledge —one hears it all, you see? One hears it all. Now, understand, it is not a thing one can do at will. It is not when one *wants* to speak in tongues—no—rather, it comes upon one.

When one makes a profession of faith, what happens?

When one makes a profession of faith, then the pastor and the brothers of the church pray for one. It is done by raising the hand. They ask, "Who among you wishes to accept the Lord?" or, "Who wants to make a profession of faith? Those who do, raise their hands." That was what I did. So one doesn't have to do anything else. One raises one's hand, and they pray; thus one comes to make himself a member on probation of the church. Then one continues listening to the services, and they go along indoctrinating one and laying down the procedure, little by little—what one must do and what one must not do, and so they educate one, teach one the doctrine.

And you visited the church often before making such a profession?

Yes. I was going to many services right here. And—I always moved to the front there, I always used to give my nickels there, when they were collecting offerings and such. And particularly when I was a boy I used to go a lot to the Evangelical church services here.

But when the Pentecostal church was in the store, did you go much before making a profession of faith?

At the last I went a lot. I'd push up front to hear; I always moved myself up to—up to the steps to hear it. And then finally they had a campaign. They brought pastors from different places to preach there; and many people came—not I alone, but many people were coming to hear them preach. I went frequently while they were having services here, and I listened to the services. I remember that at times discussions would arise among the people listening to the services outside. I recall one night when Lelé and Radamés were on the subject. I was watching the services and also listening to their conversation. And Lelé was saying, "Why is it those people are yelling and singing so?" And then Radamés answered him in this manner: he said, "Those people there feel as happy or more happy than you and I when we are drunk."

There near the outside there were always people discussing and saying something about the services. And none of these were members of the church. But Radamés is a man, as I understand it, who has studied some in the Scriptures. And so I was going to listen to the services that way, and gradually I got interested. And I believe that what it says in the Scriptures was being fulfilled. It says, "With hearing well the faith and then the word of God." So as I went on hearing the message, I was getting more interested.

And then they celebrated a campaign here and different ministers came who were well informed in the Scriptures. They were explaining the message, and I was acquiring more interest in it and more conviction. And then it was that I resolved to enter the church—not before the doubts I told you about before had been dissipated, but after my doubt was ended. Because afterward any other doubt I might have I resolved in the Scriptures.

When I decided to join the church, at first I believed I would not remain in it. One always sees certain things, especially among people who don't know. Often they gather before the doors of the church, some to criticize and others to mock, and so on. That didn't sit well with me, and I believed I wouldn't stay in because of that—the way they mock you, almost to

your face. But when I began to study the Scriptures, I came
to know that that was something that had to happen. In the
Scriptures I found the Apostle Santiago saying that the
mockers must come. So I learned that it is a part of the fulfillment of the Scriptures. Now when it happens I feel more
content. I think, good, here is the fulfillment of the Scriptures.
So before, it could have made me go away; today, it holds me
more firmly. When one has read something which he may expect to happen and then he sees it happen, then one has one
experience more. Now I know this must occur, and it doesn't
catch me by surprise. So I went along getting more interested.

Now, about how I entered the church. I don't know how
Elisabeth would explain to you how she entered. But I joined
having heard the message and possessing the most important
proof beforehand. Though I saw great things in Ponce, when
I returned I had not decided to enter in the church. It was
after that that I pushed myself forward to hear what they
were preaching.

You didn't go to so many of the meetings here?

I went to some, see, but I didn't go so frequently. As we
did that night [referring again to the night in 1949 when he
and I went and both mildly ridiculed the activities]—I would
stop and I would listen a while. I went often to listen especially when preachers from outside came. That's when one
sees the church well attended, you see? A preacher comes
from afar, and then all the people go to hear him. They announce a preacher from such-and-such a place, and then the
church is well attended—many people go, see. And during
the campaign I saw many people preaching who were well
versed in the Word. To the little that I had learned already
I added much more there; and finally that moved me to join
the church.

*Before entering, or after, did you discuss your joining the
church with some of your friends, for instance with Don
Berto?*

No, I didn't discuss it with anyone. I only recall that one

night I approached closer to the church by that door here [he points to the church down the road]. They were passing the plate and I made a contribution. And I remember that Brother Juan then invited me to come in; and I didn't want to. That night he invited me to walk in, and I don't know why, but I didn't want to. At a later date I went in seriously. But that night he urged me. He was saying, "Enter, it is good." He put before me many quotations of the Word. But—and I have noted that with the church—while one is being invited, there is always the feeling of "Later, later." And I believe the moment will come in which many are going to be left thus, "Later, later."

And you never discussed it with anyone—Cheo, Rosa?

No. I never had such discussions. They have never interfered in this. Once after I entered the church I went to work and a compadre of mine spoke up with some nonsense, but I never made anything of it. We were returning from work and he, knowing I had made myself a member of the Pentecostal Church, said to me, "Ah, now you are going to have to put up with many things here, because we are going to tell you lots of obscenities." And then I said, "Well"—this was my answer—"Well, it shall be as God wishes." But actually, nothing came of it. All to the contrary; it was a foolishness of his, because he has never said anything more to me about it.

You never had problems with your friends apart from that?

Regarding the church? No. Because since then, if any person would come to me concerning my membership, the only thing I would have to do is put the Scriptures before him—why it is that I came to join and testimony as to why I am as I am [i.e. in the church]. And if he were a little mistaken, I would explain my reasons. So I can't fall into a quarrel now [he laughs].

After you made a profession of faith the most important thing was the blessing and the speaking of tongues?

That is an important part. But all the doctrine, the education, all of that is important. Speaking in tongues is not—it is not so very important, you see. One knows that it is a prophecy one must fulfill. But as for speaking in tongues, the very Scriptures say that will save no one; it is not a question of its saving anybody. The Scriptures say it is a gift, but that doesn't mean that because a person speaks in tongues that he is saved. That would be very mistaken.

Must one make a confession before entering the church?
No [with astonishment].

One doesn't speak of one's sins or of what happened to one?
No; we do not confess our sins to any man. When we pray, then we confess our defects. We go directly there [i.e. to God]; we confess for our own part. Suppose I were to commit a misdeed and I were to believe that it was a bad thing I did. Well, right away, as soon as possible, I ought to put myself to pray. I don't go to Brother Juan to say, "I did that"; no [he laughs]. Confess here to men, no; that is not the way, you see? There is another church in which one must go to confess to a man, and then one can do whatever one pleases [he chuckles]. And I may be mistaken, but I think there could be something that a man would do, a sin so great—God knows, maybe a crime—and I'm sure he wouldn't dare confess that [he laughs].

Now, Blanca received her blessing after Elí and you?.
Yes, Blanca had it afterward; but not much time went by. I believe that something like three or four months went by, something like that. Her experience was almost the same. Oh, you would have enjoyed seeing her last Saturday. The same Scripture says that there comes a time of coolness. For a long time I watched Blanca going to services, and I saw, as we say, that she was cold in the church. And then last Saturday in the middle of the service she was greatly excited (*bien prendida*) [said with evident pleasure], speaking in tongues. Last Saturday, yes. It has been a good while that I haven't seen her—ah, I never saw her the way she was that night [he laughs]. I get

very happy when I see that because it means she feels well, understand. Immediately she feels the desire to go to church on Sunday and she feels more responsibility. For that reason I send the children for a part of the service.

Here is Eli's parallel narration.

From the time when I was little I was interested in religious matters. I remember well that when I was little my father used to take me and my brothers Mariano and Salvador to the Evangelical church. He used to tell us that we had to attend services, and he used to take us to Bible school. But afterward he lost his faith. He gave up religion. And then he began to drink. Under the influence of liquor, he gave my mother a bad life. I figure that was the cause of their separation. So when we were a little bigger and he became that way, we had to follow the same course, more or less—not drinking, but giving up church. Since he stopped going, we did too. But I always had religious feeling, you see. I knew religious things were good.

Later on, as a young woman, I began enjoying the things of the world—dances, parties, such things—and we would much sooner go to a party than go to church. I remember that as a young woman I attended some services in a Catholic church. I went to see the people kneeling. I wasn't really going to church; rather, I went to watch those who were kneeling and praying. I didn't pray at all. I went to watch. And if it were a Protestant service I might also go, seat myself, and be silent like the others. But I wasn't doing anything; I wasn't giving any service to God. As soon as I would leave we would go dancing. If there was a party we went to the party. Anything that came to our notice that we liked, we would go to. We were much more part of the world than of the things of God. I only came to have more interest in the things of God since I have the capacity of a grown woman, you see—after I had had my children.

We began to learn the Gospel when Brother Osborne came

and preached in Ponce. The first who went to those meetings was Carmen Iris. Lots of people were going from here. And there were comments made here concerning what was happening in Ponce. People were seeing miracles. They said that God—that God was doing miracles in Ponce. The lame were getting well, the blind were seeing, and the paralytics were starting to walk. Well, that girl has always liked religious things too. She didn't go to any church, but she liked such things.

Well, she left the house one night to walk around, and it seems she heard someone recounting something about the Ponce meetings. And she came back to the house and spoke with me and her father. She said she wanted to go to Ponce to see if the things she heard about were true. She wanted to do as St. Thomas—to see in order to believe. Then Taso told her, "Well, Daughter, if you want to go, go." He gave her money for the trip, and it seems to me it was Pablito Figueroa [a public car driver] who took her. He was going to take his wife Doña Fela and his sister-in-law, and Carmen went too. And Carmen, in view of what she saw and heard in the sermons —well, she was stirred by it; and when she returned she told us about it. We had already gone to sleep when she came back and she woke us up to tell us what she had seen. She told us of a child who was deaf and had recovered his normal hearing and of many blind men who had regained their sight. She came home very happy.

At that time I was already listening to the services here. I would approach the services that were then being held in the Mora family's store. I'd walk up close to the door. But I wouldn't stay long; I'd just listen a little while. The services they were giving here in the barrio were already pleasing me —they were reaching my heart; but I had still not arrived at any determination to be converted. I wanted to test something more, to arrive at a more—more serious knowledge. I wanted to test more of God's ways. I felt—I felt a desire to come closer to religious things. But at the same time I didn't quite dare. I believed that if I were converted without letting

Taso know first, then when I came back home he would say something disapproving to me.

But by the time the girl came home so enthusiastic from the Ponce meeting, with her stories of the meeting, my heart was already more with God than with anything else. I remained silent that night, just listening approvingly to everything she said. But I said to myself, "If Taso would give me the money, I would go—I would also go see." The next day some people were again preparing to go from here. And I said to Taso that afternoon, "Caramba, Taso, you know something? I'd like to go to Ponce to hear that man preaching; I feel the desire to go."

Taso has always been a serious man in these matters and respectful too toward the affairs of God. Long before he became a Pentecostal he was a man who never laughed at the work of God. He said, "Good; if you want to go, Pablito is going this afternoon. Send someone to ask if there is room for you in the car." Then I sent one of the children to Pablito's house to ask if there was a seat I could have. I was prepared to pay them to take me to Ponce. I did not dare go alone; I didn't really know where I was going. And I don't know how to walk around alone at night anywhere. On that occasion even less, for I'd get lost. And then Doña Fela sent word that Pablito had said yes. And I said, "Well, here I am; now I'm going to Ponce."

I went that night with them, and when I got there I found it was exactly the same as Carmen Iris had said. I saw the very same things, and I saw some other things besides, even more interesting. I saw for myself. It was there that I came to believe that to belong to a church is worth the effort, that to be a religious being is worth it, that one should seek out the things of God. Because of what I saw there, I had to acknowledge that there is something powerful, that there is something more, beyond the firmament one sees. There is something more. I moved forward there in the crowd.

My only doubt about the church was about the blessing, you see, which I had seen them receive in the chapel in Jauca.

The sisters dance, and here it is said that they dance in the Spirit. And I would see them dance and I would say, "That could be the truth, and it could be that it is not." But when they danced there in Ponce with their eyes closed, not opening their eyes at all for a single moment, and they went to and fro and didn't bump into anything; when they fell down and didn't hurt themselves at all, then I thought to myself, "There must be something to it." And then I returned from Ponce with this belief of mine still deeper. It was there that I confirmed my faith. It was there that I gained more faith.

Some very important things happened there. There was a girl near me with a tumor here [she points to her arm]. It was like this [she raises her hand several inches from her forearm], a very big tumor—very, very big. The preacher was way up in front on a platform they put up there. He was quite far away and the girl was near us. And he began to pray, this Brother Osborne, he began to pray there. He raised his hands and gave a beautiful sermon in English. He spoke in English, and there was an interpreter—he would say a word in English and the interpreter would say it in Spanish and we understood. While he was praying we knew what he was saying, because if he said, "O Lord," well, the other would say, "O Señor." And when he was casting out the demons, the one who was speaking Spanish said: "In the name of Jesus I order that you depart from the sick bodies."

Brother Osborne said it in English and the interpreter would say it in Spanish. And even the movements that Osborne made would be made by the interpreter. If Osborne went like this with his hand, he would do the same with his hand also. It was all easy to understand; whether American or Puerto Rican, he could understand. And as he said that prayer, well, that girl, without anyone touching her—and that tumor was really serious, so serious that she said the doctors didn't dare put her under the knife—went like this, like this [she throws her arms backward and out], and it burst. When it burst blood ran out and pus, blood and pus. Her arm was bathed in it and it dripped on her dress. And then she said, "Ai, it has burst!" She was frightened and she fell into a kind of nervous state. She was very nervous and then her family, who were walking about with her, took her to where the preacher was. He took out a very white handkerchief, a very white one, and he bandaged her arm with it. He did nothing to her, he did not cure her with anything; he simply bandaged her arm.

And I saw another thing too. I don't remember if it was the same night, because afterward I went back—I liked what I saw, and returned. There was a woman who said that she had a tumor in her stomach, and that they were unable to operate. And that night she vomited up the tumor. She vomited up blood and pus right in front of us. She made such a pool that we had to move to give her room to vomit. She was a Pentecostal, and there she was vomiting up this tumor, this foulness that she had in her stomach. And she was dancing, dancing in the Spirit. And many Pentecostal sisters were walking about with her, and all of them ended up dancing around her, and she was vomiting and going like this [imitates the sounds of vomiting] and dancing and springing in the air, as when one receives the blessing. And the sisters were all around her, speaking tongues and speaking tongues and dancing around, until finally they carried her, still under the same blessing, to where the preacher was. And when she became calm she gave testimony there. She said that the doctors had given her up because they were unable to operate. They said she would die if they operated, and there she was, cured.

And that filled me with even more faith. I returned here resolved to become converted. But I didn't tell Taso anything about how I planned to be converted. I said to myself, "It's true, it's good, I am going to become converted." And at the same time Brother Osborne was preaching he made an invitation to the people there who did not know the Saviour. He invited them with such a live faith that his words really reached one's heart. I came home resolved to tell Taso I was going to become converted. Then the next day, or two or three days later—I don't really recall how many days passed—again I approached the services in Jauca. But I know that when I came home I came with this idea of being converted. I came home, and I confirmed what Carmen had told us. Taso didn't reproach me. I told him what happened, and he didn't reproach me or say I was lying. He never doubted me.

I told him about the meeting because he was suffering from a hernia, and I told him that at the meetings sick people were getting cured. On the night we went I saw many cripples—paralytics—putting their crutches on their shoulders and walking out like that—putting their crutches high up in the air so that people might see that they were standing on their own feet. Wherever you looked one would be walking about —here one was healed, here another, and here was some other healed. One saw nothing else but crutches raised in the air, the crutches of the lame, raised up, and the cripples standing on their own two feet. And so I told Taso that he ought to go see—that the way those people were being cured of those other sicknesses, as God was curing those, he would cure the hernia also.

At the time, Taso couldn't go two or three weeks without an attack of that pain. There were times when he might go a month without feeling it, but the next month he would have it. And he would be five or six days, and sometimes up to two weeks, in bed. One time they had him in the hospital and were about to operate on him. And then they brought in someone gravely ill with pneumonia, and in order to provide a bed for the one who had pneumonia they took Taso out and sent him home for observation. The idea was to operate on him later; but he was never operated on. Then he went where Osborne was, and Osborne prayed, he prayed and beseeched heaven for the sick, and Taso was cured. He was cured, because he has never suffered from it again, and a number of years have gone by already. We are converted more than three long years now, and I have never heard him complain again of it. And yet before he could not go a month, he could not go three weeks, without being sick. And it was a matter of one foot here and one over there, because he couldn't put his two feet together when he had that pain.

I don't remember what he said when he got back from Ponce, but I know he arrived full of enthusiasm. He came back very pleased, very happy. He told everyone here what he had seen. And from then on he noticed little by little that time was passing and he didn't feel that pain. He began to comment on it, even giving testimony in the church that the Saviour cured him. Because as time went by and he didn't feel the pain any more, then he realized that from the night he went there for the first time he felt well. He has never felt the pain again.

Now, when I returned from Ponce, I remained silent. I remained silent and didn't tell him I was going to be converted. But I can tell you something; it was God doing His work upon me. They were giving services here, and as the chapel was so near, when they used to sing there I would feel a great joy, my heart rejoiced, and something told me that I should come closer, that I should get nearer to the chapel. But I was afraid that he might scold me or something. I knew he really wouldn't scold me, you see—but the wives here always are afraid to leave the house without permission, and so on. Sometimes he would go out and I would remain here alone. What I would do was sit myself down on the porch, or close to that window, which was then lower, in order to listen to the services. And no matter how softly the preacher there would preach, I used to hear that sermon as if he were right here in the house. I would enjoy every little thing in the services.

But then as the days passed, I could no longer restrain myself. I began to go out of the house. And so that he wouldn't scold me, I would take one of the children with me in my arms. Because if I go out and leave the children and they bother him a lot, then when I come back he scolds me because the children annoy him. So I would take the child on my shoulder and come about as close to the meeting as Ceferino's house. Near about there, I'd stop in front where I could hear. The services were going on, and each night I was getting closer.

Then one night I came to the very door of the chapel and sat down. I did not go with the idea of being converted that night, because I didn't dare without speaking first with Taso about it. But I went and sat down on a rock, one of those that had fallen out of the little stair wall. I sat down near the last door with Lilian in my lap. I enjoyed the service seated there, and I was waiting for the service to end before return-ing home. But when the service was ending already and the brothers were shaking hands and saying good-by, then Brother Juan Hernández, the pastor, went like this to me [a beckoning motion] from there in the pulpit. I had remained seated; I had not stood up. The service had ended. And then he went like this [motioning] to me.

And he said, "Come, Elí." When he said, "Come, Elí," to me I know I said nothing to him. But I felt as if I were being raised up and carried, as if I were being carried through the air from where I was sitting. And when I realized what was happening, he was already praying for me. There I was with Lilian, that seven-year-old child, in my arms. And then I felt as if I were carried from where I was sitting, carried to where the pastor was. But when I really understood what happened, when I realized I had been converted, I was already in front of him and he was praying. Then I myself said, "But in God's name (*Adiós*), I did not come to be converted tonight. Why is it that I have been converted this night?" I even thought that if I got home and told Taso I had given myself to this religion, he might say something in anger to me or scold me. And afterward I was frightened.

But, thank God—I say that it must have been the work of God—I got back home and told him, smiling, "Taso, I was converted tonight. I am a Pentecostal now." And he said to me, "Well, it's the best thing you could have done. Let's see if you can give up the tantrums you always have." Because I was a jealous one and bad tempered, more given to tantrums than anyone. And he said to me, "It's the best thing you could have done. Let's see if you can stop these rages you fall into." He said it a little differently, actually—"to see if you can give up a little of this that you have." And I said, "Well, then, you don't believe it." I assumed he still doubted, that he thought I was making a joke. But then when he realized I really had been converted, he took it well.

He always used to say that I had to find a religion that would calm me down. I was very irritable and very jealous, and he would say I had to stop that. I could not get fat— I was always very thin—being jealous of him and getting into rages. Whatever he would say to me, there would be a fight. There was no peace—no peace in the house, you see. And now that I am converted to the Saviour, well, there is peace, there is peace; there is a beautiful testimony for you. There is peace in the house, and there is life. Because I must speak the truth. I know that it's good because a change has occurred, God has worked a great change, in him as in me, and healed him of that sickness. And further—I also used to feel many small illnesses that I have not felt ever again, thank God. I believe this too was accomplished through means of prayer. I believe it was that. Because I took no medicine, I did nothing, and even so the illness I had has left me.

Then after that, in the beginning I used to go to church timidly, with fear, with shyness. There are many people who make fun of you, and many people here do not seek a faith because they're afraid others will mock. There are many who make fun of the work of God and have no religion of any sort; and when a person is converted to a religion there is always someone to ridicule it. And I was a woman who hardly left the house or went anywhere. But after making the profession of faith, I knew I had the obligation to attend some services, even if it were only once or twice. Well, I used to go to the chapel on Sunday, but I went timidly. I would seat myself in the seats near the front, not daring to look out at the street, because when I did that it seemed to me that the onlookers out there were making fun of me. But later on, that feeling disappeared. And little by little I was learning more about the religion. I read the Scriptures and I realized that it was prophesied that people would mock. Well, learning that ended my fear. Now if they want to mock me, let them, and I will not complain to the world.

Taso began attending services about a week or two after me. One night I didn't dare go alone. They were going to hold a service in the house of a brother named Santiago

Alicea, whom you know. He had become converted, and they were going to give a service there. This was still when I was just beginning, the first weeks that I was attending, and I didn't dare go there. People always talk. I used to hear others talking about how the sisters went off alone with the brothers. Now, one has trust in one's brothers and one dares to go anywhere alone with them. But as people always gossip, I didn't want to go to that meeting alone. I was going to the chapel here alone with the children, you see, but I didn't dare go there alone, because it was being held in Poyal [the swampy coastal section of the barrio].

Then I said to Taso, "Tonight there's a service in Poyal, in the house of Brother Chago [Santiago Alicea]; I'd like it if you would take me. Let's go, let's go together, because I don't want to go alone with the brothers. I want you to go." Then Taso said, "Well, let's go—I'll take you." And the two of us left together; he accompanied me. When they were about to end the service, then Brother Juan invited anyone who wanted to make a confession of faith—and Taso did so. He was converted right there, just as I had been before. He must have been convinced already, because he had recovered from his sickness. And who knows, perhaps he had God in his heart also. The pastor didn't have to talk much to him to convince him to seek God—he too followed in the path.

Well, now, we went on attending the chapel here. And one night the brothers began to pray. I didn't know how to pray as they pray. In the Pentecostal church they pray loudly, the majority pray in raised voices. And I was learning how to pray. I am very inquisitive—I like to ask questions—and I asked the pastor, I said to Brother Juan, "Well, Brother Juan, how does one learn to pray? I come to chapel but I don't know what I must do. Tell me how one learns to pray." Then the only thing he told me was: "Well, Sister, already you have received the Lord as your Saviour. I know you already have God in your heart. Well, when you kneel, expound all your problems so that He may hear you. I am sure that He will hear you. When you kneel, ask what you will—as if you were asking something of your mother or father. But with even more faith, because there are things you could not ask your mother or father, while you may ask what you wish of God. Ask, so that He may hear you."

And so I was getting more experience, and any problem I had, well—when I went to pray, when I knelt—I would begin to ask God about it. I would concentrate, and ask; and one night I was praying, and I felt this heat in me—but it really wasn't hot. It was—according to what Brother Juan told me afterward—it was one of the first intimations that one is going to receive the blessing. I felt it first when they were praying. It was as if there were some cooling breezes—like when one comes close to a refrigerator. One feels that cold air, that cold breeze—like when one opens a refrigerator and puts one's face up close to the refrigerator and one feels something like a very cool breeze. It was very agreeable—and *cold,* not just cool, but cold. And I felt that—that cold air. It passed over me, across my face [moves her hand in front of her face]. And later I felt it upon my legs.

And it was as I was feeling that cold breeze upon my legs that I noticed that at times my dress would move, like this, as if there were a breeze. But there was no breeze. It was only what I felt, you see? I noticed it and I looked to see if there were something moving about, something blowing about my legs. Then, after that cold breeze, then I felt several waves of heat, as if I were to bring my face close to an oven. I felt this heat about my ears, as if I were going to be burned. And I continued praying, continued praying, and continued praying. And as I prayed more, my face felt hotter and hotter. Until I realized that I was sweating, sweating, and I sweated as if—as if my face were cooking. I didn't know what it could be, I didn't know what it was, and I became frightened, and—and I stopped praying.

And later on I asked the pastor, I questioned him, what could it have been that I felt when I began to pray—first cold winds, and later that heat upon me that almost burned me. And he told me that when I felt that I shouldn't stop praying. Instead I should continue. He said those were intimations that I was receiving—that I was soon going to receive—

the gift of the Holy Ghost. For a space of two or three weeks I was receiving those—those fresh breezes, and later the hot ones, until one night they gave a vigil at Colonia Varsovia.

It was the first vigil I ever went to. They hadn't held any from the time of my conversion, and I didn't even know what a vigil was. I had heard that the brothers stayed up all night praying and singing and honoring the Lord, but so far I had not been to any. I wanted to rejoice at that vigil. I knew by then that these sensations I would get were intimations of something more, because the pastor told me they were. And I knew that when I received them, I should not stop praying, but that I ought to pray instead with more spirit, with more force, with more faith—that they meant that the Saviour was going to stamp me with the blessing of the Holy Ghost.

Well, then we went to that vigil, Taso and I. We passed the whole night in prayer and singing, and it was a lovely thing—for the vigils are beautiful, and one spends the whole night in meditation with the Saviour, and praying—praying and honoring the Saviour and singing beautiful hymns. And then about midnight, well they have an intermission—like they have in theaters, when the people go out to get a bit of fresh air, to take some air and so on. We had that part at twelve at night. We went outside then to drink a bit of black coffee, which is what they have at the vigils, and to eat crackers and things they bring. If it were a velorio or something like that, then people would be going out to drink rum and—and other things, you see. But in the vigil of the Saviour, no. There one goes and drinks a little coffee to avoid sleepiness—that is, to distract one. Because though one doesn't sleep during the night, one doesn't get sleepy either, since it is a joyful and good thing.

Then at about one or soon thereafter we began the second part. We were outside about an hour, and then Brother Juan asked us to reconvene within the chapel so as to begin the second part. And as the second part started, I felt those waves of heat coming more rapidly. In the place where I was sitting, I would feel something that came over me that was not—that was something that—I don't know, I can't explain what it was like. But I know that each time this thing approached me, it filled me—from my feet to my head—some cool thing came over me and blew upon me. And I felt at times that my body [she laughs slightly]—as if it wanted to move; I felt my body tremble—quiver. I felt as if each time something surrounded me, as when one is caught in a light shower. I felt as if my heart were growing bigger, as if my heart wanted to jump out of my chest. I was receiving those things [she moves her hands in front of her face]—thus, over one, now and again. Something comes to where one is; one sees nothing but one feels it. I was sitting there in a row of women, sisters in the church, and I had the end of the bench.

And when I closed my eyes, I saw what looked like a little light moving from here [she motions to the left at eye level] to here [she passes her hand to the right before her eyes]. And from this side it returned and passed by again. I saw it about three or four times during the second part of the vigil. I felt that cold wind, and that light passed back and forth, back and forth. And then I remained watchfully waiting, with my eyes closed, but I did nothing.

It was already getting light; morning was already coming. And we began to pray again, and when—I know that when I kneeled, there came this peculiar thing. It invaded my whole body [her voice becomes tense and excited] and I began to tremble, to move my body. I didn't want to move it—something was moving me. When I knelt they asked the brothers who were not baptized with the blessing to form a group. We did—men and women—to seek the blessing. In the prayer I was raising I beseeched the heavens—I asked the Lord to stamp me with the blessing that the pastor said He had for us.

By then my body was moving more, moving more, until at last something [her voice rises almost to a shriek] compelled me to dance, something carried me about, so that I was struggling this way and that—I could not control myself, I could not because this was a tremendous thing. This was something tremendous. And the joy one feels—because it is not a thing that frightens one, no. I didn't feel the slightest bit frightened; I felt instead that I wanted to hurry to receive it, to receive the blessing. I wanted to hurry, to be filled completely with it. And the more one danced, the more one felt it. And I know that this thing, this peculiar thing, was in me—you see—that it was in me. When one receives such a strong blessing, at times the other sisters rejoice in the same sanctification. They spoke in tongues alongside me, and they were telling me to glorify—to glorify more, and the pastor was saying to me, "Glorify! Glorify the Lord still more! You are going to receive the promise now."

And while I was glorifying, I know that at one point I wanted to say, "Glory to God, Hallelujah," and I could not. I swallowed my tongue; and then I spoke in other languages, like Hebrew or something like that. The pastor said I was going to say something in tongues; and then I heard Brother Juan say, "She has received it! She has received it! She has spoken in tongues, in spiritual tongues." And, meanwhile, while I was in that state, there were those strong movements in my body. Something comes—comes to where one is, and for the sheer pleasure of it, one goes on speaking in tongues. One doesn't know what one is saying, and one is left speaking that way without knowing how.

What I said, I could hear. But I myself did not understand what I was saying. I know that I was speaking in a tongue that was not my own, a language that was not mine. It was not Spanish; I wanted to speak in Spanish but I couldn't. I could not stop speaking those tongues. It was a beautiful thing—wanting to speak one's own language, to change, to control oneself enough to stop, to stop doing that—and not to be able to. I wanted to stop talking those tongues, so that I could ask the brethren what it was that I had. It was like speaking—like—like speaking in Latin; like the people speak who speak in Latin, and who speak in different languages. And I know that when I went to say "Glory to God, Hallelujah," I said *glori*—I know that I said *glori*—but then I stopped. I could not say *gloria*, as I say it now. And from there on I went on talking in—it was a mix-up, like the Arabs talk, and like the—well, like the Americans speak English—well, like that. I didn't understand the very things I was saying; I didn't know what it was that I was saying. I could not tell you what I said, you see?

After one has knowledge of some of this, when one has understanding of some of it, when one studies the Scriptures, then at times when the brethren speak in tongues, one may understand some of the words they use. But it is afterward, when one has been a while in this religion. One may have some knowledge and be able to interpret some of the tongues. But not everyone can interpret them; it is rare that the Lord raises up an interpreter for those tongues; indeed, one doesn't know oneself what one is saying. Well, that lasted for more than an hour. When it passed, I was bathed in such a sweat that you could wring out my clothes.

When that passes, you can stand up and leave your seat, and you are left feeling fine. One feels just the same. But during it I was kneeling and I could not stand up. The blessing came while I was kneeling, and for an hour I was in that same position. And in that same position, one—one feels a trembling that shakes one to one's very guts [she laughs slightly]. All the body is caught up in movement. And then one is speaking in tongues. Now those who have more knowledge control it, they can restrain themselves. But as it was new to me— as I was new, I really didn't know how. One can hear, and one has one's complete consciousness; but one can't stop talking until—until it passes. It comes, it invades your body, something comes over one, something peculiar. So much so that He Himself—I say this because it is the promise—so much so that if God Himself didn't want it, it would not—it would not pass.

And when I began speaking in tongues, I felt as if my face were being lighted up by a flashlight. When I sensed that light upon my face, I tried to open my eyes to see what it was; but I could not. My eyes remained thus [she closes her eyes very tight]. And I felt as if something like this were happening with my hair [she rumples the hair on the side and front of her head, suggesting the movement caused by a breeze]; as if wind were blowing my hair about, moving my hair this way. But I tell you that it was no wind; I merely felt that.

Afterward I sat down again. And then I felt fine. As I am now—here, well. I felt very happy because I had received something, and I had spoken in tongues that I had never spoken before. And I said, "Caramba, what beautiful languages I have spoken tonight—where would they be coming from?" [She laughs slightly.] And then I said, "What could it be?" Oh, I felt very happy, very happy, because I don't know how to speak English, I don't know how to speak Hebrew, and still I spoke four or five different languages that same night. I felt most happy about that.

Then when it was full daylight, then they ended the vigil, and we returned to the barrio. And I felt more alive than ever, and happier than ever, to think that I had this in me— this precious thing—which I didn't have before. It filled me with joy every time I thought of it. *Ave María*, it made me most happy. I felt full of life.

And after one receives the blessing, then each time one prays one may speak in tongues. But the strong movement occurs only when one is stamped with the blessing. And since one knows nothing about it the first time, one can't control that tremendous movement. But after one has that experience, the blessing will come and you can control it. You've already had the experience. You know it is something that comes from God. You receive it, but you receive it with more spirit, with more power. Then afterward you await it, you see? You expect it and you know it is coming. It is when one does not know— then when it comes it is very powerful, and swiftly you go toward it and it comes to you, and it comes uncontrolled, you see? But afterward one controls it, little by little.

Was it long after that that Taso received the blessing?
Taso received it afterward. When Taso received it he left his shirt without buttons [she laughs slightly and looks at Taso, who sits on the doorstep reading his Bible]. It was about two weeks later, or something like that. Taso was in the chapel here in Jauca. That night when Taso began to receive the blessing, he began the same as I. He began to—to —to dance. Then during the blessing he was using his hands a

lot—this way [she turns her hands inward, clawlike, and makes swimming movements of small compass, with hands close to the chest], going like this, but very rapidly, very, very rapidly. And he became bathed in such a sweat that you could have wrung out his shirt and gotten water out of it. And then while he was making that demonstration with his hands, his hands went this way [motioning to the front of the chest] in the—here on his shirt. And while his hands were pulling at his shirt the buttons went flying; the buttons of the shirt flew [she laughs]. They fell on the floor—I remember this from that night.

I don't believe he spoke in tongues that night. Taso always said to me that he doubted that he had received the promise, because he did not speak in tongues as I had. He was always at me with this: "Cára, Brother Juan says I have the blessing, but I don't know; I don't recall that I spoke in tongues." He was always telling me this. But one night we went to a service at Peñuelas [a settlement in the north of Santa Isabel]; I was watching, and he received a great big blessing, and I heard when he spoke in tongues. He said a word in tongues—I can't remember what it was. And the next day I said to him: "You say that you are in doubt whether you have the blessing confirmed. You know you have the blessing but you don't believe you have it confirmed. Well, when you were at the service in the house of Brother Santos, you said this word. And I recall that I told him the word—it was a mixed-up word, you see? Not Spanish; a word like in Latin—like in Latin. I kept the word in my head as he said it. And then at home I told him, not knowing if he would remember. I kept the word in my mind to show him that he need not doubt it, you see. He had the promise confirmed, because he said that word that was not his under the blessing.

In 1949 Taso was 41 years old. His economic situation was better than it had been during the preceding decades, and his political party had been confirmed in power by an immense majority in the 1948 elections. His search for a home was no more than a memory, for the family lived securely now on inalienable land, in that part of Barrio Jauca called Palmas Orillanas. In these ways life had become better.

But Taso was plainly frightened by the recurrent attacks of helplessness he was suffering due to the inguinal weakness he had acquired in childhood. Elí still harassed him with her jealousy, and there is little doubt that these things together were making him feel depressed and guilty. Though his political party was now triumphant, he derived no direct personal reward from the victory. While life was better and there was much to be thankful for, not everything was satisfactory; there were still many problems a man could not handle or understand.

I left Barrio Jauca in August 1949, and early in 1950 Taso became a member of the Pentecostal Church, surrendering the Catholic faith into which he had been born. This meant an important change in many areas of his life. It was a conscious choice, which he feels has solved many of his problems and has made the world more comprehensible and bearable. So fundamental a reorientation is dramatic when it occurs to anyone. In Taso's case, because he is a hardheaded person, intelligent and intellectually critical, and because of his bitter personal history in political struggles, such a change seems additionally significant.

The revivalist churches have grown rapidly in Puerto Rico, particularly in the past twenty years, and may be expected to continue to grow. What impels individuals to make such a religious choice during their growth was the question which motivated me, more than any other, to try to look down the path Taso had walked, to try to understand what had happened to him.

In Jauca, as in any community large or small in Puerto Rico, the majority of people are Catholics. But the term "Catholic," used to refer to a believer in a particular world religion, covers a great variation in intensity of faith and in conception of religious adherence. For the lower-class Puerto Rican Catholic, particularly in the coastal regions of the island, religious affiliation is rarely manifested by ritual participation.

The "average" Jauca Catholic, if a male, has not been confirmed, has never taken communion, has never gone to confession, is not married in the church, and has an attitude toward official Catholicism which is neither enthusiastic nor violently critical. By his measure, however, he is a Catholic—not a Protestant or an atheist, but a Catholic. The walls of his shack are decorated with saints' pictures, a cross, and a bit of palm from the preceding Holy Week. He has his children baptized, though the official baptism may take place years after the children are born. He has no objection if his wife goes regularly to church so long as it does not interfere with her household duties—though the likelihood of her going is slight. He believes in the divinity of Jesus Christ, and in the Holy Trinity, if you trouble him to think about it. He may tell you that the Catholic Church is "the church of the rich," but he is not likely to change his faith. He will expect to be buried in hallowed ground, and he does not—ordinarily—wonder whether he should be anything but a Catholic.

Such a Catholic was Taso. He could not remember ever having been in church himself, but he had been "raised as a Catholic." He had his children baptized, he gave alms if envelopes were brought to his house, and his speech was colored by religious phrases. That part of his behavior most influenced by Catholicism had to do with the baptism and choice of godparents (*padrinos*) for his children and the maintenance of respect relationships with these compadres. But though he had over fifty compadres—both godparents to his children and parents to whose children he was padrino —he did not concern himself about the connection between the godparental custom and Catholicism. And yet this area of his life was more closely bound up with the Catholic Church than any other, since he insisted on church baptism, even if years late, for all his children, up to the time of his conversion.

Beyond this Taso showed no interest in religion when I first worked with him and did not participate in any rituals besides baptism. During 1948 and 1949 he was a poor informant on religion; as I have indicated, his attitude was offhand and slightly sour. He seemed to find the revivalist churches amusing; he was mildly contemptuous, though not hostile. Once we saw several young girls in trance states at a Pentecostal service and Taso seemed to find their behavior comical, even slightly shameful. I remember that he indicated his distrust of their behavior; he disliked and suspected their lack of control. This was in the summer of 1949 toward the close of my first field trip, less than a year before Taso's conversion. It seems certain that he was reorganizing his attitudes toward religion by then, even though he never indicated this to me. It may have been because he was behaving overtly in terms of what he thought my religious attitudes to be, or because his own views were still changing on a largely unconscious level. When he finally wrote me about his conversion his letter was brief and slightly defensive.

While the material on his religious life was of particular interest to me, he made it clear near the beginning of our work on the life history in 1953 that he wanted to discuss that last. It seemed to me he felt the rest of his life story could serve as an introduction to the conversion, so to speak. And it is perhaps true that his conversion "fits," coming as it does in the flow of total life experience.

Taso's narrative raises a number of serious questions that I cannot answer. It seems obvious that by the time Taso took his trip to Ponce he was already predisposed to be influenced. He says: "I went with the faith that I could be cured." To reconstruct the changes in his thinking which led up to this proved impossible. But the succession of events does reveal something about him. His daughter Carmen Iris attends the services and returns with sensational stories. Then Elí does the same; she makes the events she has seen directly relevant to Taso. Something motivates her to urge him to attempt to cure himself through a supernatural agency and she must suppose he may listen. He goes at her urging, and experiences a strange physical sensation and a cure, which he seems almost entirely incapable of describing as a personal experience.

Just as Carmen Iris and Elí attend the important revival meetings in Ponce before him, so Blanca and Elí precede him in making professions of faith within the church. Blanca joins the church long before either of her parents but does not receive the blessing until after they have done so. When Elí joins, she first tests Taso by saying she had joined when she really had not. He says later that he was unconcerned and his tone expresses it. But I believe he acted approvingly. Elí's experience, however, was such that she could have considered herself not responsible for her profession of faith in case Taso objected.

When Taso himself finally makes a profession of faith, he says he does it as a "test." He wishes to know if the visitation of the Holy Ghost, which occurs during the trance state, is genuine. His reasoning is revelatory of the sort of character the man has. But it is plain that the test is really no test at all. Soon after he makes a profession of faith, his wife receives the blessing. And, he says, she is a serious woman; when she receives the blessing there is no further room for doubt. In a matter of weeks, he, too, is baptized by the Holy Ghost. The whole sequence has a certain unity.

Taso's conviction that he was cured before he believed is noteworthy. I am sure that he believed—or was fully prepared to believe—or the curing would not have been possible. And the authenticity of the visitation of the Holy Ghost is also proved in his mind before he tests it. He would have us believe he was not convinced at the time he made a profession of faith. Yet it seems fair to conclude from his own words that, had he not been sure he would be confirmed in his faith, the profession would never have been made.

The experience of the blessing by Elí is a "test," because he could trust her where he could trust no other. If she had this experience, then it could not be a fraud. It is possible that his profession of faith helped to trigger her receiving of the Holy Spirit. Thus at last Taso can experience the *promesa,* and know he has not been deceived—and presumably, that he is not deceiving himself, as well. He is at pains to explain that the experience is real, that it is foretold and has Biblical justification. This particular order of events bespeaks Taso's curiously hardheaded approach to nearly everything, including religion: his need for a feeling that what he does is justified, pretested, verifiable; his preoccupation with control, order, and restraint, probably put sorely to the test by his decision to be a Pentecostal; and his complementary and balanced relationship with Elí. The fact that the tests themselves are probably no more than routine confirmations of what he must have believed unconsciously already only demonstrates his need for rational support in the decisions he makes.

When Taso turned back once more to his experience in Ponce, new materials emerged. He emphasizes that the minister evoked in him feelings of guilt—the word *culpable* is best translated this way. The usual meaning of *culpable* in Puerto Rican speech is "guilty as charged," rather than "feeling guilty." The word is rarely used, anyway. It seems to me very important that Taso uses it, so far as I can tell, without any prompting from me. His guilt does not arise from his sickness, he says—he claims he does not feel guilty for being ill. It arises in connection with his friends and neighbors, and with his family; has he behaved toward them as he should? Then he shifts to Elí's jealousy of him—the minister's words "convicted" her (this translation would fit with Fundamentalist usage in the United States), as well as him. When he and Elí entered the church, her jealousy ended for good, since the jealous are not godly. And so indeed other things must have ended for him. Perhaps he is not explicit enough here; I believe his meaning, however, will be sufficiently clear to anyone who has read his story.

Against the background of his advancing years and his disillusionment with his local political leaders, the concatenation of items in this part of the story may reveal a meaningful sequence. There is his frightening illness, centered in the core of his potency—and in this context, of his potency for "evil." There is the (associated?) arousal of guilt feelings, intensified by Elí's persistent and extreme jealousy. There are Elí's urgings that he go to the revival meeting to see if he can be cured; and he goes with this expectation. The cure itself is unexplained. With the forswearing of un-Christian behavior, his consciousness of his own guilt and his capacity for dealing with it both undergo changes.

The Conversion

The conversions of Elí and of Taso are separate events, but the narrations reveal that they are also parts of a single set of circumstances. The words of the narrators reveal how different Taso and Elí are from each other. But like all people who have lived in an intimate and meaningful relationship, they subtly sense each other's moods and tempers unconsciously. For the curiously balanced and mutually gratifying partnership they have, it was right that they should both be converted to the new faith. Plainly, each was getting something for himself from the experience; but the church also became a setting within which they could relate to each other in new ways. Elí's description of her own religious background and of the steps leading up to her conversion illuminates the meaning of the experience to her alone as well as for her relationship to her husband.

From Elí's recounting, it is clear how emotionally oriented she is as compared with her husband. One gets the impression as well that Elí is a much more sensual person than Taso; it would be difficult not to read analogies into Elí's narration of her baptism by the Holy Spirit. Some of the difference between the parallel recountings, however, probably derives from the culturally determined rules for male versus female behavior.

Thus the two narrations reveal different things: both Taso and Elí joined the Pentecostal Church for the same reason, and yet each for his own reasons. Both derive some kind of general gratification out of their new status; yet each receives some particular and individual gratification. They undergo comparable experiences; but these are only comparable, not alike, and each perceives his experiences and those of his spouse in distinctive ways.

For both Taso and Elí conversion meant a new solution to old and almost unendurable problems. Taso reveals the burden of guilt he carried, and one sees the ease with which the words of the pastor could evoke Taso's guiltiness. He stands before God sick and guilty and disillusioned, and feels his burden miraculously lifted. Elí remembers the words of the Scriptures from her childhood, and from the lips of her father before he lost faith. She is drawn to religion by forces she cannot understand. Both Taso, in his description of himself and of his response to Blanca's emotional relationship to the church, and Elí, in her descriptions of her experiences, reveal a deep undercurrent of powerful human feeling which the church came to satisfy.

CHAPTER 8

History within History

THE SYSTEMATIC DESCRIPTION of the life of Taso Zayas ends with his acceptance of a new faith. It is, as I have said, both a fragmentary autobiography and an unfinished one. To fit Taso's personal experiences into the context of the vast social changes which occurred around him as he grew older is an almost impossible task. But one must begin somewhere.

A look through the lens of history shows the way a people—a social group, a subculture, a community, or a whole country—is laid open by the course of important economic, political, and ideological changes to new perceptions, new patternings of behavior and belief, new ways of seeing what is happening to them. To delineate these things as they relate to the experiences of Taso and Elí, it is necessary to look once more at Barrio Jauca against the background of the region and country of which the barrio is a part, and to see what happened to this tiny village over fifty years of rapid change.

Before the United States Occupation, Barrio Jauca consisted of several small nucleated villages or communities. These clusters of population were usually attached to large tracts of land, held as the personal possessions of wealthy landlords who provided paternalistic protection and employment for "their people." Life moved at a slow pace. Individual workers were first of all members of families and communities, largely dependent for their security and livelihood on the arbitrary benevolence of local men of power. The sugar industry which had dominated the whole region in the middle of the nineteenth century had declined, but it was still the most important source of wealth on the south coast. Most work was done by hand. Most of what workers consumed in the course of daily life was produced locally or in the home. Even though the sugar industry was capitalistic in character and oriented toward the world outside, life on the hacienda communities was turned inward, isolated and largely self-contained.

One was born to work in the cane, to come to know the feel of the dirt in every cane field on the hacienda. One made do without a formal education, used herbs or begged medicine from the hacendado when ill, stayed in the same village all one's life. One lived in a straw or wooden shack, watched one's siblings be born and die of ill-defined illnesses, ate rice and beans and drank black coffee, eloped with a local señorita at an early age, fathered children in rapid succession, and so repeated a familiar and narrowly defined cycle. Though time never stood still, the rules of life were clearly etched and the behavioral alternatives were few, or unimagined. The paternalistic quality of relationships between workers and those who were richer, better educated, more powerful and more mobile is hard for most Americans to grasp in the twentieth century. Each barrio was represented politically by a *comisario,* a sort of "sheriff" appointed by the mayor from among the local hacendados. Workers had no political power.

The haciendas were like little towns: there was grazing land for the workers' animals; woodland where they could collect tinder; a special subsistence plot where they could grow some basic foods; a grindstone for grinding their cornmeal. There were rows of shacks where they could live, often with a "group kitchen" behind. One cane field was *la pieza de los pobres,* and it supplied free sugar, and sometimes rum, to the impoverished and aged at Christmas. The foremen, mayordomos, and hacendados might serve as godparents to the children of workers (the cost was small, and workers could be coaxed to make an extra effort *por compadrazgo*). Often groups of workers would gather outside the hacendado's house to provide him and his family with music. When a worker was sick he might obtain medicine or a bit of cash from the hacendado. One's relationships with persons of power were, obviously, at the very core of existence for working people.

Some of the paternalistic context apparently had been weakened by the time of the United States Occupation, but much of it still persisted. In 1899 "the Americans" came, and then life rapidly began to change. Older people could remember another special period of change, at the time of Emancipation (1873). But even the freeing of the slaves had been a gradual process compared with what happened after 1899.

The fundamentals of the post-1899 change have already been described at length: the spread of the corporations, the capitalization of previously untilled land, the rise of industrial production in the fields, the standardization of wages and hours, the proletarianization of the worker, and the elimination of local artisan and upper classes. These changes were primarily in the economic circumstances under which Jauqueños worked and to which they had to adjust themselves. As I have indicated, there were other changes, too: medical facilities were improved; transport and communication were modernized; the educational system was enlarged and extended; political parties grew rapidly and assumed different forms; new religious ideologies were permitted to penetrate Puerto Rico in strength. While most of the economic changes that took place immediately after the Occupation were the direct result of the activity of United States capitalists in a new zone of operation, the noneconomic changes— those in political, educational, medical, religious, and ideological spheres—had a different character. They too were the concomitants of United States sovereignty over a new possession, but they developed out of the activities of the United States government or groups of American citizens, without any direct reference to economic gain.

The economic assimilation of the south coast was completed by the late 1930's. The final purchase of Santa Isabel lands by Luce and Company, landholding instrumentality of Central Aguirre Sugar Associates, was made in 1930. By that year a single corporation owned or held in lease more than 10,000 acres of land in Santa Isabel. Together with three other corporations Aguirre then controlled 98 per cent of the total area in farms in this one municipality. The sociological effects of the transformation were felt by every south coast worker. He lost many things that had meant security to him before: personal relationships with his hacendado and mayordomo, the land he used in usufruct for his own needs, the favors his personal relationships with his superiors had previously guaranteed him, and the value of most of his artisan skills. Those noneconomic advantages he was gradually acquiring—political democracy, the right to education, medical service, freedom of religion—were not yet living forces for him; and some of them, at least, had to be fought for.

But after 1930, when the full impact of the depression was felt throughout the island as it was in the United States, both the bad and the good of the conquest began to emerge in sharper relief. United States corporations built on south coast sugar paid dividends unremittingly during the subsequent years, proving financially viable when most American businesses were contracting. The profits were wrung from a labor force which had been pushed down to survival level. One result was a sharp upswing in political consciousness and political activity that finally bore fruit in 1940, with the coming to power of the Popular Democratic party. The party program, in many ways reminiscent of the Roosevelt New Deal, caught the imagination of the Puerto Rican worker, and the party lived up to its promises when it came to power. It has remained in power ever since.

Taso's life fits within the period just described. He was able to see the traditional and customary patterns of behavior of the nineteenth century uprooted and replaced, and in his daily life he participated in the vast social and economic changes which remade Barrio Jauca. Rapid as these changes were, they did not come overnight, and Taso could watch as cane fields replaced forests, pastures, and subsistence plots. He could grasp the power relationships of the past in his experiences with Don Pastor Díaz, and he came to understand the power relationships of the future in his political and union activity. In his time the company stores grew and expanded at the cost of small retailers, but they also brought before his eyes new products, new aspirations, and new motives. He felt the weight of corporate political repression, but he had known the time not long before when political repression was unnecessary, since genuine political activity by workers had been unimaginable.

When one examines the concrete and particular life experiences Taso has undergone, there seems little which makes that life unusual. Most of the major events can be paralleled in the lives of many other Jauqueños, or of people like them in the sugar zones. But as I have suggested, one event— Taso's acceptance of a new faith—seemed to me to be particularly incongruous with his other experiences. I saw this change as incongruous, or unexpected, because of what I thought I knew about Taso at the time I left Jauca late in 1949. His rather hardheaded attitude toward life, colored by considerable cynicism and backed by a fine critical intelligence; the rebelliousness which marked his political activity; his mild contempt (as I perceived it) for religion; his concern with rationality and control; and his apparent acceptance of the local norms for masculine behavior, all seemed to me to run counter to any predisposition he might have had to reorient his world view through religious conversion.

But I think Taso's religious rebirth does make sense in terms of what I have learned since. In his own way Taso sought to convince me of this, but my convictions come from insights I believe he never intended to provide. All his discussions of his religious change seemed designed to persuade me that he acted with rationality, testing his decisions objectively at each step. And—in terms of his own horizons—I accept this to be so. It is plain enough that the same mind that led him in other directions at earlier times in his life led him also to become cured miraculously of a dangerous and frightening illness, to forswear much of what had characterized his life before, and to have new and powerful emotional experiences. Yet it also seems certain that there would have to be significant changes in a man's perception before such a dramatically different life view could take final shape. In order to get some idea of these perceptual changes it may be useful to glance briefly at revivalist religion itself.

The revivalist churches have exercised a remarkable influence in recent years, particularly in underdeveloped countries and among people who are poor and subjected to rapid social and cultural change. They appear to be strongest in rural areas but also win many adherents in urban slums, whether in Johannesburg, Kingston, or Detroit. Their proselytes may be former tribesmen or former Catholics; one thing they rarely seem to be, however, is former ecumenical Protestants. The revivalist churches are the churches of the detribalized, the deculturated, and the disinherited. They fill many needs for lower-class people who, one way or another, have lost their stake in "the old ways." The revivalist churches provide an important source of recreation, and this should not be disparaged. They provide group membership, with all the psychological satisfactions such membership can give.

Since the churches themselves are usually built by the parishioners, through voluntary tithing and solicited contributions, members are able to identify very directly with the religion and with the place of worship. The decor is never awesome but always reassuringly familiar. This is fundamentally consistent with the nature of the religious belief itself, which insists on the perception of religion as an inner personal experience. The use of ritual and decor to inspire religious feeling is de-emphasized; religious thrill and intense personal feeling are played up. Contact with the Godhead is direct—and in fact, must be direct for the individual to become a full member of the church.

The pastor or lay religious leader is customarily a working man, like the parishioners. He speaks in a language—even to the dialectal details—that they understand, and they read their Bibles in the same language. In rural Puerto Rico attendance at services does not usually require a trip to town, and the pastor—unlike the ministers of the ecumenical churches and the priest—is usually a neighbor of equal class status. He may be approached directly and without class-determined deference; there is no fear one's questions may seem stupid or inappropriate, no preoccupation with an unfamiliar etiquette.

In these and other ways, the revivalist churches provide an acceptable social context for religious experience of an intense, and intensely satisfying, kind. The feeling of participation is crucial to the religion and, to some extent at least, the religious experience is dependent upon it. As Elí's narration clearly reveals, a person who is ready to have an inner "thrill of faith" is taught to do so, and the learning requires a temporary surrender of autonomy to the will of the group, as expressed in rhythmic participation, exhortation, and mortification of the flesh by fast and fatigue. Finally, the revivalist churches demand conformance and sacrifice. What may lead individuals to desire self-denial is irrelevant for the moment. What matters is the immense contemporary appeal of an ideology which insists that believers pay a price for salvation, and thereafter enables them to enjoy the sensation of paying it.

But the picture is more complicated than this. The non-ecumenical churches do not usually penetrate first in those areas which are still substantially tribal or wholly unacculturated to Western society. Rather, they tend to make their influence felt particularly in the "burned-over" parts of the colonial and rural agrarian world where Catholicism and Protestantism have already proselytized segments of the local population. The nonecumenical churches strike lower and later, at those people who are "left over"—the poorer, the less educated, the less concerned with Western conceptions of dignity and respectability, and frequently—curiously enough—the more rebellious.

On Puerto Rico's south coast the population has been traditionally Catholic for centuries. The first wave of ecumenical Protestant proselytization affected the middle-class townsmen —civil servants, professionals, small merchants—and every town plaza now boasts a Protestant church as well as a

Catholic church. But ecumenical Protestantism did not successfully invade the rural hinterlands. It has remained for the
revivalist churches to do this, as it has remained for them to
preach most successfully among the urban poor. In traditional Catholic areas, the ideological appeals of the revivalist
churches may parallel those of the ecumenical churches,
though they include many elements—such as speaking in
tongues, leading of the Holy Spirit, public attestation, uncontrolled dancing, etc.—which organized Protestantism de-
plores or, at least, firmly fails to encourage. The affect-ridden
aspects of nonecumenical Protestantism clearly have something to do with its appeal, but it is exactly the emotional attraction and the fervent response of believers which makes
such churches a source of embarrassment to some ecumenical Protestants.

Some of the special aspects of the revivalist churches are
suggested here. They carry on their missionary activity usually
well after a particular area has been saturated with other
proselytizing faiths. They direct their appeals to the poor,
particularly (though by no means exclusively) the rural poor.
They capitalize on the directness of their approach, their fit
with lower-class norms, the recreational as well as the pro-
founder satisfactions they afford, the sense of participation
they create, and the attraction of self-denial, which they first
engender and then employ.

But it should be clear that none of the appeals of revivalist
churches will succeed unless there is present a population
which has become predisposed by certain social forces to be
attracted. For this discussion, the specific psychological moti-
vation of any particular individual who joins the church
does not matter. Rather, I wish to refer to the general sociological conditions under which there will be some persons, or many, who can find in conversion a solution to their
own emotional problems. One such condition may be that
the importance and efficacy of personal relationships, particularly as between people at different levels of a social and
economic hierarchy, have been so sharply reduced that ways
of behaving have become standardized and even depersonal-

ized. When this occurs, human groupings which give more coherence to life and provide a sense of group identity can grow increasingly attractive. The revivalist churches seek to create just such groupings.

Another condition may be that the individual sense of self has been heightened by social and economic changes of the sort previously described: standardization of effort, measurement of such effort in terms of an impersonal cash standard of value, intensified economic competition, and the erosion of personal relationships with persons of greater power. When one's sense of self is intensified and this is accompanied by a growing feeling of aloneness, it seems possible that the individual capacity to feel guilt may be sharply increased. The revivalist churches are of course familiar with guilt; the individual's capacity to suffer unendurably from guilt feelings is a prime human character resource for such churches. But a heightened sense of self may lead not only to a greater capacity to suffer from guilt; it can lead equally well to a greater capacity to exult in virtue. When the attainment of virtue is made possible through the forswearing of all those things which can be turned against a man to make him feel guilty, the solution to many of life's problems can seem very clear.

What is being suggested here is that when people are subjected to changes of the kind that occurred in Barrio Jauca, they will be led ultimately to changes in their view of the world and, particularly, to changes in their view of the self. Not only in terms of economic survival but also in terms of one's general sense of well-being, individual effort and individual responsibility can emerge as more important than before. Where societies change as Jauca changed, the individual is gradually torn loose from the old personal security networks and eventually may come to see himself alone and to think of his fate as most comprehensible in terms of his own acts. Thus it may be that the broad changes in Jauca life during the first decades of this century exposed people there to new kinds of perceptions. And soon afterward, the penetrations that were occurring were also beginning to afford them new kinds of solutions. That is, the revivalist churches offer the atomized individual a new ideological medium for dealing with his emerging perceptions of himself and the effects of those perceptions.

It need not be stressed again that in Jauca people were simultaneously reorienting themselves to deal with some of their problems on an institutionalized and mass basis, through political parties and labor unions. The increase of a sense of identity with people of one's class or region need not contradict or rule out the possibility of a heightened feeling of aloneness and individuality.

The events in Taso's life run parallel to the major changes going on about him. At every point it is possible to see how he took what advantage he could of the opportunities his society offered him, in accord with his own needs and temperament. The changes themselves do not explain the *particular* trajectory of his own life; rather, they are the conditions under which his life took its characteristic shape. There is little one can find in Taso's story that sets his behavior sharply apart from that of other Jauqueños like him. His choice of jobs, his marriage, his desire for many children, his food tastes, the ways he punishes his children, his notions of maleness, even his religious conversion, all are part and parcel of the culture around him. In some ways, his acts and attitudes are in the direction of what might be called "the new"—for instance, his joining of the Pentecostal Church. In other ways—his unwillingness to emigrate, for instance—his acts and attitudes accord instead with "the traditional." But there is a cultural precedent for substantially everything Taso has thought and done in his life.

Of course, his perceptions, attitudes, experiences, and choices are to some extent his own alone; they can never be wholly explained by reference to his culture. There is a shadowy meeting place between the premises of a particular culture—the rules, the habits of mind, the values and beliefs of a people—and the unique personalities of those who live by them. Taso's life cannot be "explained" simply by reference to his culture's tenets. But also one cannot explain the culture of the people of Jauca by reference to the individual personalities of men like Taso.

In Taso's case, the crucial events which transformed the barrio affected him in the same way as they did most of his neighbors. But such deeply personal events as his loss of his father while he was still an infant; the early deaths of his mother and sister; the fact that his marriage remained stable in spite of the suffering he and his wife caused each other; his illness and its cure; and his entrance into the church—all these are special features of Taso's life, interwoven with the basic values of his social group and given in each instance a distinctive quality that is the essence of individual experience and perception.

An outstanding aspect of Taso's life would seem to be the constant search for creative ways to employ his very considerable native intelligence. During his lifetime, Taso excelled at many of the things that express underlying cultural values. He began work at an early age, acquired a reputation for being a hard and intelligent worker, and mastered all the jobs in the cane (except, perhaps significantly, cane cutting). He took a wife while still a young man, fathered children quickly, maintained a sense of romantic masculinity, chose his compadres well, paid his debts, and observed his hospitality obligations to the letter. His drive to express himself is revealed early, for example, in his struggle for the defeat of Don Pastor Díaz in the elections of 1928, before he was even of voting age. In subsequent years his political and labor union activities, together with his work and family obligations, kept him fully occupied.

Taso seemed on the threshold of a new life-period in 1948: he was very active in the Popular party local campaign, and party successes rest, much more than politicians are sometimes willing to acknowledge, on the shoulders of such men. But the 1948 campaign also disillusioned him sorely. Taso's falling-out with local political officials left him embittered, yet the supremacy of his party meant his personal efforts were no longer so important. Elí's jealous rages were still tormenting him, and the recurrent attacks of helplessness caused by his illness were frightening him. I was not sufficiently aware of these things in 1948; and I might add parenthetically that I believe we anthropologists—or some of us at least—are often quite inadequate when confronted with the intelligence and capacity for disguise, conscious or unconscious, of our informants.

Taso's conversion the following year required the deliberate surrender of certain prerogatives that seem to be tied to valued behavior items for males in his group: swearing, drinking alcoholic beverages, dancing, gambling, fornication, acquiring compadres, consensual union, delegating religious activity (if any) to one's wife, giving vent to violence in word or deed when the subculture's values for the individual are threatened, and nondeferral of gratification. But Taso's decision to become a Pentecostal was probably not hampered in any serious way by the need for these new forbearances. He had never been an enthusiastic drinker or a man who cursed freely. While he liked to gamble on the illegal lottery, the fiercely punitive laws of 1948 had taken away much of his enthusiasm—and even before, he had argued that the salesmen profited regularly, the players only rarely. As for his sexually aggressive and romantic impulses, the picture he gives is one of a man plagued by his wife's incessant suspicions and suffering simultaneously from disproportionate feelings of guilt, rather than one of a gay Don Juan.

To terminate the choosing of compadres may have been more difficult; the ritual was an old and revered one for Taso. But in the new church he seems to have seen a substitute means for planning the social relationships of his younger children. He has kept up carefully his connections with over fifty compadres since the time of his conversion. Nor was his and Eli's decision to marry after more than twenty years of common-law union a difficult one. Their group does not disapprove of sacramental union; in fact, people give such unions lip service. The denial of violence also must have come at no personal cost; Taso had never committed a truly violent act (though the record shows he may have been close on several occasions). The abjuration of "free spending" does not seem contradictory to Taso's previous mode of life. While he was gambling, his winnings were normally applied to household improvements such as building a porch or laying a concrete floor. After his conversion he undertook to raise animals on a share basis. This is a common Puerto Rican practice which Taso had ridiculed when I first knew him (he felt that the owner of the animal gets a disproportionate return, since the work of raising the animal is all done by the partner), but which he had formerly done himself as a young man.

Thus the self-denials of personal satisfaction implicit in the conversion do not seem to have been difficult for Taso to make. The crucial obstacle to conversion would rather seem to be what Taso expected it would mean to his friends and neighbors, who would witness his acceptance of a new faith, and all that went with this. To join a group which is held in mild contempt by some and regarded with outright hostility by others; to pass through the test of faith which requires a temporary but quite complete cessation of physical and mental control; and, in effect, to acknowledge the presence of a deep need for reassurance in a culture that expects men to be assured in the face of adversity—these, it would seem, were the genuine obstacles. They must have tested Taso's resolve sorely.

When Taso joined the Pentecostal Church, he was doing what many of his fellow Puerto Ricans had done in the past. I have suggested that his personal decision to do so arose from deep and intolerable feelings of guilt. These guilt feelings may have been associated with a sense of failure about his personal (especially family) relationships. The chronic recurrence of severe pain resulting from an inguinal weakness may have stimulated and intensified these guilt feelings, particularly in view of the symbolic association one may make between the nature of this illness and any past sexual "misbehavior." Moreover, it is clear that in the period I knew him, Taso was withdrawing from his social and political activities, which had disillusioned him; he was thrown back more and more upon himself and his relationship with Elí. But even if these clues do permit us to understand a little better why he joined the church, they do not explain why others like him have joined. Nor do they explain why others having very similar personal experiences have not. In short, one comes back to the point of convergence of personal and cultural "explanations" of behavior.

The question may perhaps be examined in another way. There is much in the revivalist approach to the good life that is reminiscent of early Protestantism. The church, in what it forbids and in what it encourages, provides a world view which seems to be remarkably congenial to growing mobility aspirations in a society that is becoming Westernized. Thus the injunctions against gambling, smoking, and drinking may be tantamount to enforced saving, or at least to the potential accumulation of capital for other purposes. Church marriage is more acceptable in the wider society than common-law union; and a marriage certificate is of some importance in terms of the possible future status of the children of such unions. The various tenets and taboos add up not only to forced economic saving but also to the idealization of deferral of gratification—surely a basic postulate of self-advancement in Western society. Thus conversion to a revivalist sect may be viewed as a way of increasing one's social and economic mobility, even though middle-class feelings toward such groups may obscure this.

If a society is suddenly exposed to new values by another more powerful and invading society, it seems reasonable to assume that those persons who take up the new values with the greatest speed and efficiency stand the best chance for success. This will not be true, of course, if the invading society is thrown back and the old order restored. But in Puerto Rico, United States influence has been powerful, protracted, and irresistible. There is no reason to suppose the trend will be reversed. Accordingly, more and more Puerto Ricans have been pressed to adjust their way of life to fit more successfully to new standards. In many cases such adjustment is deliberate and conscious. One may see this particularly with those Puerto Ricans who have emigrated to the mainland and who are rapidly acculturating to life here. The same process goes on to a lesser extent in Puerto Rico, varying of course in degree according to various social distinctions within the island.

The wave of ecumenical Protestant proselytization in Puerto Rico soon after the United States Occupation probably created some change in the insular social structure. The proselytes, as I have suggested, appeared to come principally from the middle class, and religious change of this sort has direct meaning for acculturation, in this case "Americanization." The revivalist churches made their penetrations at a later time, more deeply, and at lower class levels. But it may at least be hypothesized that revivalist proselytization could serve motives to acculturate among social groups which, for one or another reason, could not have been expected to move freely and easily into the ecumenical denominations.

As time passed after the United States Occupation, the culture of the conquering society posed for the lower-class Puerto Rican a set of new values and potentially desirable objectives. The cane cutter inevitably was exposed to new kinds of goods, new ideas of worth, new attitudes. And unlike remoter areas of the island where change has come more gradually, the south coast was totally revamped by the Occupation. The result at first was simply to disorient people, a fact revealed when older Jauqueños talk about the early 1900's. The new emphasis on cash income, the elimination of noncash services, the introduction of new consumers' goods, and the opportunity to earn money by intensified effort began to push aside older standards. Workers could begin to think of getting security more through material possessions or money-making skill, and less through the fulfillment of customary noneconomic obligations and the extension of personal friendships.

In the pre-Occupation situation landowners had sought above all else to avoid investing capital in their enterprises. Agriculture was extensive rather than intensive and labor-heavy rather than machine-heavy or capital-heavy. The sugar industry was contracting, not expanding. Grinding seasons were long and involved much waste of labor. Little land was used for cane. It surely would be fair to say that sugar production in Puerto Rico in 1899 was less capitalistic than it had been at midcentury. Landowners never had an accurate idea of labor efficiency. And the laborer was unable to develop an accurate idea of the value of his labor.

In the post-1900 setting there was unlimited capital available and it was to be used in the most rational (and profitable) manner possible, without reference to other considerations. Such a completely new basis for economic activity can completely upset customary modes of behavior. And people subjected to this kind of transformation, as they come to perceive the nonutility of their old ways, cast about for new ways that fit life better.

The "American way" requires that a man put his economic betterment high on the hierarchy of personal values. It pushes men in the direction of dependable daily effort, accompanied by a new conception of time—the equation "time is money." It also drives men in the direction of deferring immediate gratification in return for later reward. In the United States the premium put on a long uninterrupted period of education is a clear illustration of this; and for many young Americans all and any other personal needs must be subordinated to this goal. The American way does not so much demand that most decisions *be* economical as that one be prepared to *rationalize* them as economical. Thus it becomes "more economical" to own a big car because it will wear better; a new refrigerator is more economical than an old refrigerator; and even petty pleasures like new clothes or repainting the apartment become rationalized as economical because they improve one's job opportunities, influence people with more power, and prove one's own fitness. The direct personal pleasure such things may bring becomes secondary to the asserted motives of "practicality" and "economy."

These emphases—personal economic advancement, a time-is-money orientation, deferral of immediate gratification, the pre-eminence of the economic motive, and the subordination of pure pleasure—seem to run quite counter to the standards which must have typified life among lower-class Puerto

Ricans, particularly in the coastal zones. Yet they were embodied in what working people could learn from watching the way the men who staffed the American corporations went about their work and, by deduction, from the demands of the work itself. They found, for instance, that many of the new items in the company stores were desirable, and that the workers who made the greatest effort and used their money for personal rather than social purposes shared most in the enjoyment of material innovations. Again, they began to realize that education, which was hardly even within the grasp of lower-class people before, could emerge as the most important instrument for guaranteeing the future security of one's children if not oneself.

Perceptions of this sort do not usually translate themselves swiftly into motives to new kinds of behavior. Probably new needs are aroused frequently without any conscious awareness of the implications for future behavior. But there is no question that the attitudes of Jauqueños were being changed in particular directions by the ideological and material impact of the American Occupation. Nor is it beyond belief that people are led to new expressions of attitude and value through a new religion, even without perceiving the congruence of the new religious ideology with the social and economic changes that have already taken place. In their own way the revivalist churches make ideological imperatives out of kinds of behavior which are congenial to the new standards. The self-denials held out as moral necessities serve the simultaneous purpose of increasing thrift and teaching the deferral of gratification.

The impulse to economy is not accompanied by asceticism; those converts who are unconsciously moving toward an approximation of the new societal ideals may use their savings to further a child's education, to enjoy a higher standard of living, and in other ways, at least some of which are directly satisfying. These new uses of capital prove effective: their worth inheres in the greater future income they promise and the greater material satisfaction they afford. Such asceticism as characterizes the conversion is in the area of self-denial of spontaneous impulse *outside* the religious setting; and this, too, provides its own reward. As we see Taso relate himself in new ways to his feelings of guilt and depression, it seems as if the price of inner peace is really quite low.

A final point with regard to the possible uses of a revivalist church as a medium of acculturation may be made. It has been fashionable to assume that Westernization—crudely, the introduction of capitalistic technology and economy and of democratic ideology—leads directly to secularization among non-Western peoples. It cannot be stressed enough that this is not necessarily true. In fact, in the case of the Tasos, it would seem that Westernization has had quite the opposite effect. The new way of life seems to have brought in its wake the need for a vigorous kind of ideological dedication, and the revivalist churches may be a powerful answer. One cannot predict, of course, what may become of the intensity of belief of men like Taso when the acculturation process has moved along another half century. For the present, however, Jauca's Pentecostals are surely more fervent than Jauca's Catholics. Becoming a Protestant per se may not increase one's chances for rapid Americanization; but such a move may in its ancillary effects do just that. It may be that when Western ideology and technique are imposed on a backward people, acculturation to an easy-going secular view will come fastest if they become more religious first.

A treatment of this kind can do no more than offer in broad outline some of the possible meanings of social change against which the personal history of a single individual may be examined. The suggested relationships between social background and life history are intended to serve merely as hypotheses which might be proved or disproved or refined. The gap between the sociological explanation of a phenomenon—why people in settings such as these become members of revivalist churches—and the psychological explanation of the same phenomenon—why Taso Zayas became a Pentecostal—is perhaps unbridgeable. But through asking the preliminary questions it may become possible to make the next questions sharper and more telling.

CHAPTER 9

Epilogue

WHEN I RETURNED to Barrio Jauca in the summer of 1956 my aim was not to bring Taso's story up to date, but rather to fill in gaps and correct inconsistencies in the materials we had assembled in 1953. The story presented here goes only up to the period of Taso's conversion and the months immediately following. I realized that if I undertook to advance the story six more years, it would mean another huge task of compilation, transcription, translation, and writing, and the job might never get done. So we contented ourselves with clarifying and consolidating what had been collected before.

Inevitably, I looked about me at Barrio Jauca. I saw that the colonias where Taso had worked as a child and as a man are much the same as they were, but their populations are now almost wholly removed to public land. Alongside the main population settlement in Jauca an entire community of additional houses has sprung up. The land is held by the Insular government; it is divided into plots held in perpetuity by the residents—mainly former agregados of the colonias. The first night we walked past these houses I asked Taso how the corporation felt about this change.

"In the old days when there was a strike the corporation could make the people on the colonias work as strikebreakers," he said. "Since the Popular party, even the agregados could not be compelled to work during a strike. And the corporation had to maintain the houses in good condition, because the Popular party compelled them to. So when the government offered to buy this piece of useless land for settlement, the corporation agreed to sell it and to help the agregados move there."

"And what about the company stores," I asked him. "Who buys there now?"

He laughed. "Search me," he said. "Their agregados are gone and we, here—we have our little stores. I think those company stores will have trouble. They send public amplifiers around all during the harvest advertising sales. But we mostly buy right here."

There are many more houses in the barrio. I was unable to make a census, but I doubt that the local population has grown much through natural increase. This is because the emigration to the United States has assumed large proportions here. Barrio Jauca has its own post office substation now, and the small merchant whose charge it is ceremoniously stamps the letters before they are distributed. Most of the letters— and they were arriving at the rate of about thirty a day—are airmail, coming from the United States. Many contain money orders. Almost every day someone leaves for the first time "para el Norte," nervous, his cardboard suitcase in hand, his skin burned brown, his clothes fitting badly. And a few months or a year later he is back for a visit, this time with a metal suitcase, a cream-colored fedora on his head, swaggering a little, his face paler but fuller, bursting with stories about the tremendous cold, the Americans both good and bad, the richness and perversity of the country up there.

Work in the cane grows ever more scarce. The work of the palero, which interested me so much when I first learned of it, is now entirely gone. The ditches are made by machine. The araña now loads the cane after it is cut. People describe in awed voices how it pushes the cane into piles, picks it up in its great tentacles, and drops it into rubber-tired carts drawn by tractors. Tracks are no longer laid in the cane. The oxen get scarcer and scarcer. A new machine which cuts cane is being tried out; it works badly, but everyone says, "You wait; those Americans, they will make it work right." During the harvest men now work two shifts, the second running usually until midnight or 1 A.M. The grinding capacity of the mills has risen, and the harvest gets progressively shorter.

Wages have increased somewhat, and the Army and emigration continue to funnel wealth into the barrio. Nine of the little shacks along the road now boast television aerials. At least one house has a flush toilet. Local stores now sell, among other things, cleansing tissues and sanitary napkins, unknown in the rural barrios eight years ago. The children, and even the dogs, seem fatter, sleeker, and in better health. People deplore the decline of work in the cane, but there is always the migration. No one has come back to the barrio from the North to start a business here as yet, but at least one man—Lalo—has it in mind.

I returned to Jauca in 1956 expecting to live in the additional room Taso had put onto his house, since he had written that it would be reserved for me. Instead, I was given the use of an entire house, one of the most elegant in the barrio, and this is part of Lalo's story. Though he continues to live in the United States, working and saving, he has been sending money to the barrio in expectation of coming back some day. With the money a large lot was bought opposite Taso's house. On it there is a house which is a wealthy man's by Jauca standards. There are four bedrooms, a long living room, a kitchen with wiring for a stove and a refrigerator, and a shower. To have built the shower and kitchen as integral parts of the house is an unusual step, and suggests a change in the direction of United States culture.

Otherwise, except for its size, the house is authentically Puerto Rican. The walls between the bedrooms, and between the bedrooms and the living room, do not reach to the ceiling. The electric wiring is exposed. There are no wall electric fixtures. The living room is illuminated by two single light bulbs in fixtures on the ceiling, which is 12 feet from the floor. The windows are made of wooden slats, with jalousies cut into them, topped by tiny panes of colored glass that do not open. The floors are bare, unpainted pine. The beams show. Behind the house there is a privy. It is a Puerto Rican house, a fitting house for a lower-class coastal Puerto Rican who has struck it rich. To have built a different kind of house would have required the services of contractors from one of Puerto Rico's large cities. I am sure Lalo would not have liked it that way.

While I was there Taso's two oldest sons, Pablín and José Miguel, were painting the outside of the house with Taso's help. The main color is pale green; the trim is pink and white. If Lalo cannot re-create Puerto Rico in New Jersey, he can return to Puerto Rico and live in the style his experiences as a child urged him to aspire to. Though the house was not finished yet it was rapidly filling with furniture, shipped at Lalo's expense from the United States. There was a bed with a wooden frame finished in blond veneer, a sharp break with local culture. But there was also an iron bed of the kind people here still desire. There was a dresser and a chest of drawers, also finished in blond veneer. The drawers were full of products of United States culture that Lalo wanted for his own: sheets and pillowcases; chromolithographs of Jesus Christ; a figure of Christ on the Cross, of ivory and gold-colored plastic, cemented on a cheap table lamp; a set of records for learning English; some very bad paintings of rural scenes, in no way reminiscent of Puerto Rico, set in cheap wooden frames. In one corner was an electric sewing machine; in another a large radio. And one room was filled mainly with leatherette seats from restaurant stools, ostensibly in case Lalo should decide to open a restaurant on his return.

This is the authentic Puerto Rican harvest of six years in a casting foundry in Newark, New Jersey. At the same time, however, one of Lalo's daughters spoke fluent English and was in her second year of high school in Newark. The other children also speak more English than Spanish; the oldest daughter is married. One wonders how they would readjust to the Puerto Rico Lalo remembers and yearns to return to.

Much more, of course, can be said of Taso and his family. Things have changed in his house too, and very rapidly. There are two new rooms; and although the four very tiny bedrooms are full of beds, there is more room than before. The house is painted inside and out. Doña Elí is raising goats, a pig, chickens, a turkey, and a duck. A new china closet stands in the living room, and a new dining table—though the whole family never sat at the table at once, even in 1956. The china closet is filled with expensive Japanese china in good taste, purchased by Pablín and sent home from Japan while he was in the Army.

Pablín is married—but *casado casado,* as the lower-class Puerto Rican says when he means the marriage is not common-law. Pablín and his wife reveal the great change here when they are compared with Taso and Elí. Pablín was beginning his second year in the Universidad de Santa María in Ponce. Although the costs of his education were a drain on everyone, the massiveness of this accomplishment can scarcely be realized. Pablín's wife commuted each day to a factory in the neighboring town of Salinas. She was earning $39 weekly as an inspector of pen points—about $10 more than a fair cane cutter can make when there is work.

José Miguel is also married, but his pattern is more consistent with the older culture. He had eloped with the fifteen-year-old daughter of the deceased Pentecostal minister of Jauca; Doña Otilia, the girl's mother, said that she would take José Miguel to court if he did not marry the girl, and Taso urged him to do so. So they were married, and soon had their own little house. José Miguel was not interested in an education. He wanted to cut cane but his father told him not to bother, since the earnings were small and the work hard. So José Miguel did no more than assist his grandmother, Doña Antolina, in her store. He had hopes of emigrating to the United States. Both Pablín's and José Miguel's wives gave birth to their first children within a year of their marriages.

When I was in Jauca in 1953 Doña Elí was pregnant with her twelfth child, Noél, a boy born during Christmas of that year. In 1956 during the summer Elí was still nursing him. On one occasion I sat with Doña Elí and her daughter-in-law Nelda, José Miguel's wife, and had the—to me—strange experience of watching grandmother and mother nurse their babies together. Elí told me that Tasita, her eleventh child, continued nursing until Noél was born—a period slightly in excess of five years. Noél is a very healthy child and was the healthiest-looking of their children that I could remember.

Taso continues to be active in the church. He played an important part in the construction of a larger and more elegant chapel in the new settlement of houses in the barrio. In addition to Blanca (who was the first of the family to attend church services regularly, even before Elí and Taso) Carmen Iris has joined. The younger children also go to the services: Tasita (8), Roberto (11), and Lilian (12). Lilian has experienced her first blessing, but is not yet a regular member of the church. The only children who remain outside the church are Pablín, José Miguel, and Luis Raúl. It may be significant that they are all males and the oldest of the children, with the exception of Carmen Iris, who is the oldest of all and unmarried.

Taso's participation in the church continues in force, but I sensed some decline in his fervor. He seemed more willing than usual to talk of other things. When I asked him whether the membership had risen, he said: "The membership of the church is one of those things. It rises and it falls. The only thing that keeps growing in numbers always is the jukeboxes!" But there has been no disturbance of his faith, I believe. He suffered from prostatitis in 1954, but the hernia pain has never returned. His job pays better now than it did in 1953. His son returned safe from the Army. He has succeeded in leading more of his children into the church. He seems serene.

Perhaps some time in the future there may be reason to continue with Taso's story. He earns nearly $30 a week now, on a yearly average. He works only five days a week, usually. His work takes him into the cane, along the railroad tracks and on the spurs, eight hours a day in the sun. With what he earns he supports seven children and his wife entirely and contributes to the support of two other children. He and Elí and seven of their children live in their little house, eating their rice and beans and drinking black coffee, entertaining themselves with the Bible and the tambourine and the gossip of the barrio. Celestino carried off the daughter of Don Paco; Eusebio killed Demetrio with a knife; Don Fonso's cow was killed by the railroad train; the Republican party will never carry Ponce; when will Compadre Marcial return from the North?

Taso's story has no moral. Perhaps it is enough that his life should seem so much better to him now. Or perhaps the reader will see the waste I think I see: the waste of a mind that stands above the others as the violet sprays of the *flor de caña* tower above the cane. But the story should evoke no pity, for that is a sentiment which degrades the meaning of Taso's life to himself and to those who know and love him.

List of Characters

THIS LIST includes the names of the most important relatives of Anastacio (Taso) Zayas Alvarado and his wife Elisabeth (Elí) Villarronga Colón de Zayas, the two leading figures in the story. Their names, as well as the others listed here, are genuine. Only the names of a few minor figures have been changed, for unavoidable reasons. In Puerto Rico, as in the Hispanic world generally, persons carry the patronym of both parents. Women do not drop their own surnames upon marriage, but add *de* and their husband's patronym to their own. Normally, one's father's patronym precedes one's mother's, and children take the patronym from each parent's name to form their own. Thus the children of Anastacio Zayas Alvarado and Elisabeth Villarronga Colón take as their surname Zayas Villarronga.

Anastacio (Eustaquio) Zayas Alvarado	Taso
Elisabeth Villarronga Colón de Zayas	Elí, Taso's wife
Carmen Iris Zayas Villarronga	Taso's and Elí's oldest living child
Pablo Zayas Villarronga	Pablín, Taso's and Elí's oldest living male child
José Miguel, Blanca, Luis Raúl, Lilian, Roberto, Anastasia (Tasita), and Noél Zayas Villarronga	Taso's and Elí's other living children, in the order of their birth
Victor Manuel (Vitín), Luis (Güiso), and Moisé Zayas Villarronga	Taso's and Elí's deceased children
Pablo and Eugenio Zayas Alvarado	Taso's brothers
Tomasa Zayas Alvarado	Taso's sister

Nicasio Suárez	Tomasa's first husband, Nico
Cornelio	Tomasa's second husband
Nenita	Cornelio's second wife
Rosaura	Rosa, Taso's niece; daughter of Tomasa and Nico Suárez
Eladio	Lalo, Taso's nephew; son of Tomasa and Cornelio
Cheo	Rosa's husband
Antolina Colón	Tole, Elí's mother
Joaquín Villarronga	Tole's first husband, Elí's father
Mariano, Ramón, and Salvador Villarronga Colón	Elí's brothers
Francisco Aguirre	Sico, Tole's third husband

Glossary

Adiós A term of greeting (when passing a friend), of farewell, or of great surprise.

agregado Formerly, a Puerto Rican laborer resident on a plantation or hacienda who received part of his wages in the form of goods or services. In the period 1900–44 the *agregados* on sugar plantations were subject to political repression and control; there are very few, if any, *agregados* remaining.

aguantar Literally, "to keep in hand, to hold, to hold back." The term has a special flavor in Puerto Rico, meaning "to keep (oneself) under control, to restrain oneself."

anamú The herb *Petiveria alliacea*. It is used medicinally by rural people in Puerto Rico as an emmenagogue and perhaps as an abortifacient.

araña Literally, "spider." A newly introduced machine for loading cane onto trucks in the fields.

arregladero A gravity-feed device for supplying irrigation water automatically.

asadura Chittlings.

asopao A rice dish containing meat, fowl, or seafood (e.g. beef, chicken, shrimps) and seasoning. It is more liquid than the familiar rice-and-chicken dishes often associated with Latin American cuisine, and is a Puerto Rican favorite.

atierro The first plowing of previously uncultivated land.

bacalao Dried salt cod. This has centuries of tradition behind it in the Caribbean area, having been one of the chief foods supplied to the slaves. It is still a vital protein source in lower-class diet.

banqueo The marking-in of furrows before cane planting.

barrio An administrative unit in Puerto Rico and elsewhere in Latin America; a subdivision of a municipality. The *barrio* usually contains several nuclei of population.

bendición Literally, "blessing." A child will ask his godparents for *bendición* whenever he sees them. In the Pentecostal Church in Puerto Rico the term refers to the "outpouring of the Spirit" during a service when members of the congregation enter a trance state. To "receive the blessing" is part of the experience of becoming a full member of the Church.

bola, bolita Literally, "ball," "little ball." *La bola* and *la bolita* refer to the numbers game.

bolitero A seller of *bolita* tickets.

bombacho A loose shirt worn outside the pants, formerly used by small boys in rural Puerto Rico.

bombo A special plow for the preparation of cane fields.

botalón A long-handled shovel for ditching work in swampy ground.

bregar Literally, "to struggle." The term is used very often among lower-class Puerto Ricans to describe their lives and their work.

café macho A type of coffee used formerly to make medicine for treating malaria.

callejón A pathway in the cane fields or, more commonly, the main furrow.

canastillo A layette.

cañita Literally, "the little cane." The word is used for the illegal strong white rum drunk by Puerto Rican working people.

cará A mild expletive.

Carabaña A medicine for malaria.

caramba A mild expletive.

carey The sea turtle *Chelonia mydas virgata*. Its meat is prized.

carretero Cart driver in the cane fields.

Carta Roja Literally, "the red card." The term was used to describe the local political committees of the Socialist party in Puerto Rico.

casarse Literally, "to marry, to get married." Persons living in a common-law relationship are not usually described as *casado*. When a lower-class Puerto Rican speaks of people who have been married by civil or sacramental ceremony, he describes them as *casado casado*, that is, "really married."

central A modern sugar cane mill.

chiripear To do odd jobs, to live by sporadic labor. The word is much used by lower-class Puerto Ricans.

chisme A rumor, an item of gossip. A *chisme* may be either idle or vicious gossip.

claro de luna Literally, "moonlight." A descriptive term for a kind of dress material.

colgadizo   The rear of a Puerto Rican worker's house, containing the sleeping quarters.

colonia   Literally, "colony." The term is used by the plantation administration for its separate great farms, which formerly had large worker populations living on them. For the workers it is the place where they live or work. Each *colonia* has a name, often that of its former owner.

comadre   Literally, "co-mother."

comején   The termite *Tremes ripertii.*

comisario   Political chief of a *barrio*. The *comisario*, usually a wealthy man, was appointed by the mayor of the municipality. The post was abolished several decades ago in Puerto Rico.

compadrazgo   The system of ritualized co-parenthood associated primarily with the Catholic sacrament of baptism.

compadre   Literally, "co-father." The godfather of one's child is one's *compadre;* the father of children to whom one is god-father is also one's *compadre.*

compañía, la   Literally, "the company"; in Barrio Jauca and else-where nearby, the American sugar corporation that dominates the area.

cortarse   Literally, "to cut oneself." In the Pentecostal Church in Puerto Rico the word is used to describe a person who is moved toward conversion by the sermon, though not yet a church member. He is, to employ Fundamentalist usage, "convicted" by the message.

coquí   The small whistling frog *Glodes martinicensis* Thud.

cospe   Literally, "lump, mass." The word is used to describe the soil lifted by the ditching shovel in wet or clayey earth.

credo   Part of the prayer recited in an unofficial lay baptism.

cuarentena   A forty-day period of sexual abstention for the mother following the birth of a child. The word is cognate with Eng-lish "quarantine."

cuartero   Boy who looks after the two forward yokes of oxen in plowing.

cuerda   Puerto Rican unit of land measure, roughly nine-tenths of an acre.

culpable   Literally, "guilty," but in Puerto Rican common usage the meaning is "guilty as charged," rather than "having feel-ings of guilt."

defenderse   Literally, "to defend oneself." The term is used commonly to mean "to fend for oneself," "to protect oneself," "to keep oneself from terrible need."

embarcado   Literally, "embarked," from the verb *embarcarse*, "to embark." In Puerto Rican usage, it always means "embarked for the United States."

empachado   Colic, cramps.

encabezado   A foreman in the cane. The term was used particuarly during the early period of American expansion (1900–30) in the sugar industry, and may have derogatory overtones. *Encabezados* often misused their power. See *rematista*.

fia'o   Credit. Buying of daily necessities in rural Puerto Rico is almost always done on *fia'o*.

fulano   Fellow, any person, John Doe.

fulgón   Railway car for carrying cane.

fulgonero   A loader of railway cars.

frescura   A red wood, *Peperomia pellucida*, used for making canes and shovel handles.

frío   Literally, "cold"; in the Pentecostal Church in Puerto Rico, "not responsive to exhortation."

genio   Spirit or temperament.

gozne   Literally, "hinge"; the hinged chute attachment on trucks used formerly to carry cane to the railway loading platforms.

gran cultura   Literally, "big growth"; the sugar cane that is planted in early fall and permitted to grow for fifteen to eighteen months before cutting.

grosella   The fruit *Cicca disticha*, which has no economic importance but is used occasionally to make a compote dessert or is eaten uncooked by children.

grueso   Plump, robust, fat.

guardar   Literally, "to guard, to keep"; in lower-class Puerto Rican usage, also "to hold a grudge."

guayacán   The tree *Guaiacum officinale*, lignum vitae, and its wood.

güiro   A musical instrument, really a rasp, made from the gourd *Crescentia cujete* L.

hacendado   A hacienda owner.

hacienda   A large farm or ranch; in Puerto Rico, particularly sugar and coffee estates.

hedionda   The plant *Cassie occidentalis;* though foul smelling, it is used to make a medicinal coffee, and is used as a beverage in times of scarcity.

hoyado Literally, "hole"; a hole dug to plant seed cane.

hoyado de resiembro The digging of holes for replanting cane that did not take hold properly.

húcar The tropical hardwood *Bucida buceras.*

impacientado Vexed, nervous, out of patience.

independizado A worker who lives on his own land or Government land and is hence less subject to pressure from the sugar corporations. The term is in many ways the opposite in meaning from *agregado.*

inútil Literally, "useless." May be used to mean "disabled," or "impotent," when referring to the results of an injury or operation.

jallao An edible sea fish, *Scarus hemulon.*

jarea An edible sea fish, the mullet, *Mugil curema* (Cuvier and Valenciennes).

jugando de manos Literally, "playing with the hands." Used to mean "holding hands," as in a flirtation, or, among children, feinting, pushing, etc., which might lead to blows.

latón A big can; usually a five-gallon tin.

lechón Roast pig.

maclaine An irrigation ditch in the cane that apparently took the name of the American engineer who devised it.

malicia Shrewdness, cunning.

maliciar To divine, to infer cunningly, to suspect.

mayordomo Overseer; in Puerto Rico, particularly the overseers of the *colonias* in the cane, or of other large farms.

mero An edible sea fish, *Serramus gigas.*

modernismo Modernism, sophistication. May be used in a derogatory way.

[*nuez*] *moscada* Nutmeg, *Myristica fragrans* Houtt.

movimiento Literally, "movement." In the Pentecostal Church in Puerto Rico, the behavior of church members receiving the Holy Spirit; *movimiento* corresponds to the term "demonstration" in American Fundamentalist usage.

mozo Literally, "boy." The term, along with its diminutive, *mozito,* really means "youth" or "young adolescent."

mujer de estado Literally, "woman of status." The term means "a woman who has lived in some kind of marital union which has now been dissolved." It is conceptually the opposite of *señorita.*

mujeriego Inordinately fond of women.

municipio An administrative division corresponding most closely to "county" in American usage.

naranja The sour orange *Citrus bigaradia;* the leaves and fruit are used as medicine in rural Puerto Rico.

novenario The ninth-night religious ceremony following a death, and its accompanying prayers.

padre nuestro Part of the prayer recited in an unofficial, lay baptism.

padrinos Godparents.

pajera Oxcart for carrying hay.

pala Spade; especially, ditching spade.

palero Ditcher—the most skilled manual job in cane cultivation.

palos Sticks used for beating out rhythm at dances.

paludismo Malaria.

pasmo Literally, "spasm." The term is used in Puerto Rico to describe an illness allegedly caused by sudden contact with cold wind or water when the body is overheated.

pastel A dish made of mashed plantain, bits of pork, and seasoning, which is wrapped in plantain leaves and boiled.

pegado From the verb *pegar,* which is used in many differing senses in Puerto Rico. The hardened rice at the bottom of the pot is *arroz pegado;* well-rhymed lines of verse *pegan bien* ("stick well together"). One usage is to describe couples who are dancing very closely and intimately.

pelaillo An edible sea fish, of the genus *Chirocentrodon.*

pendiente Literally, "awaiting." The word often has a sexual or strongly personal overtone. It may be used to refer to the growing sexual interest of boys, for instance.

perniciosa A childhood disease which I have been unable to identify, characterized by sudden high temperatures, convulsions, and the passing of blood in the urine. Probably a form of malaria.

pichi pichi A small edible marine clam, probably of the genus *Donax.*

pieza de los pobres Hacienda land which in former times was used to cultivate sugar cane that was made into sugar for free distribution to the poor.

pitorro See *cañita.*

plena A typical rural dance form.

poyal Swampy lowlands, often ideal for growing sugar cane.

practicante   Male nurse.

prendido   From the verb *prender,* "to light up." It may be used to refer to states of anger, drunkenness, or exaltation, among others.

primavera   Literally, "spring"; sugar cane that is planted in the spring and cut the following spring.

querida   Mistress or lover.

quincallero   An ambulant vendor.

rascamoños   A plant used to make a medicine for the treatment of malaria.

rematista   Labor crew foreman or recruiter, during the first years of the American Occupation. The term is derogatory, since the *rematista* often exploited his position to cheat the workers.

rezar   To pray, to chant the rosary.

riego   Irrigation. *El riego corrido,* "running irrigation," refers to regular ditching work with no special payment.

robalo   An edible sea fish, of the genus *Centropomus,* probably *C. undecimalis.*

rompecabezas   Literally, "puzzles." Difficult jobs.

señorita   Literally, "virgin," "young woman." The word has special significance in lower-class rural Puerto Rico, referring to a woman who has never been in a consensual or other union and who is virginal. It is the opposite conceptually of *mujer de estado.*

serenata   Literally, "serenade." The word may mean "music sung in the evening or early morning hours to a girl one is courting." It may also mean "a meal," among other things.

serenata de viandas   A meal of boiled starchy foods and codfish.

simpático   Lovable, profoundly likable, warm.

síncope   Literally, "swooning." The climax of intensity in an illness.

tachuelo   A tropical hardwood, *Pictetia aristata.*

temor   Fear or awe.

templete   Dais or platform.

terecina   A railway handcar.

tiempo muerto   Literally, "dead time." The period, usually July to December, when there is no harvesting.

tocino   Salt pork.

trigueño   Literally, "wheat-colored." A euphemism for "Negroid," also used to distinguish a brunet from a blond person.

tronquero   Boy who looks after the two rear yokes of oxen in plowing.

uvas del mar   The fruit *Coccoloba unifera,* which grows near the seashore. It has no economic use, but is eaten by children.

vagonero   A loader of the small wagons formerly brought into the cane fields on portable rails.

velar   Literally, "to watch over, to keep a vigil." The word has a special meaning as well: "to lie in wait for," with violence implied.

velorio   A wake.

verde   Green, unripe, immature.

viandas   Starchy vegetables, green bananas, and roots such as yams, taro, and sweet potatoes, served boiled.

vieja   An edible sea fish, the parrotfish, *Scarus vetula* (Block and Schneider).

vigilia   A vigil or night watch. In the Pentecostal Church in Puerto Rico the term refers to a kind of all-night service.

virazón   A wind shift during a hurricane.

zafra   The harvest; especially, the sugar cane harvest.